NOLTE'S
SCHOOL LAW DESK BOOK

NOLTE'S
SCHOOL LAW DESK BOOK

M. Chester Nolte

Professor of Educational Administration Emeritus
University of Denver

Parker Publishing Company, West Nyack, New York

©1980, *by*

PARKER PUBLISHING COMPANY, INC.

West Nyack, N.Y.

"This publication is designed to provide accurate and authoritative information
in regard to the subject matter covered. It is sold with the understanding that the
publisher is not engaged in rendering legal, accounting or other professional
service. If legal advice or other expert assistance is required, the services of a
competent professional person should be sought.

*—From a Declaration of Principles jointly adopted by a Committee of the
American Bar Association and a Committee of Publishers and
Associations."*

Library of Congress Cataloging in Publication Data

Nolte, Mervin Chester.
  Nolte's School law desk book.

  Includes index.
  1. Educational law and legislation—United States.
I. Title. II. Title: School law desk book.
KF4119.N63   1980   334′.73′071   79-25020
ISBN 0-13-623140-3

Printed in the United States of America

To Dena Kathryn

Other Books by the Author

Guide to School Law
School Law in Action: 101 Key Decisions
    with Guidelines for School Administrators
Duties and Liabilities of School Administrators

ABOUT THE AUTHOR

Dr. M. Chester Nolte has spent a half-century in education, ranging from a teaching position in a one-room rural school in Iowa all the way to Professor Emeritus of Educational Administration at the University of Denver. Teacher, principal, and superintendent of schools for nine years, Dr. Nolte has devoted his lifetime to the improvement of the educational opportunities of all American youth. Winner four times of the coveted Educational Press Association's Distinguished Service Award, he served with distinction as President (1975) of the prestigious National Organization on Legal Problems of Education (NOLPE), as President of the DU Chapter of Phi Delta Kappa, and in other important posts in the field of education. Dr. Nolte is considered a national authority in the field of school law, and his work (150 articles and 10 other books) on school law has long been recognized as both authoritative and exhaustively researched. In 1976-77, he served with distinction as a member of the Teacher Corps at the University of Guam, providing insights into the field of law affecting organization of schools that eventually led to the complete overhaul of the island's school system. Writer, consultant, lecturer and adviser, Dr. Nolte has won unquestioned recognition in the field of school law. He earned his doctorate in school administration at the University of Denver and his master's degree at Drake University. Dr. Nolte and his wife, who live in mile-high Denver, have two grown children, CMDR James E. Nolte, M.D., now Head of Vascular Surgery at the Portsmouth Naval Regional Hospital in Virginia, and Mrs. Harriet Ann Wolford, a teacher's aide in Grand Junction, Colorado. The Noltes have four grandchildren, to one of whom this volume is dedicated.

To be
conscious
that you are
ignorant
of the facts
is a great
step to
knowledge.

Benjamin Disraeli
1804-1881

How to Use This Book

- A school superintendent who recommended the termination of a teacher for "immorality" was ordered to pay the teacher damages in the amount of $7,500 and court costs and attorney's fees, a sum in excess of $12,500...
- A 17-year-old girl, forced to disrobe because two school officials suspected her of concealing drugs, was awarded $7,500 in compensatory damages...
- A student injured in chemistry class won actual and punitive damages from the teacher and administrator who were declared negligent in providing adequate supervision to all students...
- A superintendent assigned one teacher to a teaching position at the same time that the board assigned another to the same position...
- A teacher was dismissed for "constitutionally impermissible reasons." The board was ordered to reinstate her and pay her back wages.

These are not isolated cases which occur once in a lifetime—they occur every day. Defendants are not litigation-prone; they are average, hard-working school people who are trying their best to do a good job. What has made school management a high-hazard occupation is simply that anyone with a grievance goes to court to claim his or her access to a protected right. One who works in this field must proceed as through a mine field or suffer loss of face, fortune and even career opportunities by taking one mistaken step. And there is no end in sight.

This book is designed to help those who manage schools or who participate in the making of educational decisions to avoid those mistakes and to govern themselves accordingly.

A *desk book* is just what the name implies—a book to have handy on your shelf when trouble of a legal nature crops up. You may feel secure in the knowledge that your district has a school's attorney. Or you may have access to the advice of a wise colleague or a professor of school administration. Don't be fooled: the probability of anything happening today is in inverse ratio to its desirability. The less you know about the law, the more likely you are to compound the situation, and make matters even worse.

This book will not make you capable of serving as your own attorney. Such a role is neither possible nor necessary. What it will do for you is to give you some immediate assistance on any given legal situation at a moment's notice. From that knowledge, you can then decide what course to take while waiting for the attorney to arrive.

School administrators are busy people. You hardly have time enough to keep up with the professional readings in your field, much less keep abreast of the rapidly developing field of school law. This book will help you bring yourself up to date on many cases that have been litigated that change materially the way we manage our schools in the 1980's.

I was privileged to serve for many years as a principal, superintendent, and finally as a professor of educational administration. Out of this apprenticeship grew an appreciation of the importance of knowing the rules of the game as they are used in practice. The rules most valuable to administrators today are those associated with meeting challenges of a legal nature. During my half-century in education, the rules changed many times. Only when I changed with them was I able to survive. No doubt the next fifty years will see many more changes, and the ones who survive will be those who are aware of impending change, and are able to change with the changing times.

Most of current educational law is "judge made"—that is, it depends on enunciations of courts of law from time to time. So-called "landmark" cases shape the future, and demand altered techniques in managing the schools. This book contains many such innovations, and is designed with the busy administrator in mind.

Here, for example, you will find chapters on how to deal with church-state problems (Ch. 2), how to work smoothly with parents' groups (Ch. 5), and how to keep on the safe side when dismissing school personnel (Ch. 10). Other chapters deal with child abuse (Ch. 7), teacher rebellion (Ch. 6), legally acceptable student grouping techniques (Ch. 11), and how to deal adequately with students' constitutional rights (Ch. 14). The full range of coverage extends to every phase of the administrator's legal problems, and gives actual litigated cases similar to the problems you face in your daily work in the schools.

A table of cases is included, along with a handy guide to constitutional content contained in the Bill of Rights. For your immediate reference, you will find the self-help index of topics indispensable to your daily needs. In case you find time to read further, a list of cases together with their legal citations is also included.

No one book could possibly cover all problems of a legal nature experienced by the busy administrator. This book will be helpful to you only to the extent to which you put it to daily use. You can read it like any other book from cover to cover; you may wish to go over it with your principals to bring them up to date on legal changes; or you may wish to have it handy in case problems of a legal nature arise. Whatever your strategy, the volume is timely, based on fact, not fiction, and slanted toward your daily operational needs. If you find it helpful in even the smallest way, then its preparation shall not have been in vain.

M. Chester Nolte

Table of Contents

LIST OF FIGURES

CHAPTER

1

What You Don't Know About School Law Can Hurt You

THE NEW LEGAL GAME ADMINISTRATORS PLAY

A man who had been around the world studying the laws of each country was asked what he had learned. His reply:

"I learned that in England, everything is permitted except that which is prohibited. In Russia, quite the opposite is true—everything is prohibited except that which is permitted. In France, the law is unique. There, everything is permitted—even that which is prohibited."

We Americans got our law from the English. It is no surprise then that here we look upon the law as *permissive,* that is, we think it *can be* done unless there is a specific statute prohibiting it. Even then, we have a reasonable doubt.

In the forties and fifties, school administrators were most often seen with a copy of the state school code (statutes) in hand, busily meeting each legal crisis as it occurred. The rule we followed was simple: *If a certain proposed action to be taken by the board is not prohibited, it is assumed to be permitted.* After looking to statutory law to see that an act was indeed not specifically illegal, we advised the board that there seemed to be no bar to the proposed action, and we therefore recommended it be taken. Only rarely did we resort to legal counsel in making these recommendations. Since most of the board's actions went unchallenged in the courts, this *modus operandi* proved sufficient to the times and was the one we used in 99 percent of the instances where legal issues were involved in board decision-making.

Came the sixties—often called the Suin' Sixties—a decade when court challenges proliferated as a result of the Civil Rights Movement, a time of rising expectations not only in education, but in all aspects of constitutional privilege. Boards were shocked to learn their actions were being challenged at every turn. Students challenged school rules on dress, appearance, and the wearing of armbands in school to express their displeasure with the war in Vietnam. Teachers challenged the board's exclusion of their profession in the making of decisions that affected their right to be first-class citizens. Courts even became the arena for deciding what the relationship should be between the board and its chief executive officer, the superintendent of schools. The courtroom, not the legislative chamber, became the major producer of the law. As the common law proliferated, so did the administrator's need to understand the changes that had occurred in the way Americans were managing their educational institutions.

To learn what the law is at any given time became more difficult. Whereas an administrator could look up the statutory law without too much trouble, it was quite another matter to follow the thousands of court cases that make up the body of the common law. Gradually, school administrators began to turn over their legal advisement duties to school board attorneys, who first had to be instructed in the new and burgeoning field of school law.

Law schools do not prepare specialists in any one area of the law, preferring instead to give general preparation to their graduates. Hence, the attorney who becomes at last a good school law adviser must be carefully cultivated and brought into the administrative team well in advance of litigation involving the board of education. Fortunate indeed is the school superintendent who has an effective and dedicated school attorney to help him survive legal pitfalls in his practice. Also fortunate is the school attorney who has availed himself or herself of the services of the Council of School Attorneys, sponsored by the National School Boards Association. Out of this specialization movement has come not only an effective service to the beleaguered superintendent and board, but also a ready source of instruction to these officials who must face the daily battle in a litigious social setting.

It must be apparent that the shift from statutory law to judge-made law transformed school management and widened its scope from local and state law to nation-wide, federal control. Especially in the areas of student rights and desegregation, federal courts have often become a more important factor in the determination of educational policy than local boards of education. Hopefully, the judicial tide that seemed so close to the breakwater of local control will begin to ebb in the 1980's.

Traditionally, federal courts were reluctant to interfere in the local control of education, and to some extent this is still true today. The United States Supreme Court has repeatedly expressed its reluctance to step in where local officials should be allowed to make public policy. Yet litigants have insisted that the High Court decide their constitutional rights even though education is a state, rather than a federal, function.

In 1954, the Warren Court began to extend to local school boards the constraints of the Constitution. In declaring that "the judiciary has extremely broad and flexible powers to remedy past wrongs of school authorities who have maintained segregated schools," the Court declared that thenceforth all cases involving school integration should be routed immediately to the federal district court in the state in which the controversy arose. *Brown v. Bd. of Educ.*, 349 U.S. 294, 300, Kans. 1955, sometimes referred to as *Brown II.*

THE NEW MODEL FOR SOCIAL CHANGE

Judge-made (or common) law, in contrast with statutory law, calls for an entirely different philosophical framework. Throughout most of our nation's history, legislatures and the Congress made the laws, and courts intervened only on a clear showing that such legislation was outside the power of the state, or was arbitrary or capricious. Statutory law was majoritarian, based on the will of the people, evolutionary in nature, and authoritarian to the extreme. In contrast, *judge-made* law is founded on the rights of the minority, and is subject to no vote of the people.* It tends toward revolution in the rapidity with which change can occur and is always tentative in nature, claiming no final solution to

---

*During extensive litigation to integrate the Denver Public Schools, school attorneys sought to show that the board, which rejected busing, had been overwhelmingly elected by the voters at a school election. U.S. District Court Judge William E. Doyle tersely put this argument to rest with the statement, "The shape of the Constitution is not determined by popular vote."

the problem at issue. The "impeach Earl Warren" movement in the sixties is evidence enough that such judge-made law is far from being unquestionably accepted by the majority of Americans.

Yet Americans respect the law, and in the final analysis generally comply with ruling case law over time. This has led to a new model for social change, a model having three steps:

- First, a minority goes into court and wins a decision based on constitutional guarantees;
- Second, a period of time transpires, during which the implications of the decision are widely diffused through the media; and
- Third, the minority point of view is enacted into statutory law within the several states and in the Congress.

For example, in *Brown v. Board of Education,* 1954, the Supreme Court held that maintaining separate but equal facilities for the races in public schools is inherently unequal. Some 17 states had to adjust their thinking to come into line with the decision. A period of ten years passed, after which the idea of racial equality in public schools had become sufficiently entrenched within the legal processes as to enable the Congress in 1964 to make this idea *majoritarian* in the Civil Rights Act of 1964. The process has been repeated many times over in such issues as abortion, education of the handicapped, and sex discrimination in employment. It continues to be our major engine for social change many years after the revolution began.

The intervention of the federal courts that began with desegregation soon expanded to include the religious, political, and cultural problems of local school districts. Between 1953 and 1969, the Warren Court dealt with 36 school cases, about equally divided between church-state, loyalty, and desegregation issues. Cases were decided not so much on their legal situations as on sociological, historical, psychological,* and philosophical bases. The period of judicial "activism" begun with *Brown* was to continue well into the 1980's and would change greatly the way that Americans would manage their schools for many years to come.

---

*Not generally well known is the federal court's use of experts in psychological matters in determining, for example, that black plaintiffs in *Brown v. Board of Education* were psychologically "put down" because of their assignment to exclusively black schools by the Topeka board of education. For more on this read "The Menninger Connection," Chapter 17 in Richard Kluger's *Simple Justice,* published by Alfred Knopf in 1976.

Obviously, there are practical limits to which the courts can go in solving all our problems by means of school litigation. This limitation was well stated by Judge Coleman in *U.S. v. Jefferson Co. Bd. of Educ.*, 380 F.2d 385, 419, 1967, when he wrote:

> The decree is not as I would have written it if I had been charged with sole responsibility for the effort. No offense is intended when I doubt that it is perfect ... The school official cannot win. In one breath, he is told to act; in the next, he is immobilized. ...
>
> Judges, like other human beings, do not always write in granite; they often find that they have only marked in the sand.

Temporary as their efforts may be, the decisions of federal judges are becoming increasingly more important to the practicing school administrator, not so much because they make fascinating reading—which they do—but because sometimes your very survival depends on knowing what they have to offer.

WHY YOU NEED TO KNOW THE LAW

In America, every one is presumed to know the law, and obey it. This was no great feat when our society was simple; now it has become very difficult indeed.

The English long ago refused to accept ignorance of the law as a viable defense. This is not because all men know the law, but in court, there is no really effective way to combat the defense of ignorance. If courts were to allow men to plead ignorance, everyone would use that defense, and there would be no reasonable way to refute it.

So the judge refuses to allow the defense that you did not know that this was the law. Instead, all Americans are presumed to have access to legal counsel. The more serious the charge, the more we tend to protect the right to be defended by competent legal counsel.

Ignorance of the law can land you in a slough of trouble:
- It can cause you embarrassment;
- It can cause you to think you don't need legal advice;
- It can cause you to overreact;
- It can lead to a lack of leadership on your part;
- It can lead to your firing, and (here's the *real* risk),
- It can cost you your own personal fortune.

The cases on this point (ignorance of the law) are extensive.

Following are a few that serve to illustrate the pitfalls mentioned immediately above.

Embarrassment

Your credibility as an administrator can be shaken by events that involve your knowledge, or lack of knowledge, of the law. In Iowa, a high school principal acted as chief negotiator for the teachers' union, some members of which he was obligated to evaluate and supervise on behalf of the school board. The board served the principal with an ultimatum: either give up the role as negotiator or be fired. When he refused to give up the negotiator's job, the board fired the principal, whereupon he sought reinstatement in the federal courts. His suit was unsuccessful. "State law," ruled the court of appeals, "gives the board sole discretion in the making of decisions relating to personnel. The principal showed bad judgment by acting as chief negotiator and such bad judgment can form the basis for nonrenewal of his contract." *Norbeck v. Davenport Comm. Sch. Dist.,* 545 F.2d 63, Iowa 1976.

Similarly, the supreme court of at least one state has ruled that the board may overrule the superintendent of schools with respect to the transfer of teachers. *Diefenderfer v. Budd,* 563 P.2d 1355, Wyo. 1977. "The board may not delegate away its authority over teacher transfers, even though a negotiated agreement between the board and the teachers' association may be in effect," said the court.

Some embarrassment arises where the courts hold that the board, rather than the superintendent, is the proper body for making decisions, and that this authority cannot be delegated to anyone. It was held that a board of education had the power to promulgate a regulation imposing fines on employees for tardiness. However, when that regulation was adopted by the administration, with only tacit approval of the board, it was voided. *Central Regional Educ. Ass'n. v. Bd. of Educ.,* N.J. Comm'r. of Educ. Dec., 1973.

Another court held that a local board of education had the responsibility of deciding whether a debate on abortion was proper subject matter for a seventh grade class. This responsibility could not be left to an arbitrator under an academic freedom clause in a collective bargaining agreement. *Rockaway Bd. of Educ. v. Rockaway Educ. Ass'n.,* 120 N.J. Super 564, 1972. Another board policy which gave the superintendent authority to place teachers on probation was struck down as an overreach on the board's part. *Noe v. Edmonds Sch. Dist. No. 15*, 515 P.2d 977, Wash. 1973. From these cases, the wise administrator can draw but one conclusion: failure to know the law can work to your embarrassment in your relations with the local board of education.

Legal advice

Assuming you know the law when you don't may cause you to be "blind sided" because you did not ask for legal advice before taking action. For example, a superintendent was ordered by the court not only to issue an elementary teacher an employment contract but also to reinstate him at a specified school, a judgment which the superintendent ignored. Instead, he assigned the teacher to duties for which he had no certificate and at work he had not performed for the previous seven years of his employment. The potential danger of disregarding the law would most surely have been pointed out by competent legal counsel, thus saving the superintendent considerable legal difficulty. Lacking this, the superintendent was held in contempt of court for willfully and intentionally changing the teacher's duties as ordered by the court. *Buck v. Myers*, 514 P.2d 742, Ariz. 1973.

An Arkansas board authorized the superintendent to sign all necessary forms for the federal programs in the district, but did not authorize him to enter into a lease-purchase agreement for library books, which he did, in the amount of $28,315.09. The district received the books and used them for a year. Although the board knew of the agreement, it refused to ratify it, whereupon the seller brought suit to recover the cost of the books. The court held that both parties were at fault, but that the seller could recover under an implied contract for the actual cost of the books under the doctrine of *quantum meruit* ("as much as he deserves"). The judge gave the book company the option of taking back the books or receiving partial payment of $13,500. Such an unratified action on the part of the superintendent would have been noticed by an attorney who might have warned the administrator that his actions were likely to cause legal problems further down the road. *Responsive Environments Corp. v. Pulaski Cty. Spec. Sch. Dist.*, 366 F.Supp. 241, Ark. 1973.

Administrators sometimes make mistakes in judgment which would be obvious to even the most naive law school student. In Minnesota, a superintendent was served with notice that he would not be renewed, and he sought reasons for his dismissal. The board was split 4-3 on retaining him. Without bothering to hold a legally called meeting on renewal ("The three would not have concurred anyway"), the four who favored retention wrote a letter affirming its support, and saying that there was no time to hold a legal meeting. The court held there was time. "If actions such as this can be taken by a majority of the board acting individually and outside a statutorily called meeting, almost any action could be taken by the majority without giving dissenters an opportunity to be heard. The statute says the board shall 'give its reasons for termination in writing.' The statute means what it plainly says. The letter was legally insufficient in the case. The board can refuse to renew for any reason whether valid or fanciful. Where it gave notice on February 12th, of non-renewal, and the law stipulates 'by April 1,' the contract was thus terminated and the board is entitled to summary judgment."

What this all adds up to is this: a superintendent is assumed to know the law, and abide by it at all times. In the absence of a full knowledge of the law, the wise administrator will rely heavily on legal counsel to see him/her through. Failure to so rely on your friend, the school attorney, or other lawyer, is bound to lead to failure where the law is so plainly predictable as to lead even the most naive to say, "This is the law." *Shell v. Ind. Sch. Dist.,* Dist. Court, 3rd Minn. Judicial District, July 9, 1973, Glenn E. Kelley, D.J.

Overreaction

By far the most serious effect of ignorance of the law is the possibility of overreacting to some legal problem. This may take many forms. For example, a principal was incensed when a student refused to have his hair cut. He took a braid of the pupil's hair and cut it off. In a hearing before the state commissioner of education, the latter held that dismissal was too severe a penalty in the light of the principal's overall record, but upheld a monetary fine and the imposition of a period of probation. *In the Matter of the Tenure Hearing of Dominic Parisi,* N.J. Comm'r. of Educ. Dec., 1974.

In Arkansas, some girls confessed to spiking the punch at a school function in violation of a board rule forbidding "intoxicating" beverages at such meetings. Believing that it should uphold its rules and regulations, the board expelled the girls for three months on the grounds of their confessions alone. In a suit for monetary recovery, the girls were successful. "Those students facing expulsion have both a property and liberty interest," said the Supreme Court. "When they are deprived of either without due process of law, the board members, as individuals, may be held personally liable, if they knew, or reasonably should have known, that what they were doing to the students would deprive them of a constitutionally guaranteed right." *Wood v. Strickland,* 420 U.S. 308, Ark. 1975.

Sometimes administrative action taken against teachers can be classified as arbitrary where it is taken summarily. The transfer of a principal and assistant principal, both of whom were on tenure, was held to be arbitrary and illegal where a board member got mad at them and influenced the superintendent to transfer them. *Blair v. Mayo,* 450 S.W.2d 582, Tenn. 1970. But where the action taken was for the good of the students and/or the tenured teachers, the action was upheld. *State ex rel. Withers v. Bd. of Educ.,* 172 S.E.2d 796 W.Va. 1970.

Said the court, in ruling that the board's actions were logical and without malice:

> Doubtless many, perhaps most, transfers of teachers do not involve any finding of misconduct, unfitness or anything else reflecting unfavorably upon the teachers who were transferred. There is a presumption that public officials were actuated by proper motives in the performance of their duties in conducting an efficient public school system. ... It is conceivable that many teachers are transferred by boards of education because of the mere fact that they are competent, effective teachers, and that, therefore, a proper administration of the school system dictates the basis of transfers to places and positions where the teachers' special qualifications will better promote the entire public school program. *Ibid.*

Courts are generally reluctant to intervene in the internal affairs of a school system. Any arbitrary action taken without due process or a proper regard for the rights of others, therefore, is an instant danger signal to the court that an illegal action is about to take place.

In their relationships with the board of education, school superintendents may also take actions that may be classified as "overreaction."

A board had a rule promulgated to protect the privacy of certain pupils to the effect that the superintendent was to keep the names and addresses of pupils enrolled in certain schools secret, "and not divulge it to anyone." When the superintendent interpreted this to mean the members of the board of education, the latter sued to obtain the information. The court held that the superintendent could not withhold the information sought by the board, despite the rule. *Wagner v. Redmond,* 127 So.2d 275 La. 1961.

On occasion, a local board may overreact, whether by advice of the superintendent or despite it. Following the suspension of a teacher, the board granted a hearing, but held the meeting in a room containing only 24 chairs in addition to those at the table occupied by the board. There were no seats available for the teacher and his witnesses and friends. The board refused to move the meeting to a larger room on request of the teacher. Following the hearing, the teacher was discharged, and he appealed. The Supreme Court of Michigan held that he had not had a fair and impartial hearing on the merits. "A board may not 'go through the motions' of a trial; it must adhere to basic and fundamental fairness in its judicial deliberations," said the court in overruling the dismissal. *Rehberg v. Bd. of Educ. of Melvindale,* 77 N.W.2d 131, Mich. 1956.

Lack of leadership

It is easy to see that such misguided advice from the administrator to his board may result in loss of face by the members and the board as a corporate body. Plaintiff, a teacher, was discharged after he refused to shave off his beard. No policy relating to beards had been established by the district, nor was plaintiff ever actually informed of the consequences of his failure to shave. The federal district court held that not only the superintendent but also the individual board members could be held personally liable in damages for denial of due process, lack of good faith, and lack of leadership. *Lucia v. Duggan,* 303 F.Supp. 112, Mass. 1969.

Lack of leadership may also be present where the board and superintendent are at odds. A superintendent who had no tenure was dismissed, and he complained in court. The court held that he had been amply warned of his deficiencies and afforded opportunity to protect his "liberty" interest. Since he served at the pleasure of the board, his discharge had not violated his constitutional rights. The court called his appeal "frivolous" and upheld his dismissal. *Patterson v. Ramsey,* 555 F.2d 117, Md. 1977.

Governmental employees who investigate suspected criminal activity against other employees may become "suspect" since they tend to step outside the protection they ordinarily would have and become, in effect, a criminal investigator in the eyes of the law. A government supervisor began an investigation of other employees in the course of his work. Certain desks and other effects were searched, whereupon the employees claimed invasion of privacy and governmental "snooping." The court held that when a supervisor's role is no longer that of an office manager, but that of a criminal investigator for government, in that the purpose of the surveillance is no longer simply to preserve efficiency in office but is specifically designed to prepare a criminal prosecution case against the employee, he loses the protection of his office, and must obtain a search warrant in order to search and seize materials pertinent to the case. *U.S. v. Kahan,* 350 F.Supp. 784, N.Y. 1972. And where a superintendent set up electrical eavesdropping equipment in the teachers' lounge to overhear what they were planning to do on certain items then under negotiation with the board, the court ruled that he had gone too far. "Bugging" the lounge was outside the protection of the Fourth Amendment, since he had not obtained prior clearance from the government to do so, and amounted in effect to an illegal search and seizure in violation of the law.

A board of education may not be advised to act in such a way that it can accomplish indirectly what it is precluded from accomplishing directly. A teacher was dismissed for the stated reasons that she lacked discipline and used inadequate teaching methods. At trial, the teacher showed that the real reasons she was being dismissed were her life style, her physical size, her lack of church attendance, the location of her trailer, and not her incompetency in the classroom. The court held she could collect from the board members for invasion of her privacy for compensatory damages, but in the absence of malice, she was not entitled to punitive damages and attorney's fees. *Stoddard v. School Dist. No. 1, Lincoln County,* 429 F.Supp. 890, Wyo. 1977.

Loss of your job

Ignorance of the law may cause you to lose your job. In Kentucky, a superintendent was removed from his position for cause on the grounds he had engaged in an effort to get certain members elected to the board of education. The court held he had a right to be politically "active," but that in so doing he must run the risks associated with such activity. Said the court:

> A school superintendent cannot be expected to confine his extra-curricular activities to bird-watching while a covetous rival is out campaigning for a school board to unseat him. So, if he remains within the confines of propriety, neither neglecting his duties nor using his powers to coerce those who are subject to his official influence, he is free to engage in political activity, whether it concerns school elections or otherwise.

As if in afterthought, the court also ruminated as follows:

> But... if he loses, his record of performance in office had better be above reproach, because the winners also are human, and will scrutinize his armor for an Achilles heel. *Bell v. Board of Education,* 450 S.W.2d 229, Ky. 1970.

In most states, the law says that superintendents serve "at the pleasure" of the board of education. Courts are asked to determine what this phrase means. No person, no matter how well suited through experience and training to do the job, has a *right* to work for the government. However, one who enters into government service has the right *not* to be discriminated against in fulfilling his duties. The lack of measurable standards by which the superintendent may be objectively evaluated often leads to court action which might have been avoided had the parties spelled out in advance what is meant by the phrase, "He serves at the pleasure of the board of education."

Archie Dykes pointed out that such a lack of clarity causes needless controversey, when he wrote:

> Since no legal provisions exist to indicate what the relationship ought to be, agreement on how they are to work together rests with the local board and superintendent in most states. The result, in many instances, is no agreement at all but a make-shift, spur-of-the-moment arrangement that, at best, is inconsistent and ineffec-

tive and at worst, a fertile field for controversy. Archie Dykes, *School Board and Superintendent,* Danville: Interstate, 1965, p. 71.

In a case that attracted national attention, the Board of Education of New York City suspended Superintendent Calvin Gross for 90 days without pay. Gross instituted an action to block his dismissal. The court said that the superintendent's action was premature, since he must first appeal to the commissioner of education before resorting to the courts. Anyway, boards of education may and often do remove administrators, but may do so only *for cause.* Following this decision, the board and the superintendent reached an agreement whereby he resigned from the position, but was retained at a reduced salary figure for a limited period in the capacity of consultant. *Gross v. Bd. of Educ.,* 261 N.Y.S.2d 577, N.Y. 1965.

What constitutes "cause" for dismissal of a school superintendent? In Texas, a school board was upheld in dismissing an administrator who violated the employment contract by engaging in prohibited outside employment. *Gosney v. Sonora Ind. School Dist.,* 430 F.Supp. 53, Tex. 1977. Another board was justified in terminating its superintendent, under the rubric of "unprofessional conduct," where the evidence showed that he created turmoil in the school system, and that he had misrepresented his past. *Miller v. Dean,* 552 F.2d 266, Neb. 1977. Other administrators have been removed for failure to supervise employees properly (*Hoskins v. Keen,* 350 S.W.2d 467, Ky. 1961), for filing unauthorized travel claims (*McGuire v. Hammond,* 405 S.W.2d 191, Ky. 1966), and for receiving unlawful gratuities, although the latter had an unblemished record of 21 years in the position and dismissal would result in the loss of his pension (*Chilson v. Bd. Of Education,* 341 N.Y.S.2d 143, 1973).

Efforts to improve the employment contract for superintendents have not met with success. The accountability movement will no doubt improve the contract, but this area of the law continues to be one of the major legal problems facing boards and their chief executive officer, the superintendent of schools.

Your own personal fortune

By far the most dangerous area of liability for school superintendents lies in what is called "wrongful acts," or "deprivation of a civil right" of others. There are several reasons why you should learn more about this pitfall. *First,* people are becoming more and more inclined to sue on the slightest provocation, some to make the big score, others on matters of principle. *Second,* the class action suit syndrome causes courts to sweep into the legal net those who are not directly involved in a certain case—"One does not have to be a party to a suit to be bound by the decision therefrom." It therefore becomes more and more difficult to know what your own limitations are before the law and thus defend against nuisance suits brought against you. *Third,* the U.S. Supreme Court has held that "school officials" may be held personally liable under the Civil Rights Act of 1871 (42 U.S.C. §1983) if they knew or reasonably should have known that they were depriving someone of a civil right under color of state law. *Wood v. Strickland,* 420 U.S. 308, Ark. 1975.

Prior to 1970, there was no insurance to protect board members and superintendents from the results of "wrongful acts"—that is, deprivation of someone's civil rights. In that year, several large insurance companies banded together to produce the first "indemnity" policy, a type of insurance designed to protect elected public officials from loss of their own personal fortunes in the line of duty.* The insurance "indemnifies"—makes whole again—those against whom judgments have been obtained for "wrongful" acts performed in their capacity as public officials. Although the insurance tends to be expensive, no district should be without it in the climate of litigiousness which presently exists.

The background of the problem goes all the way back to Reconstruction days following the Civil War. The Congress, dominated by liberal interests, enacted seven civil rights acts designed to win for freedmen their civil rights long denied because of slavery. Among these was the Civil Rights Act of 1871. Section 1983 of that Act reads in part as follows:

---

*See for example "The Three Kinds of Insurance Your Board Needs Right Now," *American School Board Journal,* Oct. 1971, pp. 25-27. The article identifies as minimal three types of insurance boards should have: property loss, liability (in tort), and indemnity insurance, which protects against losses due to "acts and omissions" of school officials.

> Any person who, under color of law, statute, ordinance, regulation, custom, or usage of any State, shall subject, or cause to be subjected, any person within the jurisdiction of the United States to the deprivation of any rights, privileges, or immunities secured by the Constitution of the United States, shall, any such law, statute, ordinance, regulation, custom, or usage of the State to the contrary notwithstanding, be liable to the party injured in any action at law, suit in equity, or other proper proceeding for redress; ... (42 U.S.C. §1983).

The section was never fully implemented and received legitimacy in principle only. In the early 1970's, it was dusted off by civil rights activists and put to use in the movement to obtain individual freedoms for minorities. Although over 100 years old at the time, the Act became the mainstay of the lawyers representing those who allegedly were being denied civil rights. Among the cases where Section 1983 was widely used were those involving the public schools.

You should not conclude that Section 1983 was responsible for all the many and varied freedoms gained by both students and teachers in the civil rights movement. It was *statutory* law, in contrast with the Bill of Rights, which was *Constitutional* law, and the holdings of the U.S. Supreme Court, which can be classified as the *common* law. When you add to that the propensity of Americans to solve problems through litigation, the force and effect of the civil rights movement worldwide, and the perfection of the class action suit as an engine for social change, you have an unstoppable combination militating toward gaining personal rights for each and every individual in the nation.

The key case in this area of the law is *Wood v. Strickland*, 420 U.S. 308, Ark. 1975. When three girls were summarily expelled from school, they sought monetary damages for their loss, claiming that the board had deprived them of a property right in violation of Section 1983. The U.S. Supreme Court held that where boards, acting under color of state law, deprive someone of a civil right, and know or reasonably should have known that what they are doing is a deprivation of such right, they can be held individually liable for their actions. They are considered to be "co-conspirators" under that section, and may not hide behind the board's natural immunity for what they have done.

Two other cases involving administrators and individual board members are to the same effect. In *McLaughlin v. Tilendis*, 398 F.2d

287, Ill, 1968, some teachers who were active in the union were non-renewed and they sought judgment under Section 1983. Their action was successful. And in *Lucia v. Duggan,* 303 F.Supp. 112, Mass. 1969, the plaintiff, a male teacher, was granted both actual and punitive damages as well as court costs where he was dismissed for growing a beard in contravention of the orders of the superintendent.

2

How to Keep on Top of Church-State Problems

HOW IT ALL CAME TO PASS

Persecution of the Puritan groups in England in the 17th century led to settlements in New England. The colonists were determined not to pay taxes to a state-connected church. Oddly enough, they did not provide for separation in the colonies. In Plymouth and Massachusetts, rigid conformity to the religion of the settlers was practiced, and established churches became the rule rather than the exception until the adoption in 1791 of the First Amendment to the Constitution.

As first drafted, the Constitution provided that no religious test should be required for public office under the national government. Later, a compromise was made that (a) Congress (later the states) should not establish a church; and (b) the government must not limit freedom of religion. Aside from the bar to a religious test for officeholders,* these two strictures (Establishment and Free Exercise) are the only clauses in the entire Constitution regarding the relation that should exist between church and state. The word "separation" does not appear in United States law. The idea that church and state should be separate came as a result of court action which interpreted what the Constitution meant by Establishment and Free Exercise. The Supreme

---

*U.S. Constitution, Art. VI.

Court is still the final oracle we turn to to decide those questions even today.

In the 1840's, vast migrations began from Europe. Many of the newcomers were Roman Catholics. Fear that the newcomers would seek parochial school aid from public funds caused many of the states just entering the Union to write into their state constitutions prohibitions against such use of public funds, a provision some still contain today. But where, as in Louisiana and New Jersey, the state constitutions did not contain such clauses, the Supreme Court was inclined to allow expenditures for parochial schools from public funds. In 1930, for example, a unanimous Supreme Court upheld a Louisiana law requiring that tax money be spent to supply textbooks to all children at no charge no matter what their school of attendance. *Cochran v. Louisiana State Board of Education,* 281 U.S. 370, 1930. Similarly, a New Jersey statute authorized local districts to make rules and contracts for the transportation of children to and from parochial schools. The Court upheld the law as not violative of the state or federal constitutions. *Everson v. Board of Education,* 330 U.S. 1, N.J., 1947. In both cases, the Court used as the basis for its decision the state's obvious interest in producing enlightened citizens, and held that the benefit was to the child (the "child benefit" theory) and not to the school of attendance. The point to remember here is that the Court will not go out of its way to create a right that does not already exist, e.g., that is clearly not approved by the state in question. Since neither state constitution was offended by the use of state funds for private schools, in contrast with constitutions in many of the other states, the Court could find no reason why the state should not be allowed to proceed (*Everson* was a 5-4 decision, however). Thus, where there is no direct obstruction to use of state funds for parochial schools, the Court may allow their use since to do so may be construed as neutrality toward religion rather than as support of it.

Article IX, Section 7 of the Colorado Constitution states that "neither the general assembly nor any county, city, town, township, school district or other public corporation, shall ever make any appropriation, or pay from any public fund or moneys whatever, anything in aid of any church or sectarian society...." Quite obviously, the Court would not require that Coloradoans support "child benefits" in contravention of their state constitution. In addition, the Court over the years has set up this additional constitutional test of its own: (1) the statute or arrangement by the state must have a *secular purpose* (it must promote a valid state interest, such as learning to read and write); (2) its *principal or primary effect* must be one that neither advances nor inhibits religion; and (3) the statute or arrangment must not foster "an excessive governmental *entanglement* with religion." *Lemon v. Kurtzman,* 403 U.S. 602, 1971. The quote suggests that *some* entanglement is permitted, and this indeed is the case. The Court clarified this puzzle somewhat in *Wolman v. Walter,* 433 U.S. 229, Ohio, 1977 when it approved four practices in the use of state funds for private and parochial schools: (a) loan of textbooks to parochial schools by the state; (b) administering standardized tests to parochial school children; (c) helping with treatment of speech and hearing problems among parochial school children; and (d) providing dental care for students in parochial schools. Two forms of state aid were turned down: (a) spending state money for instructional materials and equipment; and (b) permitting parochial school students to take field trips to museums and other points of interest at public expense. In the final analysis, the Court must decide on a case-by-case basis whether any scheme will meet constitutional muster in each separate instance.

Colonial parents had full responsibility for educating their children. Most children were instructed at home or in church-related schools in the colonies, but after 1840, the states began establishing their own state-wide systems under implied powers from the federal government under the Tenth Amendment. Education, like the other "police" powers of the states, became a *state* rather than a federal function, and the unit of governance for schools became the legislature. Since legislatures could not very well operate the schools directly, they chose to delegate these powers to local boards of education. Thus, each state has its own educational "system" and the national educational system is a composite of these. Surprisingly uniform in many ways, this system of education, unlike those in other countries, allows for two parallel tracks: one operated by the state, which is free, tax supported, state controlled and locally managed, compulsory, universal (for everyone), non-sectarian and racially integrated; the other privately financed and outside the direct control of the state. No state can set up a church or inhibit the operation of those already in operation. In matters of religion, the state must be *neutral.* But it can set up "reasonable" controls over private and parochial schools in the interest of seeing that *every* child-citizen is accorded an adequate education as provided for in the state constitution. (The Supreme Court ruled in 1973 that there is no such federal constitutional guarantee as "equal educational opportunity" made applicable to the states. *San Antonio Independent School District v. Rodriguez,* 411 U.S. 1, Tex., 1973. More will be said later in this chapter on the problems that arise where the state attempts to set up minimum standards for private and parochial schools.

Historically, church-state problems went through three stages. First, the colonial period was dominated by the theme of religious literacy—learn to read so that Olde Deluder Satan won't get you. The period ended when states began to take over the education of the young in their own respective state-operated systems. The second period continued the theme of religious literacy, but added the important task of educating millions of immigrants. Manifest Destiny, patriotism, and nationalism were popular themes, and the period continued until World War II. During this era, each state decided whether it would or would not require prayers and Bible reading as a condition of attending public school. When a case on this issue arose in 1962 for the first time (*Engel v. Vitale,* 370 U.S. 421, N.Y., 1962), some of the states *required* such practices, others *permitted* them, while still others *prohibited* prayers and Bible reading in their public schools. We were a nation in need of guidance. The Court held that no state may compose a prayer (even a non-denominational one) and require all children to recite it as a condition of attending public schools.

The following year, the Court strengthened the decision by holding that the principle applies to school boards and state legislatures. *Murray v. Curlett, Abington School Dist. v. Schempp,* 374 U.S. 203, 1963. (The earlier case had been a test of a state board of regents' requirement of prayer in public schools.) The key here is "compulsion" —requiring children to pray or read the Bible in school amounts to an "establishment," hence is constitutionally unacceptable. Prayers of a voluntary nature are not outlawed but are suspect if there is even a hint of board compulsion. *Hunt v. Bd. of Educ. of County of Kanawha,* 321 F.Supp. 1263, W.Va. 1971.

The third period in the development of church-state relations features some problems which will be taken up in the next section.

SOME PROBLEMS IN CHURCH-STATE RELATIONS

As a general rule, private and parochial schools are not subject to the constraints of the Constitution. However, the courts have recently ruled that private schools may not discriminate against minority children in their admission policies. *Runyon v. McCrary*, 427 U.S. 160, Va. 1976. In 1925, the Supreme Court ruled that the state may not require that all children receive instruction from public school teachers only. *Pierce v. Society of Sisters*, 268 U.S. 510, Ore. 1925. "The child is not the mere creature of the state," said the Court. "Those who nurture and direct his destiny have the right coupled with the high duty to direct his feet in paths which lead upward." Parents may decide to send their children to schools other than public schools—but those schools must be "equivalent" to the public schools in the same state. The word "equivalency" has no specific legal meaning, so the courts must rule on a case-by-case basis what legal meaning should be given it in each instance. Given the disenchantment of parents lately with the public schools, litigation related to the "equivalency" concept has been on the increase. The problem from the state's standpoint is the extent to which it may set up minimum standards for private and/or parochial schools in lieu of attendance at a public school. The states have been facing stiff resistance from fundamentalists who insist that any regulation of teacher certification, curriculum or building standards for private schools violates their religious freedom rights. Particularly enigmatic is the extent to which the state may go in controlling so-called "Christian academies." *Kentucky State Board of Education v. Hinton*, D.C. Ky., 1978.

Another issue is whether home instruction in lieu of attendance at a public school is "equivalent" to public school attendance. Here again the court must proceed on a case-by-case basis, since each state law is different and each particular situation carries different fact situations. Thirty-two states permit home instruction in fulfilling the compulsory attendance laws. Some of these, including Massachusetts, require that children who are instructed at home must be taught "in a manner approved in advance by the local superintendent or school committee." When a parent challenged the statute because he failed to get his plan for home instruction approved, the case aroused interest from many parents who would like to instruct their children at home but have been denied that privilege. The courts ordinarily do not approve such an arrangement unless the parents are certificated teachers, or provision is made for certificated teachers to teach the children. One thing is certain—this rule of law will continue to be challenged so long as parents are dissatisfied with the options facing them in educating their children.

The options facing parents, especially those who are poor, leave much to be desired. Lacking money to pay tuition to private schools, they complain that they should have access to several different options in educating their children. A suggested solution is for the state to provide parents with "vouchers" —sight drafts on the public treasury which can be spent in the school of the parents' choice. See for example Coons and Sugarman, *Education by Choice,* Berkeley: Univ. of Calif. Press, 1978, a pro-voucher argument. The church-state issue continues to block the voucher plan, and there has been little testing of the plan in practice. Those who support voucher plans say that there will be no true education "in the marketplace" until parents have realistic options on the way in which they will educate their children.

A related problem mentioned above is whether the state should support part or all of the secular portion of the private school curriculum through use of state funds. The position of the Supreme Court has been that it is better to restrict religious freedom in schools than to establish a religion.

Another problem is released time for religious instruction. The Supreme Court ruled in *Zorach v. Clauson,* 343 U.S. 306, N.Y. 1952 that students may be excused during school hours to receive religious instruction with parental approval so long as little money is spent by the district or there is no use of school facilities in the program. The test for constitutionality of a released time program has three parts: (1) Is the location of the instruction near or on school property? (2) Is there an expenditure of public funds to support the program?, and (3) Does the board promote either directly or indirectly the practice of religion among students? Any released time program which provides for meetings off school property, which expends little or no money and which does not constitute a "promotion" of religion will stand constitutional muster.

An example may be helpful. The Harrisonburg (Va.) School District maintained a released time program where students were released during school hours to attend religious instruction in a mobile unit parked across the street from the school on a public street. Religious classes were integrated into the regular schedule so that children could be dismissed to receive instruction throughout the school day. The plan was challenged on the grounds that it amounted to "an establishment of religion." The federal district court agreed— "it created an impression of tacit endorsement of the program by the school district" —but the circuit court reversed the court below, and held that school cooperation was "a largely passive and administratively wise response" to the secular wishes of the students and their parents. *Smith v. Smith,* 523 F.2d 121, Va. 1975.

Another legal problem in the church-state area is whether a school board must allow the use of school facilities by religious groups, or groups of students who want to hold religious meetings. It is well-settled law that the use of school facilities by outside groups must not interfere with the on-going program of studies, but here again, the guidelines are vague and the word "interfere" has no recognized legal meaning. Usually, the courts allow local boards wide discretion in such matters. But if you allow one group to use the school facilities, you must allow all groups to do so. In *Hunt v. Bd. of Educ. of Kanawha Co.,* 321 F.Supp. 1263, W.Va. 1971, some students sued to force the board to permit them to meet on school property for prayers and other religious services, a request which the board denied. The court held that the legislature's failure to include "religion" or "religious groups" in a statute describing the permissible use of public school property precluded such a use of school premises.

The point to remember is that state laws vary on use of school property, and the board is bound by the state's statutes on the subject, as well as the state board of education's regulations. You should seek the advice of your school's attorney in such matters and work carefully to create the "neutrality" toward religion that is mandated by the Supreme Court.

Other problems of church and state will be discussed below under the heading, "Teaching Moral and Spiritual Values." There is a noticeable revival of interest in church-state problems and litigation on this subject will continue to plague school personnel for some time to come. The Supreme Court has diligently avoided allowing any state to establish a church, or official religion, which may cause some observers to say that it has taken a hard stand against freedom of religion under the First Amendment. That is a debate too complex to get involved in here.

THE ESTABLISHMENT CLAUSE AND YOU

Neither Congress nor the states may found a church, or favor one religion over another. The interpretation of what that First Amendment prohibition means has resulted in much litigation. The Supreme Court has ruled that "we are a religious people whose institutions presuppose a Supreme Being ... but in matters of religion the government must remain forever neutral." *Zorach v. Clauson,* 343 U.S. 306, N.Y., 1952. Neither the state nor the federal government can aid one religion, aid all religions, or prefer one religion over another. *Everson v. Board of Education,* 330 U.S. 1, N.J. 1947. The government may not make a religious observance compulsory. *Zorach, supra.* Neither the state nor the federal government may set up a church. No tax in any amount, large or small, can be levied to support any religious activities or institutions, whatever they may be called, or whatever form they may adopt to teach or practice a religion. In the words of Thomas Jefferson, the establishment clause was intended to erect "a wall of separation" between church and state. *Everson, supra.*

In our zeal to avoid breaking down that wall, school people have done children a disservice. Intent on keeping church and state separated, schools have avoided facing up to the need to teach moral and spiritual values, good sportsmanship, and ethical character in the schools. The Constitution does not require that church and state should never mix. The state, of course, has a vital interest in religion, at least to the extent that schools are expected to teach those values which have their roots in some religious doctrine. The Supreme Court did not "outlaw" God in the schools; what it said was that no state may compose a prayer and require all children to recite it in public schools. The ruling was misinterpreted to mean that there shall be no prayers or Bible reading in schools at all—not at all what the Supreme Court said or meant. But the public schools are expected to inculcate in children those qualities of character and ethical behavior which will help them to function as good citizens. We look on our schools as our first line of defense against foreign or cultistic ideologies. By failing to do anything to build appreciation of the finer things of life in children, educators often do worse than nothing—they give the impression that religious matters are altogether taboo and should not be mentioned in schools at all. Nothing could be further from the truth.

To avoid the cult of "secular humanism," the schools should proceed to do what can legally be done to teach those social creeds that will produce fine citizens. Thus, whether or not we have an establishment violation will boil down in all cases to "a matter of degree."

Justice Douglas wrote, "The First Amendment does not say that in every and all respects there shall be a separation of church and state. Rather, it studiously defines the manner in which there shall be no concert or union or dependency one on the other. That is the common sense of the matter. Otherwise, the state and religion would be aliens to each other—hostile, suspicious, and even unfriendly. This we do not want to happen." *Zorach v. Clauson, supra.* The government must be neutral when it comes to competition between sects. It may not thrust any sect on any person, nor elevate one over the other. We must not read into the Bill of Rights, said Douglas, "such a philosophy of hostility to religion."

Clearly, both church and state are entitled to live in detente together. While the state may not establish a church, it also may not inhibit the free exercise of religion by coming down hard on religions already operating in the social milieu.

School administrators should seek to provide ethical values to children because children are entitled to such services from the state. Saying that because the Supreme Court has overruled prayers and Bible reading in the schools we cannot do anything about religion in public schools is a cop-out. There are many ways to do indirectly what we cannot do directly—e.g., help children build sufficient moral bases for their future lives as citizens by ministering to their needs in school. We turn now to how that may be done.

TEACHING MORAL AND SPIRITUAL VALUES

Parents who do not wish to send their children to public schools may (a) enroll them in private or parochial schools of their choice, or (b) teach their children at home. School administrators in public schools then have three options: (1) released time for religious instruction; (2) shared time where church and state cooperate; and (3) in-school curricula that contain the elements of moral training and self-discovery appropriate to the developing citizen. Each of these options will be considered in turn.

Released time

In *Illinois ex rel. McCollum v. Bd. of Education,* 333 U.S. 203, 1948, the Supreme Court ruled that a released-time program in the Champaign schools was unconstitutional. The reason for its decision was that religious classes met on school grounds in school facilities, and the services of the public school teachers were being used to promote the program. But in *Zorach v. Clauson, supra,* 1952, the Court approved a plan that allowed children, with the consent of their parents, to attend, during school hours, religious classes in their own churches or synagogue. Thus, no moneys raised by the state were being used, and where the classes met off school grounds, there was no "establishment" of religion. Since that decision, many districts have tried and still use released-time programs where religious training can be had without violating the Establishment Clause of the First Amendment.

Shared time

Shared-time programs require the cooperation of church and state in a plan which "shares" the children's time between religiously supported and state supported schools. The plans vary widely, and are difficult to categorize. Shared time is not as widely practiced as is released time. The reason is not difficult to find: states tend to award school funds on the basis of the school of attendance. Where the district has the children half a day and the parochial school the other half, the district gets only half the state aid it otherwise would get for the same child. However, where there is no serious "entanglement" between church and state, the courts are inclined to allow the practice. As in other litigation, each case must be judged on its own merits. The test: (a) there must be a *secular purpose* being served; (b) its *primary effect* must be neither to advance nor to inhibit religion; and (c) there must be no *undue entanglement* between government and religion. Even using the public school for religious meetings may in and of itself be considered "establishment" if there is any hint the board is either promoting or inhibiting religion in any way.

In-school teaching of moral values

More than nine out of every ten American children receive instruction through the public schools. Some of the plans that have been tried in an effort to inculcate moral and spiritual values are as follows: In Salt Lake City, the district developed the Ethics Education Program based on moral principles contained in the great American documents—the Mayflower Compact, the Declaration of Independence, and the Emancipation Proclamation. Another approach is that advocated by the Public Education Religion Studies Center (PERSC) at Wright State University in Ohio. The Center has developed curricula containing such courses as *the Bible as Literature* and *Comparative Religions of the World*. All religions are taught, not one. The plan has court sanction, and is widely used in the mid-western states.

The American Bar Association's Special Committee on Youth Education for Citizenship also has a "law-related" curriculum to teach children respect for the law. Finally, there is the values clarification movement based on the use of cases involving moral judgments that must be made by the children who participate in it. Values are taught as operational guidelines to the solution of moral dilemmas. There is also emphasis on self-discovery and understanding.

Silent meditation in schools for one minute a day is specifically required in four states, and several others have such a plan under study. In *Gaines v. Anderson*, 421 F.Supp. 337, 1976, a Massachusetts law was challenged that required one minute of silence daily "for meditation and prayer." The case was dismissed because children were not required to "pray" but only to remain silent during the meditation period. However, in *Malnak v. Maharishi Mahesh Yogi*, 440 F.Supp. 1284, N.J. 1977, the practice of Transcendental Meditation (TM) was declared to be an establishment of religion because TM contains religious principles not present in other meditation techniques of a secular nature.

Where prayers are offered voluntarily as a part of a secular meeting, such as at commencement or baccalaureate, they are protected because they are secular rather than sectarian in nature. Where the church building is used because it is more suitable for seating the audience, there is no church-state violation according to most courts of law.

When presented in the name of art, even religious presentations may be protected by freedom of expression. In New Jersey, the Commissioner of Education held that offering the rock opera *Jesus Christ Superstar* on stage by a group of students passed constitutional muster when offered as a work of dramatic art and music. *Jacobs v. Bd. of Educ. of Town of Phillipsburg,* N.J. Comm'r. of Education Dec., 1975.

FREEDOM OF WORSHIP IN THE SCHOOLS

The Supreme Court is more concerned that state and church should not mix than that there be freedom of worship in public schools. Thus, even voluntary prayers may be considered "suspect" if the schools use compulsion to achieve participation in them or in the program of ethical studies.

Parents may exercise freedom of religion by sending their children to private or parochial schools. They may even exempt their child from participation in some aspects of the curriculum they find objectionable, but this cannot be carried too far. For example, where the schools provide sex education classes, parents must show good cause to have their children exempted. And where parents objected to the use of movies, television, and other audiovisual projections as "worldly" and "evil," the school board was upheld in requiring that the children must be educated in this way despite the religious objections of the parents. *Davis v. Page,* 385 F.Supp. 395, N.H. 1974. The state, said the court, has a very real interest in providing its youth with a proper and enabling education. Also, the child has a right to receive it, a fact that outweighs the parental right to inculcate and mold their children's religious beliefs to conform to their own. A key factor in the decision was the pervasive use of audiovisual equipment in the school system, a technique approved by the court.

In Oklahoma, an Arapahoe Indian child was expelled from school for wearing his hair in traditional braids in contravention of a school regulation. The parents brought action alleging a violation of their religious freedom. The court ruled in favor of the school. *Hatch v. Goerke,* 502 F.2d 1189, Okla. 1974. Similarly, a male student who refused to enroll for R.O.T.C. on religious grounds was held to have a lesser interest than the state in teaching leadership, hygiene and first aid. *Sapp v. Renfro,* 372 F.Supp. 1192, Ga. 1974.

An Amish farmer objected to having to send his child to school in town, which was against the Amish religion. The Supreme Court upheld his right to an exemption from the compulsory attendance law. *Wisconsin v. Yoder,* 406 U.S. 205, 1972. And where the parent objects to the flag salute and will not allow his child to participate in it, the Supreme Court has ruled that "compulsion as here employed is not a permissible means for achieving national unity." (We were at war, and it was argued that refusal to salute the flag could be considered a subversive act). *West Virginia State Board of Educ. v. Barnette,* 319 U.S. 624, 1943.

Said the majority, "We think the action of the local officials in compelling the flag salute and pledge transcends constitutional limitations on their power and invades that sphere of intellect and spirit which it is the purpose of the First Amendment to our Constitution to reserve from all official control." (Reversing *Minersville Sch. Dist. v. Gobitis,* 310 U.S. 586, Pa. 1940.)

Because local boards are educating the young for future citizenship they must be particularly careful, said the Court, lest they "strangle the free mind at its source and teach youth to discount important principles of our government as mere platitudes." Even though we were at war, there were more important considerations than governmental unity—to wit, the right to freely practice one's religion without interference by the state.

CASES TO ILLUSTRATE CHURCH-STATE RELATIONS

The following cases make up the Ten Commandments governing the separation of church and state. They apply to all governmental bodies, not excluding local boards of education, "who have important, delicate, and highly discretionary functions, but none that they may not perform within the limits of the Bill of Rights." *W. Va. St. Bd. of Educ. v. Barnette, 1943.*

1. Thou shalt not require that all children be taught by public school teachers only. *Pierce v. Society of Sisters,* Oregon 1923.

2. Thou shalt not require a salute to the flag or the pledge of allegiance as a condition of attendance in the public schools. *W.Va. St. Bd. of Educ. v. Barnette,* 1943.

3. Thou shalt not use state funds for private and/or parochial schools if there is a prohibiting clause in the state constitution. *Cochran v. La.St.Bd. of Educ.* 1930; *Everson v. Bd. of Educ.,* N.J. 1947.

4. Thou shalt not make a practice of using the public schools for religious instruction. *McCollum v. Bd. of Education,* Ill. 1948.

5. Thou shalt not compose a prayer and require all public school children to recite it daily. *Engel v. Vitale,* N.Y. 1962.

6. Thou shalt not require daily reading of the Bible and the recitation of prayers on school grounds during school hours and under the supervision of school personnel. *Chamberlin v. Dade County Bd. of Pub. Instr.,* Fla. 1964.

7. Thou shalt not choose only that theory of the origin of man contained in the Book of Genesis as the exclusive basis for teaching children in public schools. *Epperson v. Ark.,* 1968.

8. Thou shalt not use public funds for the promotion of any religion. *Lemon v. Kurtzman,* Pa. and R.I., 1971.

9. Thou shalt not use public funds for the purchase of instructional materials and equipment for parochial schools nor for transportation of private school pupils on field trips. *Wolman v. Walter,* Ohio, 1977.

10. Thou shalt not require unreasonable "equivalency" of private and/or parochial schools in order for them to qualify for state approval. *Ky. St. Bd. of Educ. v. Hinton,* 1978.

3

Coping with Civil Rights Activists

YOU ARE VULNERABLE TO PERSONAL DAMAGE SUITS

Following the Civil War, the Congress passed seven civil rights acts to help in reconstruction of the South. Among these, two are still in active use by civil rights leaders and others who want to take advantage of the language contained in those acts to nail somebody who is "depriving anyone of a civil right." Unfortunately, you, as a school official, or even as a teacher, are vulnerable if you do deny someone a civil right protected under the Constitution or under the two viable acts. This chapter explores your vulnerability to personal damage suits, and what you can do to lessen your chances of being held responsible (hence liable) for deprivation of civil rights in the line of duty.

Civil Rights Act of 1866

The first Reconstruction Act of importance to school personnel today is the Civil Rights Act of 1866 (42 U.S.C. §1981). The Act provides that any person, no matter what his race or previous condition of servitude, "shall have the same right as white citizens," to "make and enforce contracts, to sue, be parties, and give evidence, to inherit, purchase, lease, sell, hold, and convey real and personal property," and be entitled "to the full and equal benefit of all laws and proceedings for the security of person and property." The Act also provides that such persons shall be subject to like punishment as whites, "and to none other, any law, statute, ordinance, regulation, or custom to the contrary notwithstanding." In practice, the law means that all persons have the right to own property, to buy and sell same, and to enjoy its occupancy, and to enforce contracts no matter what their social, economic, racial or personal circumstances may be.

The potential of the Act has not escaped the attention of civil rights activists, who are inclined to use it for such leverage as equal housing, employment opportunity adjustment, and similar purposes. It is particularly useful in "reverse discrimination" cases where contracts are involved. A case in point arose in Pennsylvania, where white teachers of the City of Erie sought compensatory and punitive damages because they were laid off in an order favoring minority employees rather than according to the district's seniority list. The furloughs were due to declining enrollments. Claiming the lay-offs denied them their right under Section 1981 to make and enforce contracts and deprived them of a property interest without due process of law, plaintiffs were able to convince the court that they were entitled to the protection of the Civil Rights Act of 1866. *Bacica v. Board of Educ. of School Dist. of City of Erie,* 451 F.Supp. 882, Pa. 1978.

Awarding of attorney's fees in Section 1981 cases is discretionary with the court. In denying paintiff *Bacica* attorney's fees, although he was clearly the prevailing party, the court pointed out that the mountains of evidence presented by plaintiff's attorney failed to clearly outline the controlling facts, causing the judge to make his determination "only after considerable effort and prodding." This lack of evidence so hindered the court that it became a "burden on the court which delayed the resolution of the matter." Also since there was insufficient evidence on which to fix damages of those plaintiffs found to be entitled to damages, the court merely issued an order fixing liability and providing for later assessment of damages (presumably to be negotiated).

Similarly, the Supreme Court of South Carolina held that termination of a white teacher on the grounds that she would not accept transfer to another school did not constitute "reverse discrimination." *Riggs v. Laurens Dist. 56,* 248 S.E.2d 306, S.C. 1978. The teacher maintained that the board's action in requiring that a white teacher transfer to another school and in picking a white teacher rather than a black teacher for such transfer in order to satisfy the requirements of a Department of HEW order denied her protection under the Civil Rights Act of 1866. The court, however, refused relief, and held that the transfer, which did not involve loss of pay or benefits, was not a violation of her constitutional rights.

Civil Rights Act of 1871

By far the greater engine for social change in relation to individual rights is the Civil Rights Act of 1871 (42 U.S.C. §1983). The pertinent section is quoted earlier in Chapter 1 (see page 35) and can be summarized here in a few words: *Any person who acting under the aegis of the state deprives another person of a civil right is liable to that party injured in any action at law, suit in equity, or other proper proceeding for redress.* The Supreme Court has ruled that individual board members may be held personally liable if they knew or rightfully should have known that what they were doing under color of state law would deprive a person of a civil right. *Wood v. Stickland,* 420 U.S. 308, Ark. 1975. There is always the tendency once your actions are challenged to overreact—to push back against any initial actions by civil rights leaders and activists. The courts, however, are constantly reminding school boards that their decisions must be fair and impartial because biased action by the board members can be considered a "conspiracy" to deny a civil right for which the individual board member must pay. Wrongful action on the part of the board may cause stigmatization of the reputation of an individual, or deny to that person a right guaranteed under the constitution. Nuisance suits continue to plague boards because there is the potential danger that a plaintiff may collect, if not against an individual board member, at least against the board as a corporate body. In 1978, the Supreme Court reversed an earlier stand and held that boards as corporations may be held liable if their policy or custom forms a pattern of discrimination. *Monell v. Department of Social Services,* 98 S.Ct. 2018, N.Y. 1978, reversing *Monroe v. Pape,* 365 U.S. 167, Ill. 1961.

The key words in determining whether you or your board will be liable in damages for deprivation of a civil right are these: (1) *For individuals acting in concert as a conspiracy*—if you knew, or reasonably should have known, that your actions, taken under color of state law, would deprive someone of a civil right; (2) *For your board as a corporate body*—if board policy or custom caused deprivation, the board may be liable. Just whether or not you are within these limits is of course a matter of judgment. That is why you should avail yourself of a better-than-average school attorney to turn to in times when civil rights activism runs rampant in your district.

SOME SAMPLE SECTION 1983 CASES

Whether plaintiffs in actions against the board shall name the board or individual members as defendants rests with plaintiff's attorney. Now that the Supreme Court has decided that boards in their corporate capacity can be considered "persons" for purposes of Section 1983 actions, plaintiffs may join both board and individual members in the suit. It will then be up to the court to decide whether the deprivation complained of is due to the board's policy and custom or whether it was the result of some employee's zeal. The Court made it clear that *Monell* does not mean that the plaintiff can rely on *respondeat superior* (the master is responsible for the acts of his servants). Therefore, if the deprivation is the result of the board's failure, then the board as a body is liable; if of the individual employee, then that person is liable on his or her own. This will raise some interesting discussion as to whether an individual employee, say an administrator, was acting under a policy or custom of the board's, and the board must therefore bear the responsibility for his actions taken in good faith and in line of duty. On the other hand, is the action complained of that of an individual who deliberately and maliciously violated the civil rights of some individual? For example, the Wyoming Supreme Court ruled that a local superintendent "maliciously" violated the civil rights of a teacher he recommended be fired "for immorality" and assessed him $4,600 in damages under Section 1983. Despite his claim of a "qualified, good faith immunity" against personal liability, the superintendent was held liable. The court ruled that to qualify for a good faith immunity, the superintendent must demonstrate by a preponderance of the evidence that he acted without malicious intent, and that he was not aware that his conduct would deprive the teacher of a constitutional right (here the property right to his job; he was a tenured

teacher). Since he was unable to bear the burden of proof, the superintendent was assessed damages and attorney's fees under 42 U.S.C. §1983. *Albert v. Holso,* 584 P.2d 1009, Wyo. 1978.

Figure 3-1

SECTION 1983 CASES LOST BY THE BOARD

- A teacher who was dismissed for being active in the teachers' union sued for damages. The court held that the board could not punish a teacher for exercising a constitutionally protected right. Individual board members had to pay from their own pockets.

- A male teacher was told to shave off his beard or lose his job. When he refused to shave, the board dismissed him. Individual members of the board had to pay not only back salary but also punitive damages (the teacher developed an ulcer) and attorney's fees, a total of $600 each for the superintendent and five board members.

- A 27-year-old New Yorker who was locked into a mentally retarded class throughout 12 years of public school was awarded $500,000 by the court on the grounds that the board was negligent. The court emphasized that the injury was not due to malpractice.

- A girl who was thought to be concealing marijuana paraphernalia was required to strip down to her underwear. The search was unproductive. She was suspended for five days. The court held school officials liable in damages for deprivation of the girl's right to be free from unreasonable search.

The large number of Section 1983 suits demonstrates the importance of this "sleeping giant" which was revived after 100 years to turn the engine of social change. The *Monell* decision will surely not cause these numbers to decrease—quite the contrary. It behooves the board member and the school administrator to learn more about this potential hazard, and to govern themselves accordingly.

One threshold question in a court action is that of jurisdiction—does the court have the right to step in? Before *Monell,* some federal district courts declined jurisdiction on the ground that the board was not a "person" under Section 1983. Now that the bar has been removed, courts will accept cases that they otherwise would have rejected on the basis of lack of jurisdiction.

Figure 3-2

SECTION 1983 CASES WON BY THE BOARD

- The board banned some books from the curriculum, whereupon the teachers claimed denial of academic freedom. The court ruled that since the teachers had bargained away their right to control the selection of textbooks, the board had not acted unconstitutionally in banning the books.

- A teacher was non-renewed and it was discovered that her performance evaluation forms had been altered. She claimed that the implication that she was dishonest was sufficient to "stigmatize" her reputation, but the court could not agree.

- A student who was graduated from high school with minimum reading and computation skills sued the board for $5 million, charging malpractice. The case was handed down by the same court that held a board negligent for failure to discover and remedy a normal boy's assignment to a mentally retarded class for 12 years. The court denied his claim.

- A teacher's suit against the board for dismissal alleged to be in violation of Section 1983 was thrown out because the court held that the statute of limitations specifying three years in which to file a suit for damages had run out.

Nor is it always necessary for a civil rights activist claiming deprivation of a civil right to exhaust administrative remedies before turning to the federal courts. The weight of judicial authority is that these administrative avenues do not invariably have to be traversed before the federal courts will claim jurisdiction.

In deciding whether the statute of limitations has been exhausted, the federal courts will make that judgment on the time period specified in the appropriate state statute. Where the statutory limit of "the most analogous state statute" is one year, the courts will adopt that period of time as the guide to determine whether the statute of limitations has run out.

It appears that the Eleventh Amendment no longer furnishes immunity for school board members or other state officials. As you may recall, the Eleventh had been interpreted by the courts to apply immunity of citizens of one state against suit from another state without the former's consent. The deciding case was related to the death and injury of students on the Kent State University campus on May 4, 1970. *Krause v. Rhodes*, 416 U.S. 232, Ohio 1977.

You may defeat a suit for damages under Section 1983 if you can show that you acted in good faith and did not violate "settled, undisputed rights" of an individual that you "knew or reasonably should have known" existed. One who acts with malice loses his good faith immunity forthwith.

WHERE LIABILITY ORIGINATED

The controlling case relating to individual liability under Section 1983 was *Wood v. Strickland*, 420 U.S. 308 Ark. 1975. The question before the Supreme Court was whether school board members, as individuals, could be held liable for deprivation of a civil right. Plaintiffs were girls who had spiked the punch at a school function and were expelled from school without full recognition of their due process rights. Justice White delivered the reasoning of the majority, using in part these words:

> ...In the specific context of school discipline, we hold that a school board member is not immune from liability under Sec. 1983 if he knew or reasonably should have known that the action he took within his sphere of official responsibility would violate the constitutional rights of the student affected, or if he took the action with the malicious intention to cause a deprivation of a constitutional right or other injury to the student. That is not to say that school board members are "charged with predicting the future course of constitutional law." ... A compensatory award will be appropriate only if the school board member has acted with such an impermissible motivation or with such disregard of the student's clearly established constitutional rights that his action cannot reasonably be characterized as being in good faith.

What those historic words mean is only now becoming clear. Gone are the days when the board could dismiss teachers or expel pupils with impunity. Where the deprivation is slight, minimal due process is needed, such as in the suspension of a student from school. Where the substantive rights are more pronounced, such as the loss of three-months' schooling as in *Wood*, the Court has said that more substantial due process rights are due. In general, the more substantial the rights involved, the more careful the board must be in according the individual his or her full constitutional rights. This rule of thumb places a distinct responsibility on school officials to determine how substantial the threatened right is, and to guard it accordingly. While lawyers may differ on how substantial the right may be, the board still must act as the conscience of the situation—must recognize where an act you take may be considered to be arbitrary, capricious or illegal. This does not exactly "charge you with knowing constitutional law," but merely warns you that where constitutional rights are at stake, you should ask the question, "Is what we are doing fundamentally fair?" If there is a doubt, you should not proceed, or at least not with the alacrity with which you had been accustomed to proceeding in the past.

THE CATEGORIES FOR SUING UNDER SECTION 1983

Problems involving civil rights of others break down into eight categories:

1) contract questions regarding bids and pension or insurance benefits;
2) constitutional questions regarding race, sex, age, native language, dress or hair codes;
3) constitutional questions on such matters as union activities or confidentiality of school records;
4) program deficiencies where malpractice or negligence may be involved;
5) personal torts such as defamation, libel, slander, assault and battery;
6) bodily injury and infliction of pain and/or emotional distress;
7) taxation questions, such as unfair rates or illegal levies; and
8) miscellaneous "wrongful acts" including, for example, dismissal, failure to promote, and school closings.

These general rules apply in Section 1983 cases:

1. The action taken must be "under color of state law." Since the board is in charge of a subdivision of state government, the school district, it is likely that any action taken by the board will be considered "state action." Where, on the other hand, an

internal church conflict arises, the courts will declare no jurisdiction under Section 1983 and will leave the parties as it
found them.

2. Whether a grievance is real or imaginary is for the court to
decide.
3. Whether the injury or deprivation is intentional or unintentional is not the issue—whether in fact a deprivation has occurred is more to the point.
4. Plaintiffs must show that a constitutionally guaranteed right
has been denied.
5. The burden of proof then shifts to the state to show that what it
did was (a) necessary under the circumstances and (b) not
discriminatory in any way.
6. If the state cannot show that it took the action to fulfill a valid
state purpose, and that it could do it in this way only as the
best and most equitable means of doing justice, the plaintiff
will prevail.
7. If the state can show that it was meeting a valid state purpose
in the action taken, and that there was no deprivation of a
protected right, the board/administrator will prevail.

"Wrongful acts" are those board actions performed under color
of state law which deprive someone of a constitutional guarantee without due process of law. The Supreme Court held that board members
and administrators lose their normal immunity protection where they
knew or reasonably should have known that what they were doing in
depriving someone of a civil right was unconstitutional. Plaintiffs may
recover either damages or other benefits where the action taken is
unconstitutional, depending on the way the suit is filed.

LOWERING YOUR LITIGATION PROFILE

The best hedge against possible unwanted litigation is to shore up
your own establishment—lower your litigation profile so that when
litigation comes you can say you have done what you can to lessen the
probability that damages will be awarded. The following actions taken
well in advance of civil rights litigation will prove helpful not in eliminat-
ing litigation entirely but in lightening the blow when it does fall.

Develop litigation-proof written board policies. Check your policy
against the due process standard: (a) that no person shall be con-

demned unheard; and (b) that *every* judge (sometimes the board is the judge) must be free from bias. Where the board sits in judgment, can it act in an impartial way? Would it be better for due process fairness if you were to appoint a panel to hear the factual evidence, leaving the ultimate decision to the board? The National School Boards Association can help, and your state association very likely will assist in developing defensible policies. All you need to do is contact these organizations for help.

Rely more on legal counsel. Being forewarned is being fore-armed. Don't wait until litigation arises, then try to stamp it out. Get a good school's attorney and tell him or her you want a report on your district's vulnerability to civil rights actions. Assess your vulnerability to suit; after all, life is a game of playing the odds. Then try to reduce the odds you will be sued successfully by anybody that walks in the door.

Keep your cool. Count to ten. Don't try "to show those guys you mean business." Many court cases would never reach litigation if boards could learn *not* to overreact.

Establish due process procedures. Do students facing suspension or expulsion have machinery to file grievances? Do teachers insist on adequate procedures to get it out in the open? Be sure that the ma-chinery is there and in place *before* a suit is filed. When you wind up in court, it may be too late.

Communicate. Keep avenues of communication open. Play it all out in the open. Take the initiative in making decisions, and let the people know what those decisions are. Assess responsibility for com-municating. Make individuals accountable for certain parts of the plan. And have a plan that is discussed, tried, and implemented all along the line. But the greatest of these is *communication*.

Involve others. Arrange for input from all public(s). Invite help from the community. Insist on feedback from outsiders. Practice joint problem-solving, insist on shared decision-making, play down the "es-tablishment," play up the people.

Bargain. One means of avoiding court action is to negotiate. Bargaining can often settle potential conficts in-house where other action may lead to litigation. Procedures for handling reductions in staff, salaries, discipline and control of students, and civil rights of employees can often be negotiated out of existence. Be willing to bargain.

Use your conscience. Always ask, "Is it fair to all concerned?" Does it protect both the individual and the state's interests? Is there need to be so authoritarian? Do we have to show everybody we're running the show? Sometimes a word of caution can head off reams of litigation. Fair is fair. "State-operated schools may not be enclaves of totalitarianism," is the way the Supreme Court said it. "School officials do not possess absolute authority over their charges. Children both in and out of school are 'persons' under our Constitution, and they do not shed their constitutional rights at the schoolhouse gate."

That's plain enough. The smoothing hand of caution is better than the rough boot of expediency. Keeping your head when others lose theirs may spell the difference between your being held liable in a Section 1983 suit and being home free.

The cause you save may be your own.

4

You and Tort Liability

YOUR LIABILITY FOR TORT

Every individual is liable for his or her own negligence. This principle of law came down to Americans from the English, who held that each person must bear the burden of his or her own wrongful acts. Ordinarily, no one can be held liable if he or she does not owe somebody a duty, since that is the first requirement. School board members and administrators owe children a safe place in which to study and play. The state, it is reasoned, has taken children away from their natural parents, and placed them in a state institution, the public school. There, the parents can rest easy in the knowledge that the child is protected against injury—that the school is "a safe place." But sometimes the opposite is true—schools are large, impersonal places with any number of opportunities for injuries to occur. Adults in charge of the child are liable for two reasons: (1) the school is considered to be a "safe place," and (2) the state has created a legal fiction which makes adults liable—the doctrine of *in loco parentis* (in place of the parent). This doctrine of law states that if a person owes a child a duty and breaches the duty owed, and an injury occurs that "but for" the breach would not have occurred, that person can be held liable for damages in tort. A look at these conditions will help you, the administrator, to avoid needless litigation and protect your own personal interests and those of the district against possible erosion of your resources.

School is a safe place

The state has undertaken the education of all children within its borders, and has set up public schools for that purpose.

Figure 4-1

FACTS ABOUT TORTS

- A tort is an actionable wrong other than breach of contract that results in an injury.
- The injured party has to demonstrate that he or she has suffered a loss.
- Tort suits are civil rather than criminal actions in a majority of cases.
- Torts include both intentional and unintentional injuries to others.
- You can be liable for injury to others only if negligence is proved.
- Courts will seek only to restore an injured party to the same position he or she had before the injury occurred.
- The law imposes a duty on all individuals to refrain from injuring others.
- Courts will award damages in tort action suits for actual loss, for punitive reasons (to punish the tortfeasor), and/or for compensatory reasons (attorney's fees).
- Relief to the injured party, besides monetary damages, may include mandamus (court order to do something), injunction (cease something which is being done), or habeas corpus (produce the person for trial).
- An individual is responsible for his or her own torts and not ordinarily those of others.
- Negligence is gauged by one's ability to foresee that injury may result unless some action is taken to prevent it.
- The standard of care needed is that of an average, prudent person under the same circumstances.

Since the child is away from home—away from his natural parents—someone must be found to look after the child and protect him or her from harm. Obviously, school boards are responsible for seeing that the schools are safe. However, in practice, this duty is turned over to the employees—superintendent, principals, teachers, and others.

Figure 4-2

THE COURT TEST FOR NEGLIGENCE

In order for a person or persons to be liable in tort where an injury has occurred, all three of the following conditions must be present:

- *First,* the defendant must have *owed* the plaintiff a *duty*. Ordinarily, the board owes students in public schools the assumption that the school is a safe place in which to study, work, and play.

- *Second,* the defendant must have *breached the duty* owed the plaintiff, that is, he or she must have done something that he should not have done, or he failed to do something that he should have done to cause the injury complained of.

- *Third,* the breach of duty must form the proximate cause of the injury, that is, there must be a link between the doing of something or the failure to do something out of which grows the injury and without which it would not have occurred.

It is the plaintiff's burden to show that (a) he or she has suffered an injury, and (b) that the injury suffered is the direct result of the plaintiff's breach of the duty owed. Whether or not as a matter of fact the proof has been established is for the jury to determine on instructions from the judge. The jury handles matters of fact (negligence), while the judge handles points of law (instructs the jury). School board members and administrators are not immune from tort liability if it can be proved that they owed the injured party a duty, that they breached the duty owed, and that the breach of the duty owed was the proximate cause of the injury.

Where an injury occurs, it is then the duty of the courts to decide, on the evidence, who is at fault. In Colorado, a child was injured when hit by a rock thrown on the school grounds by an unknown individual. Parents brought suit against the district, joining the teacher, principal, local superintendent, county superintendent and members of the school board as defendants. The court ruled that none of the others would be liable unless there was negligence on the part of the teacher in charge of the playground. Since she could not have "under constant and unremitting scrutiny the precise spots wherein every phase of play activity is being pursued," the injury was an accident for which the teacher was not liable. Inasmuch as the teacher had not been negligent, the others were likewise not at fault. The case was dismissed. *Carroll v. Fitzsimmons*, 384 P.2d 81, Colo. 1963.

A tour of the school plant with the reasonable individual reveals many areas of possible tort liability. Most litigation arises from such hazards as those associated with the gymnasium, the chemistry laboratory, shop classes and buses. School cafeterias come in for another share of suits for damages, followed by athletic events and school grounds. Many of these involve legal questions related to whether the school has provided sufficient supervision for a particular activity. Being somewhat removed from these hazards, boards and superintendents have been held not liable where they have instituted a program of supervision, so long as it can be established that a teacher or other school employee has been put in charge. Also, in cases where the district has been declared negligent, the board members are protected from personal liability either through a state immunity to tort liability, or through the purchase of liability insurance. Consequently, the threat of loss of personal funds by school board members and administrators is slight, provided the district is not maintaining a nuisance, and school officials are acting without malice. The potential dangers for libel and slander and malpractice are more compelling, and these will be taken up later in this chapter.

In loco parentis

Some adult must be in charge, and the administrator and board usually fulfill their legal duty by assigning this responsibility to a member of the staff. The standard of care for that individual, who can be held personally liable where negligence is proved, is that foresight which the ordinarily prudent parent would have shown under the same or similar conditions. Since this standard is different under different circumstances, it is for the jury to decide, as a matter of fact, whether the teacher's actions would compare favorably with that of a prudent parent, given the set of circumstances in each case.

Like the "safe place" doctrine above, the *in loco parentis* responsibility is not of major concern to the administrator and school board member so long as these individuals have assigned supervisory duties to competent employees. Ordinarily, superintendents are not liable for the negligence of other employees—each individual is liable for his or her own wrongful acts and no others. There is one notable exception, however—where a superior officer, such as a superintendent, knowingly assigns a subordinate who is found to be incompetent, to a position of responsibility, and injury occurs due to that subordinate's negligence, the door may be open to the claim that the superintendent's lack of care was a breach of the duty owed the injured party. We turn now to a consideration of the possible defenses against charges of tort liability.

DEFENSES AGAINST TORT LIABILITY SUITS

School personnel have several defenses available in case a court action is brought claiming negligence. Only a few states have not abrogated the governmental immunity doctrine, and still hold that school personnel, in their official capacity, cannot be sued since they are performing a state-approved function. The number of such states, however, is down to less than seven, so that it can be said that governmental immunity has almost disappeared as a defense against tort liability claims. Another defense is that you have given the responsibility to another employee, who can then be sued individually for damages. Other defenses are as follows.

Assumption of risk

You can defend against negligence charges by saying that the injured party assumed a risk. This is most often used where a student, injured in interscholastic sports, brings suit against the district or one or more individuals. One who goes out for a sport assumes some risk, and unless it can be shown that another individual such as the coach was negligent, the student must bear (must assume) the risk involved in going out for the sport.

Contributory negligence

Some injuries are so obviously foolish that you can say that the student—or other individual—brought it on himself or herself by allowing the injury to happen. The younger the student, the less likely is this defense to work. Where, however, the student is old enough to foresee, or reasonably have been anticipated to have the foresight to see, that what he did would result in an injury, the student may be called on to bear the burden because of his own contributory negligence.

Comparative negligence

Several states have comparative negligence statutes, which pro rate the negligence among those involved. Thus, the jury might find that the student was 40 percent negligent and the teacher 60 percent negligent in assessing damages. Inasmuch as not all the states have adopted comparative negligence statutes, you will need to become acquainted with your own jurisdiction to determine whether this defense is available to you.

Unavoidable accident

You can say that the injury was the result of an unavoidable accident, and that to expect you to foresee that an injury would result from the situation here involved would amount to clairvoyance. The law does not require superhuman foresight, only that possessed by someone of average intelligence and prudence. When you have done what you could, the courts will generally decree that teachers and others in charge cannot reasonably be guarantors of student safety, and give you the benefit of the doubt.

PERSONAL TORT LIABILITY

School boards and superintendents sometimes become polarized, leading to inevitable charges of tort liability. In New Jersey, for example, the president of a local board wrote an open letter to a newspaper about another member of the board. The letter, addressed to the member, and signed by the president, expressed surprise "that the truth concerns you," and declared that "you have become so desperate in your destructive drive to divide and conquer that you now twist and distort your previous untruths, half-truths and inferences." The member filed a tort action suit against the president claiming libel. The president countered by saying she was only defending her own

---

Figure 4-3

SOME SAMPLE TORT LIABILITY SCHOOL CASES

- A mother took her elementary school son and his schoolmate away from the site of a wrestling tournament. The latter was injured while refueling the car when the son intentionally ignited some gasoline on the other's clothing. Parents of the injured boy brought suit against the district in failing to supervise the tournament properly. The court held for the school district. Alaska 1977.

- A student fell 18 feet from the top of a slide fire escape on the outside of his school. The fire escape was not functional and the court held that the district had been negligent in not removing it from the building. Oregon 1976.

- A high school student was killed when he fell backwards during a bout of "slap boxing" in the school gym at noon, although the district had posted rules against such an activity. The court held the district liable for failure to supervise. "Even high school students need supervision now and then," said the court in ruling that lack of supervision caused the accident to happen. Calif. 1970.

- A student was injured when in a school play someone unknown substituted loaded cartridges instead of blanks. The school principal was not held liable. N. Mex. 1969.

- A student was injured by a pencil tossed by another student while the teacher was absent from the room. Parents of the injured student brought suit against the teacher and the school district. The court held that if the jury could find that the teacher's presence would have prevented the injury, then her absence from the room could be considered the proximate cause of the injury. N.Y. 1962.

---

reputation "against numerous charges and allegations published by the plaintiff." The board met and enacted a motion to use public funds to defend the suit on the grounds that the action was taken on behalf of the entire board. The court ruled that the action complained of was not the action of the entire board, but only that of the president acting alone. Said the court, "When a board member does a wrongful act, whereby injury to another results, he or she is liable therefor, not because he is a school official or board member, but because he is the person doing the act." *Errington v. Mansfield,* 195 A.2d 670, N.J. 1963.

Two board members came to the school and questioned one of the students, a 15-year old girl, and made accusations in the presence of others of her unchastity, and threatened to send her to reform school if she did not confess the rumors. The board members were held liable for assault. *Johnson v. Sampson,* 208 N.W. 814, Minn. 1926. And in California, a superintendent published an open letter in the community newspaper in which he accused two boys of wrongdoing and of "serious violations of manners, morals and discipline" while away on a band trip. The board was held liable for the damage to the boys' reputations. *Elder v. Anderson,* 23 Cal.Rptr. 48, Cal. 1960.

Also in Califorina, a group of school trustees asked questions of various people in the community about the superintendent's fitness. Later, they discussed such matters with the district attorney and the county superintendent. The superintendent brought an action for libel, claiming they had made disparaging remarks against her. The court pointed out the distinction between the actions of the board, as a corporate body, the acts of the trustees individually, and acts of the school officials, here the county superintendent. Concerning the immunity of the school board as a corporate body, the court said, "The district is immune from tort liability for the alleged acts of the trustees within the sphere of their authority."

The acts of the individual trustees, however, were a different matter. The court held they could be sued "because their remarks would obviously make it difficult and burdensome for the superintendent to perform her contractual obligations." It was for the jury to decide whether the trustees, acting as individuals, had stepped outside their normal immunity protection and thus had become liable for defamation of character. *Lipman v. Brisbane Elem. Sch. Dist.,* 359 P.2d 465, Cal. 1961.

CONSTITUTIONAL TORTS

A recent newcomer to the field of tort liability is the so-called "constitutional tort," or wrongful acts or omissions tort. School board members, say the courts, can be held liable for any actual or alleged errors, misstatements, misleading statements, acts, omissions, negligence or breach of duty in the discharge of their duties, both individually and collectively. These torts are related not so much to physical injury caused to others, as to a deprivation of some rights guaranteed under the Constitution, the state constitution, or any statute, ordinance, or board regulation. Discussion of the implications of this tort (sometimes called errors and omissions) has been divided here. See Chapter 3, "Coping with Civil Rights Activists," and Chapter 5, "Working Smoothly with Parents' Groups." Recommendations were given in Chapter 3 on how to avoid needless litigation in the errors and omissions area. The best defense, an indemnity policy for the entire board and employees, will be discussed here.

Most cases fall into eight categories of the law. The boxes on these pages include at least one sample case from each of the litigation areas. These are not at all exhaustive, only illustrative of the kinds of cases that may arise in each category. Literally hundreds of cases have been filed in which school boards are involved, and new ones are being filed daily. You will want to look these over and familiarize yourself with the potential areas of litigation in the daily operation of the schools.

Figure 4-4

SAMPLE CASES INVOLVING CIVIL RIGHTS

CATEGORY ONE: CONTRACT MATTERS

- A superintendent was actively engaged in supporting some friends for office on the board of education. Unfortunately, his candidates lost, whereupon the incumbent board dismissed him. Claiming denial of a constitutional right, the superintendent sued to be restored to his job. The court ruled against him. "In the game of politics," said the judge, "one who supports this candidate or that must realize that his choice may lose, and be prepared to suffer the consequences that may eventually occur."

- Bids were taken on construction of a schoolhouse. The board, however, refused to accept the low bid, and the low bidder sued, claiming that in concluding that the low bidder "was irresponsible," the board had defamed his character. The court held that the board had acted in good faith and within its realm of authority. The lowest bidder must be the lowest "responsible" bidder, not necessarily the lowest money bid. So long as the board had not acted in a malicious fashion, the court would not intervene to make it change its mind.

Figure 4-4 (continued)

CATEGORY TWO: CONSTITUTIONAL QUESTIONS INVOLVING DISCRIMINATION

- School children wore black armbands to protest the war in Vietnam. They were told they must remove the armbands or go home. They contested the board's action in court. The Supreme Court ruled that in its zeal to eradicate black armbands, but at the same time allowing other insignia to be worn, the board was guilty of discrimination against the children who were acting within their constitutional rights in wearing black armbands to school.

- A high school girl was denied the right to play on the boys' tennis team, although she was ranked third in the state. She brought suit challenging the board's decision. The court ruled that since there was no comparable girls' tennis program in her high school, and she could demonstrate an ability to compete on an equal footing with boys, the board's action was discriminatory, hence illegal.

CATEGORY THREE: CONSTITUTIONAL QUESTIONS OTHER THAN DISCRIMINATION

- A teacher's contract was non-renewed, whereupon she sought reinstatement in a federal district court. The teacher had been active in the teachers' union and she claimed her dismissal was in retaliation for such a protected activity. The court agreed, and held that her civil rights had been denied her.

- Children "sat in" in a public school but their actions were peaceful and did not substantially disrupt the on-going program of studies. When they were expelled for their activities, the students brought suit against the board. The court ruled that the board could not take such an action in the absence of disruption or riot.

CATEGORY FOUR: TAXATION

- Disenchanted taxpayers brought suit against the board, claiming it had illegally used public money to influence a state-wide election of the Proposition 13 genre. The court held that the board had indeed used moneys for a specific purpose not authorized in the law, and issued a cease and desist order against further use of school moneys for this purpose.

Figure 4-4 (continued)

CATEGORY FIVE: PROGRAM DEFICIENCIES

- A student claimed he had been denied his rights when he failed to get a job or gain entrance into a college upon high school graduation. Charging "malpractice," he brought suit under Section 1983. The court, however, said that he had had the same opportunities to learn as other students, and that the failure had been due in part to his own lack of motivation.

- Crippled children who were excluded from the "mainstream" brought a Section 1983 suit against members of the board of education, claiming program deficiencies. The court examined the charge and held that the board had not been at fault since there was a program of sorts for them, and that they would probably do better in segregated classes than in the regular "mainstreamed" classrooms.

CATEGORY SIX: BODILY INJURY AND EMOTIONAL DISTRESS

- A girl who told her principal in private some intimate details about herself was later moved to sue on the grounds that the information became "common knowledge around the school." The court held that if she could prove it, she would have a cause of action against the principal, if not the school board.

CATEGORY SEVEN: PERSONAL TORTS

- A teacher who had been denied renewal of her contract sought for and received a hearing before the board of education. At the hearing, certain facts were brought out by the school's attorney which the teacher claimed were slanderous. She sued each of the board members as individuals. She was unsuccessful. When she requested an open rather than a closed hearing, ruled the court, she had opened the door to whatever facts might come out at that hearing. She could not have her cake and eat it too.

Figure 4-4 (continued)

CATEGORY EIGHT: MISCELLANEOUS CLAIMS

• A teacher in a small rural community lived in a trailer near the schoolhouse. In the fall, her boyfriend moved in with her and they lived together until the board, finding this an embarrrassment in a small town where everyone in the district knew what was going on, asked her to change her living arrangements. When she refused, they fired her. The court ruled that the board's action was not a denial of her right to work inasmuch as the board had held numerous meetings at which the teacher had had ample opportunity to present her side of the controversy.

5

Working Smoothly with Parents' Groups

A NATIONAL CREED

If there is any fixed star in the educational firmament, it is that the schools belong to the people. The "common school" has a long and impressive history—it helped the westward course of history, it educated the young of millions of immigrants to our shores, and finally, it put men on the moon. No one can argue with success—and as an institution the public schools have been just that—successful far beyond our fondest dreams.

Yet public schools as they were known during the past 200 years have become an enigma if not indeed an anachronism. Where do we go from here? Obviously, some new direction is needed, one that will give the people a hand in the making of decisions that affect their children in school. The problem is not that parents want a piece of the action—they have asked for and been granted that voice all along. What is new is that better ways must be found to turn up that voice so that its volume is equal to that of boards and administrators. Despite a long history of parent involvement, there has now occurred a massive "erosion of lay control." One reason is related to size: in 1900, there were some 110,000 local school districts each having a board of education. In this set-up, one board member represented 138 citizens. Today, with less than 17,000 school districts, each board member represents nearly 2,500 people. An obvious result of that change is that the individual citizen seems less able than before to influence decision-making in the public schools.

Another trend is toward polarization in education. School board members, like their counterparts in city government, have been elected to office on promises to handle certain issues. One superintendent who had been the head educator in a large city for 20 years said on retirement that he could count on one hand the divided votes on the board during that time. Today, one has to dig back into records to find that many *unanimous* votes, illustrating that board members are less willing to compromise their promises to the electorate and get on with the business of educating children. These are "hard" issues they face, and one does not compromise on principle. It is not uncommon to find board members suing other members of the same board—for fraud, misrepresentation, withholding of vital information, you name it. In such a political climate, it is no wonder that the good of the average student is sometimes forgotten and the schools made a battleground for adult differences and for ideological confrontation on issues facing boards of education today.

Parents are the natural advocates of their children. In school situations, however, their wishes come into conflict with rules and regulations of the board of education. Mothers and fathers are not always familiar with the laws under which the board operates. They hesitate to seek their rights for fear of possible harm to their children. Suits in equity are serious steps for parents to take, especially where the process is costly, often lengthy and exhausting, and by the time the case is decided, the issue is moot. Yet most wise administrators want and actively seek the participation of parents, not only to get feedback but also to "run a democratic ship." However, sheer size often defeats their purpose. Bureaucracy sets in, and schools often are run like a factory or business. Teacher militancy has created a louder voice for employee involvement. State legislatures have tended to usurp powers earlier enjoyed by boards of education. Memberships in voluntary associations have tied the boards' hands. The result is that boards, long the strongest governmental units in existence, have become one of the weakest in terms of their ability to deal realistically with any particular problem requiring their discretion.

By far the greatest erosion of law and board power came through the intervention of the courts. Beginning with the *Brown* desegregation decision in 1954, and continuing down to the present, the Supreme Court and lesser courts have limited the right of a local board to operate the schools apart from intervention by outside agencies. Despite repeated efforts to decentralize schools, demand accountability in their operation, and cut their budgetary demands, the local board has less power today than it did at the turn of the century. Such emasculation of board power has been interpreted by citizens in various ways— as capitulation, apathy, neglect, or insensitivity to educational needs of children. Quite the opposite can be and often is true; board members are not sure of their authority, tend to think that whatever they do will be insufficient, too late, or too little to solve the problem. But there is an old saying in schools: *If you don't use your power, you lose your power.*

This "vacuum" theory of power assumes that where no action is taken to solve a problem, a vacuum is created into which flow other forces that seek to take over the power left hanging. The procrastinating board is the helpless board. It is the board's duty to act—not act wisely, but act. Failure to act is a signal to outsiders to organize and to

---

Figure 5-1

WHAT ARE THE RIGHTS OF CHILDREN?

What are these rights? In brief, they are:

1. The right to a free education.
2. The right to be protected against harm.
3. The right to inspect student records.
4. The right to special education for students with special needs.
5. The right to due process of law.
6. The right to equal educational opportunity.
7. The right to freedom from unreasonable search and seizure.
8. The right to freedom of expression.
9. The right to freedom of religion and conscience.

From D. Schimmel and L. Fishcher, *The Rights of Parents in the Education of Their Children,* Columbia, MD: National Committee for Citizens in Education, 1977, p. 1.

---

descend on the board with all kinds of weird ideas, and the board is acted *upon* instead of acting *in* and *through* the powers it already has.

The best plan therefore is to act in concert with others—citizens, parents, taxpayers, the state department of education, the legislature, and any and all parties to the educational scheme. But it must be declared at the outset that the board is going to have the last word, come hell or high water. The legislature in its wisdom has designated the school board as the local decision-making body and that is good enough for the courts. It is only when the board fails to exercise its power that it loses it entirely.

This "authority by default" gives away power that rightfully belongs to the board. The problem then is to design a plan that will work smoothly and harmoniously with parents and other groups in providing the kind of education they want for their children now living in and to live on in the future in a democratic form of government.

SOME CASES IN POINT

If parents and others want a piece of the action and don't get it, we can learn a lot from the litigation that has come up in which board actions have been challenged. Here are some representative cases in which groups have come up against the board and challenged its wrongful acts or its acts of omission in the performance of its duty to educate. Read them, and apply them to your local situation. The limits of the law can be discerned from what the board could or could not do in any given situation.

- A Mississippi school board, distressed because public school teachers were not sending their children to public schools but had enrolled them instead in a racially segregated private school, passed a resolution that it would terminate all public school teacher-parents who sent their children to private schools. Three of the teachers who were later dismissed under the resolution sued to regain their jobs, claiming parental prerogative. The federal district court ruled that their First Amendment rights had not been violated, especially since the district was under a desegregation order. The U.S. Circuit Court of Appeals for the Fifth Circuit affirmed. The U.S. Supreme Court subsequently dismissed the teachers' appeal because of an earlier decision that private schools cannot be legally segregated. *Runyon v. McCrary*, 427 U.S. 160, Va. 1976. The Mississippi legislature in the meantime had enacted a law prohibiting school boards from dismissing teachers solely because of their choice of schools. "Few familial decisions are as immune from governmental interference as parents' choice of a school for their children," wrote Chief Justice Burger for the majority, "so long as the school chosen otherwise meets the educational standards imposed by the state." The decision (to dismiss) "intimates no view on the question of when, if ever, public school teachers—or any comparable public employees—may be required, as a condition of their employment, to enroll their children in any particular school or refrain from sending them to a school which they, as parents, consider desirable. *Cook v. Hudson*, 511 F.2d 744, Miss. 1976, 429 U.S. 165, 197.

- The proposition that parents have a constitutional right to instruct their own children on family life and sexual matters at home and that this right was exclusive came up in California. The schools had instituted a sex education and family life course which was required of all students except those whose parents objected on religious grounds. The court found that the program met a valid secular purpose and since any child was free on request to take another course in lieu of the sex education course, the board's action must be upheld. *Citizens for Parental Rights v. San Mateo Cty. Bd. of Educ.*, 124 Cal.Rptr. 68, 1975.

- Parents in Hawaii complained that a board rule requiring children to help in the cafeteria amounted to "involuntary servitude," a violation of the Thirteenth Amendment. The rule required children to participate in cafeteria duty one day per month up to a maximum of seven days per year. The federal district court concluded that such mandatory cafeteria duty could not rise to a constitutional level. *Bobilin v. Bd. of Educ.*, 403 F.Supp. 1095, Hawaii 1975.

- In the absence of state law prohibiting corporal punishment, the U.S. Supreme Court has ruled that a parent may not veto corporal punishment for his own child when, in the opinion of professional personnel, such a course of action is justified. The Court did say, however, that the parent, if he so requests, is to be provided with a written account of any corporal punishment administered to his child, together with the name of the adult witness required in each case. *Baker v. Owen*, 395 F.Supp. 294, 44 L.W. 3235, N.C. 1975.

- "However strong the state's interest in universal compulsory attendance," ruled the Supreme Court, "it is by no means absolute to the exclusion or subordination of all other interests." Parental requests on the grounds of religious belief, where reasonable, said the Court, that the child be excused from compulsory attendance at a public school, must be honored. *Wisconsin v. Yoder,* 406 U.S. 205, 1972.

- "School rules specifying a period of detention after school for unexcused absenteeism and tardiness and for skipping school are not unconstitutionally vague." *Fielder v. Bd. of Educ.,* 346 F.Supp. 722, Nebr. 1972.

- Parents challenged a practice of one district of knocking down a student's grades for truancy. The New Jersey State Commissioner of Education held such a rule was improper punishment. *Minorics v. Bd. of Educ.,* N.J. Comms'r. Dec., 1972. Similarly, a board rule denying academic credit for failure to fulfill attendance requirements was likewise declared illegal. *Gutierrez v. School Dist. #R-1,* 585 P.2d 935, Colo. 1978.

Figure 5-2

PARENT RIGHTS CARD*

From the National Committee for Citizens in Education, 410 Wilde Lake Village Green, Columbia, MD 21044 Dial *toll-free:* 1-800-NET-WORK for further information.

Dear Parent:

This card lists 21 rights you may have as a parent of a child in public school. The rights are grouped under four headings: *Student Discipline, Student Instruction, Student & Other Records,* and *Other Rights.*

STUDENT DISCIPLINE

You have the right as a parent in any of the states listed...

- To take legal action against a school official if your child has been disciplined with "excessive or unreasonable" physical force. ALL STATES

- To appeal the suspension of your child. ALL STATES

- To appeal an administrator's decision to place your child in a class for students labeled "disruptive" or "troublemakers." ALL STATES *except* CA, DC, GA, KY, MO, NB, ND and WA.

Printed with the permission of the NCCE. See also NCCE's The Rights of Parents in the Education of Their Children @ $3.50 from the address above.

Figure 5-2 (continued)

STUDENT INSTRUCTION

You have the right as a parent in any of the states listed...

- To see instructional materials used in research programs funded by Dept. HEW and Natl. Science Foundation. ALL STATES
- To have your handicapped child placed in an "appropriate" public school program. Parents also must be consulted about the evaluation and placement of their handicapped children. ALL STATES
- To appeal an administrator's decision prohibiting your daughter from trying out for and playing in male-dominated sports. ALL STATES *except* CA, IA, IL, IN, KS, KY, MN, NB, ND, NM, and WY.
- To visit your child's classroom(s) *at any time* during the day, providing you first notify the school office. AL, AK, AZ, CO, DE, DC, FL, IN, IA, LA, MD, MI**, MS, MT, NB, NV, NH, NY, NC, ND, OH, OK, SC, SD, TN, TX, UT, and VA.
- To attend a minimum number of conferences with your child's teacher(s). AL, AK, AZ, CT, DC, DE, FL, LA, MD, MI, NB, NV, NH, NC, OH, OK and TN.
- To educate your child at home, providing you meet conditions and standards set by your state. AL, AK, AZ, CA, CO, CT, DC, FL, GA, HI, IL, IA, ME, MD, MA, MN, MS, MO, MT, NV, NH, NJ, NM, NY, NC, OK, RI, SD, TX, UT, VA, and WV.
- To request that your child be excused from studying subjects you object to on religious, moral or other *reasonable* grounds. AK, AZ, CO, DE, DC, FL, ID, IL, IN, IA, LA, MD, MI, NV, NH, NY, NC, OH, PA, VT, VA, WV, and WI.

**Resident parents of the school district have the privilege of visiting the school and/or classroom where their child or children are in attendance, provided prior request is made of and granted by the building administration.

- To request that your child be excused from reading assigned books you object to on religious, moral or other *reasonable* grounds. AL, AK, AZ, CO, DC, FL, ID, IL, IN, LA, MD, MI, MS, NV, NH, NY, NC, OH, VT, VA, and WV.
- To request that your child be excused from school activities you object to on religious, moral or other *reasonable* grounds. AL, AK, AZ, CO, DE, DC, FL, ID, IL, IN, IA, KS, LA, MD, MI, MS, NV, NH, NY, NC, ND, OH, OK, PA, RI, VT, VA, WA, WV, and WI.

STUDENT AND OTHER RECORDS

You have the right as a parent in any of the states listed...

Figure 5-2 (continued)

- To look at *all* your child's school records. You may challenge any record you believe to be untrue or unfair. School officials must respond to your challenge within a "reasonable time." If still dissatisfied, you may request a hearing. ALL STATES
- To look at all official school policies. ALL STATES *except* IL.
- To look at other official school records, such as research and planning reports (but not personnel records). AL, AK, AR, CO, CT, DC, FL, HI, ID, IN, KS, LA, ME, MD, MN, MO, MT, NB, NM, NV, NH, NY, ND, OR, SC, TX, UT and WI.

OTHER RIGHTS

You have the right as a parent in any of the states listed...
- To appeal a school policy or decision that prevents your child from expressing controversial views, so long as they are not obscene, slanderous or libelous, and do not cause serious disruption. ALL STATES
- To speak at all public meetings of the local school board. AL, AK, AR, CO, CT, DC, FL, GA, HI, ID, IN, KY, LA, ME, MD, MI, MN, MS, NB, NM, NV, NH, NC, ND, OH, OK, SD, TX, UT, VT, WV, and WY.
- To appeal some local board decisions to a higher state authority (other than a court). AL, AZ, CO, CT, DE, FL, GA, IL, IN, IA, LA, MD, MA, MN, MS, MT, NB, NV, NH, NJ, OH, OK, OR, SD, TX, UT, VT, WV, and WI.
- To appeal a policy or decision that prevents your child from joining a club or activity that is controversial but otherwise lawful. AL, AR, CO, CT, DE, DC, FL, GA, ID, IA, LA, MD, MI, MS, MO, MT, NB, NV, NH, NJ, NY, NC, OH, OK, OR, RI, SC, SD, TX, WA, WY and WV.
- To appeal a policy or decision that allows school employees to search your child or his property without a legal warrant or your permission. AL, AR, CO, CT, DC, FL, GA, IA, LA, MD, MS, MO, MT, NB, NH, NJ, NY, NC, OH, OK, OR, PA, RI, SC, SD, TX, UT, WA and WV.
- To be a member of any parent/citizen group and have your group recognized and heard by school officials. AL, AK, AZ, AR, CO, DC, FL, HI, ID, IL, IN, LA, ME, MI, MS, MT, NB, NM, NV, NH, NY, NC, OH, VT, VA and WV. ***

***The rights listed above were current as of the date of publication of this book.

GETTING DEPENDABLE FEEDBACK

How much citizen power is enough? That question must be answered in terms of how much feedback from parents and other patrons the board wishes to include in its decision-making process. Boards are often "spooked" by idle rumors or seemingly critical remarks they overhear and tend to read too much into them. The problem is to get dependable feedback from those factions in the community that should be heard from in order that a wise decision can be made. Believe it or not, there is a standard way in which this can be done. With careful control, the local board can provide the feedback you need without the possibility that these groups will take over. The citizen group is *always advisory,* and the board, no matter how much it may like to do so, cannot abdicate its responsibility to have the last word in all decision-making. These suggestions are important as you set up the machinery to provide much-needed information from your district. Here are the pointers:

1. *Select a citizen group that represents a true cross section of your school district.* It should include persons from every racial, economic, political and ethnic group in proportion to their pro rata share of the total population. Only a committee that is carefully and scientifically selected can provide the full-voiced feedback that you will need, so plan and execute this part of the plan meticulously.

2. *Allow nobody but board members to appoint citizen committee participants.* There are two reasons: one, official board selection clothes appointees with a mantle of quasijudicial authority; two, the board as a whole is mandated to appoint the group as representative of all points of view in the community.

3. *Define a specific task and purpose for the committee.* Prepare a formal charge you want the group to accomplish—and keep the focus narrow. List your objectives in measurable terms. Make plans to check on the work of the committee from time to time during the duration of the study.

4. *Emphasize that the committee holds advisory status only.* Inform them from the outset that they are helping you, but will not be making decisions, only recommendations which the board will act on

as it sees fit. The board cannot legally sidestep its obligation to have the last word, and a word now will help them understand that they are advising the board only on this one task which you have set before them.

5. *Assure full cooperation from the board.* The committee will need facts and figures, a place to meet, secretarial help, other aids. No holds should be barred in providing these to the committee in order that they may complete their assignment as soon as possible. Deadlines should be set, and progress reports decided upon.

6. *Keep an open mind until all the facts are in.* Don't second-guess the comittee. Don't indicate what you want them to find. Nothing will kill the initiative and thrust of the committee more quickly than telegraphing in advance what the board hopes they will find. Citizens who work diligently and in good faith should have the assurance that the board will accept their findings without telling them the way you think it will all turn out in the end.

7. *Disband the committee quickly after its objective has been accomplished.* Few activities drag on with such leaden certitude as the work of a citizens' committee. Speed up the work, and then thank the committee for its services. Some boards have learned to their regret that citizens committees formed for one purpose have survived to work on other things. Take care, therefore, that the committee comes to grips with one issue and one issue only. When that task is accomplished, the work is done; thank them and disband them quickly.

8. *Boards have an obligation to make decisions—a duty you cannot shirk.* Remember, when voters don't like your decisions, they have a recourse—they can cast their votes for others to take your place. Vote your convictions, but do vote them on the basis of the factual findings of the committee of citizens. Thus, you have had input on an issue by a cross section of citizens advising you what they think should be done. What could be more democratic than that?

The clamor by some citizens to join boards at the bargaining table sounds reasonable on paper, but it has a pitfall—groups in open meetings where bargaining is going on tend to play to the media, instead of trying to reach acceptable resolution to conflict. So know and protect your negotiations' privacy, even though a sunshine law may be at stake. Certain things, like laundering dirty linen in public, just aren't done within the range of the television cameras.

Also, be careful how you handle textbook selection. Because texts and other instructional materials are potential pitfalls for the board and parents, a system should be carefully devised for this purpose. Failure to have such a mechanism may lead to the formation of a censorship committee in the district, but perhaps no more likely than if you have no machinery for textbook selection at all. In one case, the board won its battle when it banned ten books from the reading list when the judge decided that the teachers' association had bargained away its right to the board in exchange for other considerations. The case is an example of how groups can trade away a prerogative which they otherwise would have, thinking they certainly won't need it in the future. *Cary v. Bd. of Educ.*, 427 F. Supp. 945, Colo, 1977.

Finally, citizens' groups operate best in settings where expansive goals are set, such as those related to the curriculum or to accountability mandates. If they are given a panoramic-type guideline, citizen committees can advise the board about the basic direction in which it should move, while leaving precise procedures to the teaching and administrative staff. Any other structural arrangement tends to plunge the public in over its head, leading inevitably to self-appointed censors among those individuals who may espouse admirable purposes but who have potentially dangerous gaps in essential knowledge of the considerations at issue.

CHAPTER

6

What to Do When Teachers Rebel

HOW THE GAME IS PLAYED

Americans have a built-in prejudice against worker groups that make demands on management. This bias, inherited from the English, is associated with the protection of property and capital goods growing out of the Industrial Revolution sweeping across Europe in the 18th century. Organizations of workers were considered by Adam Smith (1723-1790), the inventor of Economics, to be "conspiracies in restraint of trade," hence to be outlawed. In 1769, the English Parliament made the destruction of machinery a capital crime. Smith counseled that the law of supply and demand, like the law of gravity, was a hard and fast principle that should not be tinkered with, else it would upset the system. Labor was not a capital outlay, to be amortized over time, but an "expenditure." The worker who balked could be replaced with another worker who would do the work because of the financial incentive—"If you don't do the work as I say, then I will fire you and get somebody who will." The net result was an English jurisprudence that protected the property of owners, but gave little consideration to the rights of the workers.

In America, organizations of workers, following the English pattern, were thought to be engaged in a criminal conspiracy. In 1806, the U. S. Supreme Court ruled that workers who sought to raise their wages were criminals who were on conviction sentenced to jail. *Phila-delphia Cordwainers Case,* 1806. By 1840, the labor movement was upgraded when the Supreme Court held that the mere act of combination did not make a labor union an unlawful body. *Commonwealth v. Hunt,* 4 Met. 111, 1842. Rather, whether a combination of workers was criminal depended on the nature and purpose of the concerted activity. If the workers threatened to strike, an injunction would lie to prevent it. An employer could go into court and ask the court to prevent the strike on the grounds that it would create a clear and present danger to the peace. In 1935, the Congress enacted the Wagner Labor Relations Act, which requires employers to permit their employees freely to organize and to bargain with them collectively. The Act was subsequently declared constitutional by the Supreme Court. Union membership stood at 2.75 million in 1916 and rose to more than 17 million by 1960. Collective bargaining became the accepted way of reducing conflicts between labor and management during WWII—so much so that labor unions became quite powerful when compared with management. In the Taft-Hartley Act of 1947, the Congress sought to restore labor and management balance and cut back the power of the unions, to open up somewhat the right of all workers to work free from union dominance.

Although collective bargaining became public policy for workers in the private sector of the economy, the Wagner Act specifically excluded workers in public (governmental) employment. In 1951, in *Norwalk Teachers' Ass'n. v. Bd. of Educ.,* 83 A.2d 482, Conn., the state supreme court held that teachers did not have the right to strike absent specific authority given by the legislature. Rising militancy by teacher groups in the 1960's, in which other public employees joined to demand a "piece of the action," precipitated a crisis in the ranks of public employees everywhere. Confrontations, strikes, slowdowns, and sick-ins caused many boards to capitulate to the teachers' demands to join the board at the bargaining table. Today, more than 90 percent of all teachers in the nation bargain with their boards of education.

In Pennsylvania, public employee strikes are not prohibited unless or until such a strike "creates a clear and present danger or threat to the health, safety or welfare of the public." The law was ruled not to apply to school teachers, because it would unconstitutionally disrupt and interfere with a governmental function, and would place the interests of the teachers above those of their students. *Butler Area S.D. v. Butler Educ. Assn.,* 97 L.R.R.M. 2925, Pa. 1978. Until 1978, Pennsylvania was one of seven states that allow some public employees to strike under certain limited conditions specified in the law. Wisconsin amended its law to allow for strikes on a trial basis for a three-year period beginning January 1, 1978. The other states that allow strikes under limited conditions are Vermont, Montana, Hawaii, Alaska, Minnesota and Oregon, listed here in the chronological order in which they permitted strikes.

Figure 6-1

ELEMENTS OF UNION SECURITY

Exclusivity. An arrangement wherein the union is agreed upon as the exclusive and only bargaining unit recognized by management in that company or industry for a particular classification of workers.

Dues check-off. Management agrees to deduct union dues from workers' pay and turn them over to the union.

Closed shop. An arrangement whereby the management employs, and retains in employment, only persons who are members in good standing of a specified labor union. It is the most extreme of all the "union security" arrangements.

Union shop. Employer may hire a nonmember of a union provided the new employee joins the union within a specified length of time.

Preferential hiring. Employer agrees to hire union members if they are available; if not, employer may hire nonmembers.

Agency shop. Employees do not have to join the union but must pay as a condition of work a certain "agency" fee for being represented by the exclusive bargaining agency.

Master contract (in education, the "agreement"). When the parties reach accord, they reduce negotiated items to writing; this agreement becomes binding on the parties.

The bargaining table

The model for collective bargaining is the table, which stands on four equally important legs. (See Figure 6-2.) Without any one of the legs, the table could not stand; hence, each is essential to the success

Figure 6-2

THE BARGAINING TABLE STANDS ON FOUR LEGS

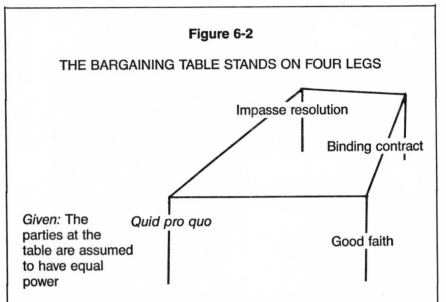

Given: The parties at the table are assumed to have equal power

LEG ONE: *Good faith bargaining mandated.* The parties must agree at the outset to deal with each other in good faith and try honestly to reach resolution of their differences. Failure to do so constitutes bad faith and/or an unfair labor practice.

LEG TWO: *Quid pro quo* (something for something). There must be something to bargain away for something gained. One cannot go to the table and demand something, without being willing to give something in return for that something.

LEG THREE: *Impasse resolution.* Third party intervention in case of deadlock is provided for. (1) Mediation—an advisory procedure to bring the parties back to the table (2) Fact-finding—third parties establish facts and recommend solutions to the impasse (3) Arbitration—may be either advisory or binding depending on what the parties agree to. Neither party must be allowed to paralyze the negotiations process.

LEG FOUR: *Binding agreement.* The process of negotiations results in a meeting of the minds, the essence of which is then reduced to writing and becomes binding on the parties over the life of the agreement.

of the process it represents. The parties begin bargaining with certain ground rules spelled out in advance—that they will deal in good faith, that they will honestly promise to come to the table in the spirit of true

---

Figure 6-3

WHAT THE SUPREME COURT HAS SAID ABOUT COLLECTIVE BARGAINING

- The agency shop in the public sector is not constitutionally impermissible. However, there is a point in a union's political activity beyond which the individual employee may restrain the union from expending the "agency funds" which he has contributed to the system. *Abood v. Detroit Bd. of Educ.,* 431 U.S. 209, Mich. 1977.
- When the board sits in session to consider public business, it need not distinguish whether one who speaks on an issue, even though it may involve negotiated matter, is an employee of the district, or a non-employee. The right to speak out on public issues cannot be limited to non-employees alone. *City of Madison v. Wisc. Empl. Rel. Comm.,* 429 U.S. 167, Wisc. 1976.
- A city ordinance prohibiting persons to assemble "in or upon public streets, sidewalks, highways, public parks, or public buildings" without a permit is a violation of a union's right to meet peaceably and to associate with others. *Hague v. Committee for Industrial Organization,* 307 U.S. 496, N.J. 1939.
- A board's prior role as negotiator does not disqualify it to decide that the public interest in maintaining uninterrupted classroom work required that teachers striking in violation of state law be discharged. *Hortonville Jt. Sch. Dist. No. 1 v. Hortonville Educ. Ass'n.,* 426 U.S. 482, Wisc. 1976.

---

conflict resolution in mind, that they will avoid unfair labor practices, that they will not allow the bargaining process to be paralyzed by impasse, and any other considerations they feel important to initial negotiations. Each understands that if he is to gain something, he must be willing to give up something of value in order to gain it. Nothing will so hamper the bargaining process as intransigence on the part of one or both of the parties. Also, time limits are set and deadlines established in the initial stages of the process, so that realistic goals can be met. In the absence of a state statute governing bargaining by teachers and boards of education, there may be a question at the outset on what is negotiable. Normally, the range of negotiation is "wages, hours and conditions of employment," but this term can be interpreted either *narrowly* (money matters only), or *broadly* (everything we talk about is a "condition of employment"). The rules governing negotiations in the

---

Figure 6-4

WHAT THE LESSER COURTS HAVE SAID ABOUT
COLLECTIVE BARGAINING

- In Cook County, Illinois teachers who were active in the union were dismissed. The federal Circuit Court of Appeals for the Seventh Circuit held that teachers have the right to organize and engage in union activity and that any illegal constraints on this right may be enjoined and the perpetrators made to pay damages. *McLaughlin v. Tilendis,* 398 F.2d 287, Ill. 1968.
- It is not clear whether teachers' unions have the power to surrender constitutional rights of teachers to select instructional materials for use in the classroom. *Cary v. Bd. of Educ.,* 427 F. Supp. 945, Colo. 1977, aff'd., 10 CA July 10, 1979.
- A California appellate court has ruled that a school district may recover money damages under either a tortious inducement to breach individual teacher contracts or a theory of liability resulting from unlawful acts where teachers strike. *Pasadena Unif. Sch. Dist. v. Pasadena Fed'n. of Teachers,* 140 Cal.Rptr. 41, 1977.
- Union officials and employees who had defied court orders to end a strike were punished by the courts for criminal contempt, with fines of $75,000 and incarceration for periods ranging from fifteen to thirty days. *Bd. of Lakeland Cent.Sch. Dist. v. Lakeland Fed'n. of Teachers,* 399 N.Y.S.2d 61, 1977.
- Termination of striking employees by the local board of education has been held by the federal district court for Alabama as not interfering with the First Amendment rights of such employees. *United Steelworkers of America v. Univ. of Alabama,* 430 F.Supp. 996, 1977.

---

public sector were borrowed from the private sector, and are much the same except that the public employees are not generally allowed the right to strike, or if they do have this right, it is so limited that a strike by public employees is virtually eliminated. Confrontations are part of the process, and any unilateral action by one party without informing the other is considered an unfair labor practice. Two-way communications are the essence of the process; nothing must be allowed to stop the on-going dialogue between the parties. Each recognizes a mutuality of interests and interdependence one on the other. Both parties may be represented at the table by agents of their own choosing, but in such instances, the parties must ratify any tentative agreement for it to become binding. Costs are to be shared equally between the parties. The bargaining process is—

Bi-lateral	rather than	uni-lateral
Democratic	rather than	authoritarian
Cooperative	rather than	paternalistic
Face-to-face	rather than	behind-the-back
Aimed at resolution	rather than	aimed at blocking action

At the table, the parties agree that with every offer, there must be a counter-offer. Failure to make a counter-offer can be an obstructionist tactic, if not indeed an unfair labor practice. This is the way the game is played, and it has been played this way since bargaining began.*

While you may question whether teachers without the right to strike are actually equal in power to the board of education, the fact remains that the threat to strike, a work slowdown, or a sick-in can be as effective as a strike. Thus, although teachers have gone to jail for illegally striking, the fact remains that teachers' groups can effectively disrupt if not close down the schools entirely, even without the right to strike. This means that although the board must have the last word, if it agrees to enter into a bi-lateral process for decision-making, it must honor the wishes of the other party in reaching that decision, or face a charge of bad faith in so doing.

TEACHERS AND POSSIBLE BOARD BIAS

One due process guarantee is that the accused shall be accorded a hearing before an *impartial* tribunal. Teachers sometimes claim that the board, which is deeply involved in community affairs, cannot serve as an impartial body, since it has a function to perform and may make up its mind without considering both sides of an issue. The issue of

---

*A somewhat cynical view of the claim that both sides must of necessity win in the bargaining process is illustrated by the story of the bear that was hungry and the man who was cold who met in a neutral cave to negotiate their condition. After some hours of negotiations, so the story goes, the man emerged from the cave wearing a bearskin coat. He was no longer cold, and the bear was no longer hungry.

board bias was at stake in the case of *Hortonville Joint School Dist. v. Hortonville Education Ass'n.,* 426 U.S. 482, Wisc. 1976. Prolonged negotiations between the teachers and the board failed to produce a contract and the teachers went on strike, which was against the law. The board invited the teachers to return to work without penalty, but most refused, whereupon the board held a hearing for the striking teachers and voted to terminate their employment. The teachers claimed they had been denied due process of law (the board dismissed them at 20-minute intervals) because the board had already made up its mind and was not therefore impartial. The case eventually reached the U.S. Supreme Court, which held that absent a showing of bias or malice, a local school board may validly conduct a hearing to terminate illegally striking teachers even though the board was negotiating labor questions with the teachers at the time. See Figure 6-3.

Striking teachers who come into court to seek equity do not come into equity "with clean hands," said the Court. They can hardly expect the courts to justify what they have done—broken the law. Furthermore, the Wisconsin legislature, in its wisdom, has seen fit to place the running of the schools in the hands of local boards in each community. The Supreme Court and lesser courts should not interfere in this operation unless it is clear that a constitutionally protected right is being denied, a condition not present here. The board's action in the case was not disciplinary in nature, except incidentally. Its main interest was in fulfilling its function as an agent of the state intent on the education of the young. The policy question for the board was what choice among the alternatives to the teachers' strike would best serve the interests of the parents and children who depended on the system and the interests of the citizens whose taxes supported the system.

The Court ruled that the state's interest in providing a good education for children outweighed the teachers' interest in being protected against an erroneous deprivation of their property interest. In holding for the board and against the teachers, the Court said in part:

> ...The state legislature has given the board the power to employ and dismiss teachers, ... Permitting the board to make the decision (to dismiss the striking teachers) preserves its control over school district affairs, leaves the balance of power in labor relations where the state legislature struck it, and assures that the decisions whether to dismiss teachers will be made by the body responsible for that decision under state law.

Bias, as applied to a judge or tribunal, is often "sensed," as in a case in which a mayor sat as a judge to try persons accused of speeding. The fines from those cases constituted a significant part of the city's income. The U.S. Supreme Court held:

> The situation is one which would offer a possible temptation to the average man as a judge to forget the burden of proof required to convict the defendant or which might lead him not to hold the balance nice, clear and true between the state and the accused. *Ward v. Village of Monroeville,* 93 S.Ct. 80, Ohio 1972 .

Temptation must be put aside by the judge or tribunal in the interest of justice. A U.S. District Court in California, in response to a contention that the board was not impartial, wrote:

> The question ... is not whether the board was actually biased, but whether under the circumstances, there existed a *probability* that the decision-maker would be tempted to decide the issue with partiality to one party or the other. *Gonzales v. McEuen,* 435 F.Supp. 460, Cal. 1977. (Emphasis supplied.)

In deciding that the confidential relationship between the attorneys for the district and the members of the board of education, reinforced by the advisory role played by the attorneys for the board, created an unacceptable risk of bias, the court concluded that bias "can be presumed to exist."

Apparently, board members must eschew *any appearance of evil* in their handling of a case; they must use kid gloves at all times. Bias can be presumed where the board members may have a *pecuniary* interest, or where it is clear that they had their *minds made up* ahead of time. The temptation factor seems to be present in both instances, and board members will do well (and this applies to superintendents too) to avoid serving in a judicial capacity where there is a chance that bias will be presumed because of the relationships involved in the case.

Bias can be presumed because of pecuniary or personal interest, but there is still another view of impartiality—that of *separation of functions.* Boards make rules, enforce those rules, and sit in judgment when the rules are broken (legislative, executive and judicial functions). To be truly "impartial," the judge must be one who has not been involved in the case, that is, one from outside. Several states have provided that boards should have available to them a "panel" or "tribunal" from outside the system to hear the evidence, then turn it over to them for final determination. Colorado has such a provision in its teacher tenure act. In Denver, the board dismissed a tenured teacher, and she asked for and received a hearing before a tripartite panel, which after hearing the evidence, recommended that the teacher be retained, a recommendation that was not honored by the board. Instead, the board, maintaining that the panel's findings were "sketchy" and "incomplete," substituted findings of its own, and fired the teacher, who then brought action to be reinstated. Her suit was successful. The Colorado Supreme Court held that the board was bound by the findings of the panel, and that it could not substitute its own findings for those of the panel. "To permit the board to overrule the panel's findings would defeat the purpose of the tenure act by placing the decision to hire or fire in the hands of a body which has not actually seen and heard the witnesses," said the court in holding that the board had acted illegally—in a biased way—in making its decision to fire the teacher notwithstanding the recommendation of the panel to keep her. *Blair v. Lovett*, 582 P.2d 668, Colo. 1978.

The case illustrates the principle of law that the court will determine the intent of the legislature if at all possible, and follow that wish in its implementation. Where there is no controlling statute, the courts fall back on the fundamental fairness doctrine—the board must avoid the very appearance of evil in making its decisions within the sphere of its jurisdiction.

However, prior involvement in some aspects of a case will not necessarily disqualify board members and the superintendent from acting as a decision-maker. Impartiality must be judged from the evidence in each case. Did the judge have a monetary interest in the outcome? Did he or she have a biased point of view, that is, a prejudgment? Would he or she stand to gain something by the outcome? Said one court in holding that board members had not been partial in their decision:

> The mere exposure to evidence presented in non-adversary investigative procedures is insufficient in itself to impugn the fairness of the board members at a later adversary hearing. Without a showing to the contrary, state administrators are presumed to be men of conscience and intellectual discipline, capable of judging a particular controversy fairly on the basis of its own circumstances. *Withrow v. Larkin,* 95 S.Ct. 1456, 1486, 1975.

The courts have distinguished two stages in any case: (1) the investigative stage, and (2) the trial or hearing stage. A substantial pre-hearing familiarity by decision-makers with the facts of a case—if they try the case during its investigative stage—can bias their judgment when the case comes before them for a decision. That is why you must not reach a decision during the early stages of the case, but must reserve your decision until all the facts are in, and then base your decision only on the evidence presented at the hearing. Failure to reserve judgment may open the way to a charge of bias on the grounds that the board had already made up its mind in advance, and the hearing was a mere sham.

Teachers have the right to form unions and to be active in them. However, laws denying teachers the right to strike have repeatedly been upheld in the courts. You could well argue that teachers, who are role-models for the young, should not be allowed to thumb their noses at the law. It is doubtful that respect for law and order can be taught by those who do not practice it. Particularly reprehensible would be a court ruling that teachers who illegally struck should receive pay raises as a result of a strike. A teacher works in a sensitive area in the class-room. There he shapes the attitudes of young minds towards the society in which we live. In this, the state has a vital and defensible concern. Fitness for teaching depends on many things. Boards would do well to remind teachers that they are not in the same position as workers in the private sector but that their behavior may trigger similar behavior in their charges. This limits the rights of teachers as against other workers and makes them a special case.

7

The Mounting Problem of Child Abuse and Neglect

SCOPE OF THE PROBLEM

When the history of childhood is finally written, it will be a sorry story indeed. Between 1900 and 1979, the study of childhood became routine for the psychologist, the sociologist and the anthropologist. However, childhood has only recently become of interest to historians, in part because of the alarming increase in the incidence of child abuse and neglect. Were it not for the intervention of the judiciary, children might still be considered "chattels," "infants," "dependents," or "changelings" before the law. With the help of the Supreme Court in 1969 and before, children are now considered "persons" under our Constitution, and their rights are being rapidly elevated to an equal plane with those of adults. Just what it means to call children "persons" will have to be worked out, since children have been systematically excluded from economic and political decision-making, to full constitutional status equal with adults, and to representation in proportion to their numbers in the total population. With the aid and support of the judicary, children have moved in our time from the position of chattels to full person-hood principally through changes in the common law.

In colonial days, one half of all children died before the age of ten, and those who survived were continually reminded they were born in sin and were doomed to hell if they did not conform. Puritan parents were admonished, "Once a day, take something away from them." Children early were hastened into adult responsibility, learning Latin by school age, many graduating from college at 16. Not until the Enlightenment was any attention paid to childhood as a phenomenon worthy of study. A tendency to over-idealize childhood led to a mythology that even today has not entirely disappeared. Yet children are no longer economic assets to their parents; quite the contrary, they are a decided economic disaster to some, since it costs over $100,000 to raise a child to maturity today.

Advice Columnist Ann Landers polled some 50,000 parents on whether given the choice they would again have children. Over 70 percent said they would not, it wasn't worth it. Since children are not the inevitable result of marriage, many couples elect not to undertake parenthood. More women are working than ever before; of those women who do have children, more than half have jobs outside the home. Such a major *dis*adjustment in the social machine must be of necessity cause *mal*adjustments in the way children are treated.

WHAT *IS* CHILD ABUSE AND NEGLECT?

Child abuse may be physical, such as shaking, beating, burning, or failure to provide the necessities of life, such as adequate food, shelter and clothing. Or it may be emotional, a failure to provide warmth, attention, supervision, love, and concern for the child as a person. Many children today are emotionally disturbed, that is, they are concerned so deeply with their own relationships that they cannot free their minds to study in school. Child abuse may be verbal, such as excessive yelling, belittling, or teasing children. More recently, cases of sexual abuse have come to light, including incest, indecent sexual activity in the family, or exposure to pornography and obscenities. In Los Angeles, for example, the police estimate that 300,000 children, many of them under the age of 5, are used each year as objects of pornography. Child abuse can happen anywhere, in poor, middle-class, or well-to-do homes, in rural areas or in the bustling cities, and may involve one or both parents, as a recent study shows.

Early estimates were that more than one million children suffered child abuse and neglect or both each year, with at least one in 500 victims dying. Now that estimate has been doubled. The Department of Health, Education and Welfare calls it "a national epidemic and a very serious social problem." Over 2,000 children a year die as a result of abuse and neglect, a serious problem if only considered from the standpoint of their loss. Those who live may have life-long emotional problems, and are more likely than other children to abuse their own children if they have some later on.

We know now that child abuse is a symptom of a deeper malady that can be successfully treated if caught in time. But first, more people must know and understand child abuse and neglect, and care enough to want to do something about it, before its incidence can be reduced or eliminated entirely.

The American Humane Child Protection Association of Englewood, Colorado 80110 lists the following as possible reasons why parents abuse their children: immaturity, unrealistic expectations, unmet emotional needs, frequent financial, legal, or illness crises, lack of "parenting" knowledge, social isolation of the family, poor childhood experiences, and/or abuse of drugs or alcohol. Most abuse parents are "normal"; relatively few are "criminal" or mentally unbalanced, according to the Association. Since parents are the most frequent child abusers, it stands to reason that schools can do much to alleviate the problem, and most boards of education now have positive board policies to deal with child abuse and neglect within the schools of the district.

Child abuse and neglect affects us all—it's a social burden that costs undue amounts of money to carry, a legal burden for the overloaded courts and society in general. Since the majority of troubled parents can learn how to be good mothers and fathers, to feel better about themselves, and to enjoy their children, local boards are taking more than a passing interest in reducing child abuse and neglect in their own jurisdictions.

Between 250,000 and 300,000 children each year wind up as "throwaways"—children who run away from home or get into trouble, and the parents say, "I can't do a thing with that child; keep him away from me." In November, 1978 a judge in Milwaukee was baffled when parents of a 16-year-old girl who broke family rules, smoked marijuana and misbehaved in school "divorced" her. The judge tried to get the parents to keep the girl, but was amazed at how easy it is legally for parents to avoid dealing with their errant children. In Boulder, Colorado a 24-year-old man sued his parents for "malparenting"—raising him with plenty of material comforts but little love. The son claimed that because of their alleged lack of parental guidance, he is classified as a paranoid schizophrenic who may need psychiatric care for the rest of his life.

The rate of child abuse and neglect among out-of-wedlock children is more than twice as high as for those of married couples. Many states have enacted legislation aimed at stemming the tide of abuse and neglect even in the face of a national realization that the state cannot legislate morality. Many are adopting the Standard Children's Code. Although the first child abuse and neglect case was reported in 1874, it was not until the 1960's that states enacted reporting statutes. Now all 50 states and the District of Columbia have some statutory provision for mandatory reporting of non-accidental injury and neglect of children cases in their jurisdictions.

The best of these contain three provisions: (1) a workable definition of reportable conditions of abuse and neglect; (2) a class of persons required to make reports of existing conditions and injury to children; and (3) a required public response to offer services to the child so identified. Thus, there are three steps: (1) identification, (2) investigation, and (3) intervention in the battle to bring a halt to child abuse and neglect at the local level.

Four principal classes of reportable conditions now appear in these state statutes: (1) non-accidental physical injury, such as bruises, broken bones, and burns; (2) neglect, normally failure to provide the necessities of life for a child; (3) sexual molestation, including incest, rape, and/or molestation; and (4) emotional or mental injury, such as secondary effects of rape, but this latter class has not been well defined in most of the states. Eighteen states now require reports for cases that are "threatened" or are likely to occur, while 45 states have separate sections in their laws that define reportable conditions in more detail.

REPORTING AND FOLLOWING UP

In 46 states, physicians along with other medical professionals are required to report any incidences of non-accidental injury they encounter in the line of duty. Teachers are required in 42 states to report

---

Figure 7-1

COMMON SIGNS OF CHILD ABUSE AND NEGLECT

- A child has repeated bruises, welts, burns or marks on the body and the parents seem unconcerned, or deny that anything has happened, or give unlikely explanations, such as "He fell in the bathtub," or "She fell down stairs."
- The child may exhibit signs of undernourishment, inadequate clothing in cold weather, or is left alone to wander at all hours. (Sometimes, though, *over*-neatness may be a sign of abuse, according to the American Humane Child Protection Association.)
- The child exhibits disruptive behavior, such as aggressiveness, negative behavior, constant need for attention and adult help.
- When children are excessively shy, friendless and withdrawn, it may indicate that there are serious problems at home.
- Parents who are "super critical," and who discipline their children frequently and severely, may begin to abuse them when their unrealistic expectations are not met.
- Families that are extremely isolated, that don't share in school or community activities, and that resent friendly offers for help may be distrustful of people, and may tend to abuse their children by keeping them out of contact with other children.
- Children who are occasionally disciplined are not necessarily abused or neglected. One must look for a pattern of continuing—perhaps worsening—abuse and/or neglect before it is time to call for help.

---

child abuse and neglect, while day care workers must do so in 32 states. Social workers, who do much of the investigative work and intervention, are required to report child abuse and neglect cases in 42 states. Law enforcement personnel also must report in 32 states, while the statutes of 22 states require "any person" who knows of a case to report it to authorities.

Most state statutes require that the report be made "immediately," which raises a question when school people, for example, decide to handle the case in-house and days pass without an official report having been made. Penalties for failure to report such cases are generally both criminal and civil, although it is generally accepted that one who reports a case cannot be held liable if he or she is wrong, or is right and an action is brought against him or her. Many states require that a guardian for the time being (*guardian ad litem*) be appointed if the child is to be taken from the parents pending disposition of the case. Most states now have central registry of all child abuse and neglect cases but these vary somewhat in effectiveness as clearinghouses for state cases. Most states provide for termination of parental rights, with many states defining in detail which acts will lead to termination of parental control.

LEGAL STATUS OF CHILDREN

While children may be "persons" in the eyes of the Supreme Court, their individual legal status depends on the relationship between the child, the parent and the state. Over the years, Latin terms have come to describe these relationships; these terms are three in number.

In familia

Colonial parents were charged with the complete upbringing of their offspring. Failure to bring up a child properly or to teach him or her according to the scriptures might result in parental punishment. As a member of a family circle, the child has certain recognized rights, or more exactly, expectations—food, shelter, clothing and persons concerned with his present and future welfare. The family circle has been recognized by the law for centuries. It is a closed circuit into which historically the law hesitates to intervene unless absolutely necessary to do so. One of the most cherished American traditions is that the parent has the right to raise his children according to his personal dictates. Law sanctifies that tradition by granting to parents legal custody of their children and by the legal presumption that parental love and concern will provide the child with all necessary care and protection. It is only when evidence to the contrary reaches a court or a startled public that the privacy of the parent to raise his child as he pleases is questioned.

In *Wisconsin v. Yoder*, 406 U.S. 205, 1972 the Supreme Court upheld the right of a parent, one Amish farmer, to exclude his child from the compulsory attendance law on religious grounds. And in 1925, the Supreme Court in *Society of Sisters v. Pierce*, 268 U.S. 510,

Ore. 1925 held that the child is "not the mere creature of the state. Those who nurture and direct his destiny have the right and the high duty to direct his feet in paths that lead upward." Judges today do not wish to intervene in family matters, often ruling that the child must be placed back into the home where the incident occurred rather than break the magic of the family circle.

In loco parentis

In other portions of this book, we have indicated that the teacher stands in place of the natural parent when the child is undergoing instruction in an institution operated by the state. *In loco parentis* teachers have both the rights and the responsibilities of the parent, only on a smaller scale. The parent still retains the same control of the medical assistance, the religious upbringing, and the privacy of the child's mind he has always possessed, even though the child is absent from the home in schools operated by the government. This shared ownership of the child's education is often confusing, and is based on the legal fiction that someone must be in charge of the child at all times for its own good. When that concern for the child's welfare is missing or altered in any way, the state is involved, since it has a prominent interest in the health and welfare of each of its citizens, even though they may be below the age of eighteen.

Parens patriae

Literally, "The state is the parent." The child is entitled to attention to his needs; if this is not forthcoming the state may be required to step in and provide it, or see that it is provided for the child. This can be handled through the various social agencies and the juvenile court system, which underwent vast changes following *In re Gault*, 387 U.S. 1, Ariz. 1967, in which the Supreme Court held that due process of law "is not for adults alone." The juvenile courts were ordered to provide due process and equal protection in handling juvenile cases. These courts, however, are frustrated at times by heavy loads and lack of money or facilities to rehabilitate the errant youngsters they must process. The whole change in our handling of juveniles since *Gault*, together with the rising misuse of drugs, alcohol and a rising crime rate have overloaded this time-honored legal concept so that it suffers from overuse and underfunding—to the detriment of many of our youthful offenders.

Figure 7-2

ON THE SCALES OF JUSTICE THESE INTERESTS MUST BE BALANCED

The Individual's Interest	The State's Interest
1. Equality of treatment	1. Right of peaceful, on-going school system
2. Right to know and learn	2. Right to require reasonable obedience
3. Right to succeed in school	3. Right to expect steady attendance and reasonable punctuality
4. Right against discrimination	4. Right, within reason, to control individual's behavior
5. Right to be one's self	5. Right of corporal punishment
6. Right against stigmatization	6. Right of suspension and/or expulsion following due process procedure
7. Protection against invasion of privacy	7. Right to expect assumption of some responsibility for student's education
8. Right to attend school is both a "liberty" and a "property" right	8. Right to require certain subjects and a reasonable level of performance
9. Right to due process of law and equal protection of the laws	9. Right to group students for instructional purposes
10. Right of freedom of speech and of the press	10. Right to transmit information on students under limited immunity
11. Fundamental fairness in all dealings with the school	11. Right to put down disruptive intrusions into the schools

In order for the state in the person of school officials to justify prohibition of a particular expression of opinion, it must be able to show that its action was caused by something more than a mere desire to avoid the discomfort and unpleasantness that always accompany an unpopular viewpoint. *Tinker v. Des Moines Comm.Sch.*, 393 U.S. 503, Iowa 1969.

Child abuse or neglect can be a civil or a criminal misdeed. As a crime it will be heard in a local district court. As an alleged violation of a civil code it will fall under the jurisdiction of a juvenile or family court. Occasionally it can be both a criminal and a civil action, and concurrent actions in both district and juvenile courts will be possible. The exercise of juvenile court jurisdiction is a matter of judicial discretion.

WHAT CAN SCHOOLS DO?

In recent months, there has been a significant increase in school programs to identify and prevent child abuse and neglect. What can schools do? Most districts start with adoption of policies setting forth the board's desires to abide by the appropriate state and federal laws and to deploy personnel to that end. Many districts sponsor instructional programs for staff members. Others enter into partnerships with other community agencies, while still others offer courses for their students to help them become better parents. Such a movement to abate child abuse and neglect is long overdue, since over two-thirds of all cases of this kind involve children between the ages of 5 and 17—children of school age. Yet in most states, schools have accounted for less than one-third of the reported cases.

Why have schools been reluctant to report child abuse and neglect cases? To some, it is outside the school's area of concern, or viewed as an imposition on an already overworked staff. Those schools that have shown a willingness to assist in this endeavor and who cooperate willingly with social workers and others have been able to cut the incidence of such abuse while at the same time being rewarded by better opportunities for those they assist.

NATIONAL PICTURE SHOWS INCREASES

Child abuse and neglect are on the increase, according to a study conducted by the American Humane Association in 1978. All 50 states, the District of Columbia, and three U. S. territories were included in the sample. A total of 357,533 reports of child abuse and/or neglect were submitted in the base year 1976. The following are a few of the findings from the study:

- 58.3 percent of the reported cases were neglect only; 26.5 percent were child abuse only; and 15.1 percent were both abuse and neglect.
- There were substantiated cases of child abuse/neglect at all income levels. However, most cases reported involved lower socioeconomic families.
- In families where child neglect and abuse were substantiated, the median income on all cases was $5,050 per year. Median income is substantially higher in abuse cases ($6,890 per year) than in neglect cases ($4,250 per year). The median family income for all U.S. families in the base year 1976 was $13,900.
- Alcohol dependence was considered a factor in 17 percent of the families in validated cases of abuse and/or neglect in 1976.
- The involved children of abuse and/or neglect remained in the home with the family in 82 percent of the validated cases.
- Females were the alleged perpetrators in 61 percent of the validated cases of child abuse and/or neglect. This predominance, however, is related to the neglect area; only 45 percent of the alleged perpetrators in validated cases of abuse only were female.
- Natural parents were perpetrators in 86.9 percent of all validated cases. The myth of the cruel stepparent is thus put to rout, since only 7.1 percent of the cases were due to the stepparent.
- Boys tended to be victims more often than girls among younger children, but from age 12 on, girls are more likely to be the victims. Overall, the number of male-female victims is about equal.
- 71.8 percent of all abuse/neglect cases reported required no treatment; 21.4 percent required moderate treatment; 6.1 percent required hospitalization, with 0.2 percent resulting in permanent disability, while 0.5 percent were fatal.

POLICY IMPLICATIONS FOR SCHOOLS

School boards and administrators need to anticipate the mounting problems in child abuse and/or neglect, and take such actions as these:

- Districts need to institute a full complement of parenting courses for both adults and students in the schools, with particular attention to state figures on child abuse and neglect.
- The board should adopt written policy showing the district's willingness to abide by the state statute on child abuse and

neglect and pledging the board's cooperation in reporting, investigating and intervening in such cases in the future.

- Appropriate procedures to implement the board's policy on child abuse and neglect should be developed by the superintendent's staff and widely publicized.
- In-service programs to acquaint the teaching and classified staffs with the problem should be scheduled periodically.
- A school team to which cases of child abuse and/or neglect can be referred should be formed, with the responsibility of investigating reported cases, visiting the homes, and evaluating family conditions, as well as cooperating with other agencies interested in the problem.

In schools where these recommended practices have been instituted, there is a significant reduction in child abuse and neglect despite the fact that more cases are brought to light than theretofore. The resulting help to troubled families and to their battered children has been well worth the risk. If only one child were to be helped to succeed, that alone would be a compelling reason for school systems

---

Figure 7-3

A CASE IN POINT

- A distraught girl of 13 sought out her school counselor and asked for help. She told the counselor that she had been raped several times by her stepfather. It was his habit to awaken her each morning, she explained, but two weeks ago he suddenly got into bed with her and sexually assaulted her. It had happened twice, most recently that morning, and she was frightened. The counselor called the welfare department, only to be met with indifference. The counselor pressed for action and reluctantly the agency agreed to make a home visit "to see whether the child is enjoying this."
- A school district which had reported several cases of suspected child abuse and neglect received a letter from the local department of social services stating that they were over-reporting. The letter instructed the district to report only "serious" cases and made clear that the agency's position was that bruises were neither indicative of serious abuse nor painful to the child.

From "What Schools Are Doing About Child Abuse and Neglect," by Diane D. Broadhurst in *Children Today,* Jan.-Feb., 1978, pp. 22-23.

---

everywhere to be involved in alleviating the problem of child abuse and neglect.

Figure 7-4

CHILD CAN EMPLOY AN ATTORNEY

May a child employ legal counsel when his/her interests are hostile to those of the parents? The Supreme Court of Alaska says so.

A girl of 14 who ran away from home repeatedly was hauled into court by her parents, and the judge was requested to order her to stay at home. The parents were represented by legal counsel, so the girl requested an attorney, one Wagstaff, to represent her. He appeared in court, but was escorted from the premises. The judge held that the parents were represented by counsel, and that that was sufficient for the juvenile hearing at hand. Wagstaff appealed.

The Alaska Supreme Court held that a child of 14 whose interests are hostile to those of her parents, where the penalty would have been to be declared a "juvenile delinquent," is entitled to her own attorney. "It is urged," said the court, "that a child should not lose his cloak of love, nurture, and guidance when he enters the halls of justice. In answer to that, it must be pointed out that in most instances the child would not be in court unless a serious problem in the parent-child relationship has developed. We assume that with the benefit of hearing arguments on both sides of the controversy, the court will be able to give substantial consideration to the need for parental love, nurture, and guidance, in deciding the future welfare of the child." *Wagstaff v. Superior Court*, 535 P.2d 1220, Alaska 1975.

8

Some Rules to Follow in Obscenity Cases

ACADEMIC FREEDOM

In its narrow sense, academic freedom refers to the liberty the teacher may take in handling subject matter within the classroom. In its broader sense, however, it may also refer to speech and expression outside the classroom which may have a logical bearing on the teacher's credibility as a teacher. There is no doubt that the state has a right to investigate the competence and fitness of those it hires to teach in its schools. "A teacher works in a sensitive area in the classroom," said the U.S. Supreme Court. "There he shapes the attitude of young minds toward the society in which they live. In this, the state has a vital concern." *Adler v. Board of Education,* 342 U.S. 485,N.Y. 1952.

Courts have tended to use the broader definition of academic freedom in determining how far boards of education may go in limiting academic freedom. Board scrutiny of the teacher's work is not limited to a teacher's classroom conduct, but may, and often does, extend beyond the schoolroom door. Said the Supreme Court, "There is no requirement in the federal Constitution that a teacher's classroom conduct be the sole basis for determining his fitness. Fitness for teaching depends on a broad range of factors." *Beilan v. Bd. of Public Educ.,* 357 U.S. 399, Pa. 1958.

Nobody knows exactly how many lawsuits teachers file against local boards of education challenging their dismissal or non-renewal of the teaching contract. One thing is certain, however: the number of lawsuits involving teacher dismissal is far greater than all other educational lawsuits put together. The volume of such litigation tends to confuse boards in dismissing teachers, since one must read the cases to keep up with this expanding area of the law.

In general, a teacher works for the state not under the conditions he might choose to see there, but under the terms laid down for him by the state. This was true in 1927, and still obtains even today. *State of Tennessee v. Scopes,* 289 S.W. 363, 1927. Some enlightening changes have occurred, however, which bear repeating. For example, during the 1950's (the McCarthy years), there were attempts made to weed out "communistic influences" from the public schools. The Supreme Court was called on to decide whether a New York statute (the Feinberg Law) barring from employment in its schools any member of an organization on the "subversive" list was unconstitutional. The Court, by a 6-3 decision, held that it was not. "It is clear that such persons (teachers) have the right under our law to assemble, speak, think and believe as they will. It is equally clear that they have no right to work for the state on their own terms. If they do not choose to work on such terms, they are at liberty to retain their beliefs and associations and go elsewhere. Has the state thus deprived them of any right to free speech or assembly? We think not." *Adler v. Bd. of Educ.,* 342 U.S. 485, N.Y. 1952. Teachers under *Feinberg* could be released or refused employment merely because they knowingly belonged to an organization that was on the state's subversive organizations list.

But what of those who belong *unknowingly* to a subversive organization? In 1952, the Court decided that an Oklahoma statute that made innocent membership in such an organization basis for dismissal was unconstitutional. *Wieman v. Updegraff,* 344 U.S. 183, Okla. 1952. The state denied teachers equal protection of the laws where they were penalized without actual knowledge that their oganizations were on the banned list. "Indiscriminate classification of innocent with knowing activity must fall as an assertion of arbitrary power," said the Court (5-3) in holding for the teachers.

Teacher loyalty was tested in two other cases in the 1950's. In *Slochower v. Bd. of Higher Education,* 350 U.S. 551, N.Y. 1956, a teacher took the Fifth Amendment when called on to testify before a federal legislative committee. The board fired him for his lack of cooperation with the committee. The Supreme Court ruled that this was guilt by association, since no inference of guilt can be drawn from one's refusal to testify, and ordered him reinstated. Constitutional protection extends to a public servant "whose exclusion from such employment pursuant to a statute is patently arbitrary or discriminatory."

To the opposite effect was *Beilan v. Board of Public Education,* 357 U.S. 399, Pa. 1958. A Philadelphia public school teacher refused to answer his superintendent's questions about his communist activities even though the superintendent stressed the importance of his inquiry to the teacher's fitness to teach. After a hearing, the teacher was dismissed for "incompetency," whereupon the teacher challenged the board's action in court. The Supreme Court held that the school board may constitutionally inquire into an employee's fitness to teach, and such inquiry need not be limited to the employee's in-school activities. Nor is such an inquiry an infringement of the employee's First Amendment rights of freedom of speech, belief, or association.

Following the ruling in *Scopes* that a state law banning the teaching of Darwin's theory of evolution was not unconstitutional, the *Scopes* rule applied in public schools for more than 40 years. Arkansas had a law prohibiting teachers in any state-supported school from teaching the theory, and in Little Rock in 1968, the statute came up for a test. Mrs. Epperson, a biology teacher, sought to have the statute invalidated on the grounds that it was too narrow and interfered with her right to academic freedom The United States Supreme Court agreed with her and declared the statute unconstitutional. Instead of exploring the academic freedom (speech freedom) implications of the case, however, the Supreme Court based its ruling on religious grounds, holding in effect that a statute that limits teaching in public schools to that theory of the origin of man contained in Genesis alone amounts to an establishment of religion. *Epperson v. Arkansas,* 393 U.S. 97, 1968. "Such a limitation of teaching rights is not within the bounds of neutrality towards religion required by the First Amendment," said the Court in holding that the new biology book containing a chapter on Darwin's theory could legally be used in the public schools of Arkansas.

Figure 8-1

THE SUPREME COURT SPEAKS ON TEACHER LOYALTY OATHS

- A public employee may be discharged pursuant to a state security law where he refuses to answer questions relevant to his/her employment. *Lerner v. Casey,* 357 U.S. 468, N.Y. 1958; *Beilan v. Bd. of Public Educ.,* 357 U.S. 399, Pa., 1958.
- A statute requiring teachers as a condition of employment to list all organizations to which they belonged or contributed in the past five years is unconstitutional. *Shelton v. Tucker,* 364 U.S. 479, Ark. 1960.
- A state statute requiring all public employees to swear in writing that they have never lent their "aid, support, advice, counsel, or influence to the Communist party" is unconstitutional. *Cramp v. Bd. of Public Instruction,* 368 U.S. 278, Fla. 1961.
- A statute that requires teachers to swear "by precept and example ... to promote respect for the flag and the institutions of the U.S. ..." is so vaguely written as to be unconstitutional. *Baggett v. Bullitt,* 377 U.S. 360, Wash. 1964.
- A loyalty oath that attaches sanctions to membership without requiring the "specific intent" to further the illegal aims of the organization is unconstitutional. *Elfbrandt v. Russell,* 384 U.S. 11, Ariz. 1966.
- To be valid, a loyalty oath for public employees must be limited to knowing, active members who help to pursue the illegal goals of the subversive organization. *Keyishian v. Board of Regents,* 385 U.S. 589, N.Y. 1967.

TEACHERS AND FREEDOM OF SPEECH

In Illinois, a teacher was dismissed for writing and sending to a newspaper for publication a letter criticizing the board for allocating school funds to athletic programs rather than the academic program. The letter contained some inaccuracies, but in general was temperate and on point. The board, after a hearing, dismissed the teacher for speech "detrimental to the efficient operation and administration of the schools of the district," but failed to show that such disruption had in fact occurred. The Supreme Court held that in the absence of malice or fraud, the teacher was protected in criticizing the board on issues of public interest. The teacher's right to freedom of speech and of the press must be balanced against the state's interest in efficient public schools. Since there had been no actual disruption of the schools as a result of the letter, the Court held that the dismissal of the teacher had been improper. *Pickering v. Board of Education,* 391 U.S. 563, Ill. 1968.

"A teacher is entitled to the same protection under the First Amendment as any member of the general public," said the Court. The Court, however, did not set down a general standard against which all critical statements might be judged in future, choosing instead to base its holdings on a case-by-case basis. The statements were in no way directed towards any person with whom the teacher would normally be in contact in the course of his daily work as a teacher, so there was no threat to the working relationship. The statements were not *per se* libelous, and even though some of them were false, there was no indication that the falsification was deliberately made. Aside from the fact that it made the board angry, the letter had little effect on school operation, and was therefore protected by the Constitution.

"Teachers as a class are the members of a community most likely to have informed and definite opinions as to how funds allocated to the operation of the schools should be spent. Accordingly, it is essential that they be able to speak out freely on such questions without fear of retaliatory dismissal," said the Court in upholding the teacher's right of free expression, and ordering his reinstatement.

In *Perry v. Sindermann,* 408 U.S. 593, Tex. 1972 a teacher in a community college was dismissed because he publicly criticized the board of regents. A press release by the board stated that insubordination was the cause of dismissal, but it provided the teacher with no official statement of reasons. There was no pre-termination hearing. Although he had no formal tenure, the Supreme Court held he had *de facto* tenure based on language in the college's official faculty guide providing that teachers who had been in the system seven years could be dismissed only for cause.

"A person may not be denied a government benefit because of the exercise of a constitutionally protected right," said the court. "An objective expectation of continuing employment is created where a teacher, as here, has been in the system for a length of time sufficient to build up a vested interest in the job. The state may not impair a life, liberty, or property interest arbitrarily without affording the injured party appropriate procedural protections."

SEX EXPRESSION AND TEACHER FITNESS

One area that continues to raise the hackles of parents is where the teacher mentions sex in his classroom, or otherwise gives the impression that he or she is unfit to teach because of "suggestive" remarks in class. A teacher who, for example, discussed matters relating to sex in his speech classes was suspended and later discharged. He sued for reinstatement on the grounds that his dismissal had been arbitrary, oppressive and unreasonable. The court, however, refused his request for relief, holding that he was paid to teach speech, and not biology. "Bringing up the topic of sex in his speech classes exceeded the bounds of propriety. We deem that it constituted bad conduct which would warrant a discharge even though there was no express rule prohibiting it and he had received no warning to desist therefrom. As an intelligent person trained to teach at the high school level, the teacher should have realized that such conduct was improper." *State ex rel. Wasilewski v. Bd. of School Directors of City of Milwaukee,* 111 N.W.2d 198, Wisc. 1961.

In Florida, a public school teacher was offered another contract on the condition that he refrain from discussing his personal sexual exploits in class. He refused and filed suit charging denial of academic freedom. The court said that such expression as talking about masturbation, prostitution and homosexuals in class was not protected by the First Amendment. *Moore v. Sch.Bd. of Gulf City,* 364 F.Supp. 355, Fla. 1973.

New Jersey law authorizes local boards to require employees to undergo psychological examination "if the need arises." A male teacher in that state was elected president of the Gay Alliance of New Jersey and he announced his intention to publicize the Gay Movement even though warned by the board that this might lead to an investigation of his job potential. When he persisted, the board then sought to have him examined by a psychiatrist. "The state has an interest," said the court," in protecting school children from the influence of unfit teachers, and teachers who deviate from the normal conduct expected of teachers may be unfit for teaching." *Kochman v. Keansburg Bd. of Educ.*, 305 A.2d 807, N.J. 1973. In a similar case, a teacher appealed to the Commissioner of Education. The latter upheld as lawful the board's directive that the teacher submit to an examination, and his decision was affirmed by the State Board of Education. On appeal, the court held that while one has the right to speak out, such a right must depend on its timing, its substance, its purpose, its truthfulness and other factors. The board was merely contending that the teacher's actions were evidence of "deviation from normal mental health which may affect his ability to teach, discipline and associate with his students." A teacher's fitness may not be measured "solely by his or her ability to perform the teaching function and ignore the fact that the teacher's presence in the classroom might, nevertheless, pose a danger of harm to the students for a reason not related to academic proficiency," said the court in holding that the board's requirement of a psychiatric examination was reasonable under the circumstances. *Gish v. Bd. of Educ. of Borough of Paramus*, 336 A.2d 1337, N.J. 1976, *cert. denied*, 46 L.W. 3220, 1977.

Another form of "sexual expression" may be a sex change, as in the case of *In the Matter of the Tenure Hearing of Paula M. Grossman*, 316 A.2d 39, N.J. 1974. The court was faced with determining whether a sex change from male to female made the teacher unfit to teach. In holding that it would, the court noted that the children had known the teacher as a male, one Paul Grossman, and that his/her presence in the classroom following a sex change might have a negative effect on the mental health of the children that might result in the teacher's loss of control over the children. The Supreme Court of New Jersey refused to review the finding (321 A.2d 253, 1974).

In Maryland, a junior high school science teacher received some notoriety for his advocacy of the Gay Rights Movement. The question before the court was whether the actions of the teacher, in publicizing his dispute with the school board, impaired his teaching effectiveness. The court found no evidence that his activity had disrupted the school, and held that his statements made in public were protected by the Constitution. The court did rule, however, that the board could find sufficient grounds for the dismissal in that the teacher, in filling out an application to teach in the district, had fraudulently denied that he was

Figure 8-2

A CASE IN POINT

Jane, a single high school girls' p.e. teacher, was rated satisfactory or better during her two-year stint on the job. After the board had offered her a third contract, and after she had signed it, she notified her principal that she was pregnant. Despite her signed contract, the board met and moved to dismiss Jane on the grounds that her "condition" reflected adversely on the school, and that her conduct was "immoral" and that her continued presence in the gym "would have a detrimental effect on her students." The board also claimed that because of her duties as a p.e. teacher, Jane's pregnancy would make her unable to teach. She appealed to the state board of education, which upheld the board. She then appealed to the courts, pointing out that the board had not taken similar action against five other unwed pregnant teachers in the same school system. To her aid came several teachers, administrators and parents who sought her reinstatement. The board, however, refused to reverse its decision.

Should the court rule that the teacher's dismissal had been illegal?

The court ruled in favor of Jane, the teacher. Based on undisputed facts in the case, the board had failed to move against five other pregnant single teachers, an action that was "arbitrary, unreasonable, and not supported by substantial evidence." Furthermore, the board had failed to demonstrate that Jane's "condition" would in any way adversely affect her teaching duties. "One does not come into court with opinions only," said the court (in reference to the board's claim of "immorality"), "but with hard evidence that a teacher's effectiveness is destroyed as a matter of fact." The court ordered her dismissal reversed, and reinstated her to the position of teacher of p.e. *New Mex. State Bd. of Educ. v. Stoudt*, 571 P.2d 1186, 1977.

a homosexual. *Acanfora v. Bd. of Educ. of Montgomery County*, 491 F.2d 498, cert. denied, 419 U.S. 836, Md. 1974.

Sexual aberrations may form the basis for teacher dismissal if there is a tendency to destroy the professional achievement of the teacher in question. A teacher in Illinois challenged his dismissal as a result of his involvement in a magazine in which a picture of him together with a woman nude from the waist up appeared. The court upheld his dismissal since the evidence showed that the magazine in question was obscene and that the conduct which resulted in his termination was not constitutionally protected. In arriving at its conclusion that the magazine was "obscene," the court offered these indicia: (1)

the average person applying contemporary community standards (Chicago) would find that the work, taken as whole, appeals to the prurient interest in sex; (2) the dominant theme of the magazine is morbid interest in nudity, sex, bondage and discipline, and sado-masochism; in addition, it depicts sexual conduct in a patently offensive way; and (3) the magazine is utterly without redeeming social value and the work, taken as a whole, lacks serious literary, artistic, political, or scientific value. *Weissbaum v. Hannon*, 439 F.Supp. 873, Ill. 1977.

Figure 8-3

IS A TEACHER'S PRIVATE CONDUCT HIS OWN BUSINESS?

"The private conduct of a man, who also is a teacher, is a proper concern of those who employ him only to the extent it mars him as a teacher, who also is a man. When his professional achievement is unaffected, where the school community is placed in no jeopardy, his private acts are his own business and may not be the basis of discipline."

Quoted in *Erb v. Iowa State Bd. of Public Instruction*, 216 N.W.2d 339, Iowa 1974 (finding that plaintiff teacher's fitness to teach was not irreparably harmed by a single adulterous act).

A teacher of some experience was observed by a neighbor, a policeman and the school superintendent to carry, dress, fondle, undress, and examine a mannequin on his own property. Although he admitted the bizarre behavior, he sought damages for his dismissal, claiming the behavior was protected. His psychiatrist testified in his behalf and opined that his behavior would not undermine his effectiveness with children. His dismissal was upheld on the grounds that his manifestation of sexual aberration would constitute conduct unbecoming a teacher. *Wishart v. McDonald*, 500 F.2d 1110, Mass. 1974.

FOUR-LETTER WORDS IN THE CLASSROOM

Academic freedom consists of two parts: the student's right to know and the teacher's right to teach. The former is virtually without legal limit, the latter must in the nature of things be limited by the state's interests expressed through the local board of education. More will be

---

Figure 8-4

A CASE IN POINT

A 51-year-old teacher who had been married to the same man for 29 years told a judge her membership in a wife-swapping club had nothing to do with her competency to teach. She was supported by her principal, who testified that her classroom teaching was adequate, and that the board had offered to rehire her for the following year. She was challenging revocation of her credential to teach by the State Board of Education under a state statute permitting the State Board to revoke certificates of those teachers it thought should be weeded out "for obvious unfitness for service." A hearing examiner had found that as a member of the "Swingers Club" she had engaged in acts of sexual intercourse and oral copulation with men other than her husband and had appeared on television programs (while facially disguised) to argue for unconventional sexual behavior. She sued to regain her credential, maintaining that her private life was her own business.

If you were the judge, would you rule in favor of the teacher or for the board of education?

The board won. With two justices filing dissenting opinions, the state supreme court ruled that the teacher had not been unconstitutionally deprived of her license to teach. "The intimate and delicate relationship between teachers and students," said the majority opinion, "requires that teachers be held to standards of morality in their private lives that may not be required of others." *Petit v. State Board of Education,* 513 P.2d 889, Cal. 1973.

---

said in Chapter 15 on the right of the student to know; here we are concerned with the teacher's right to teach.

Academic freedom may not be a negotiable item. For example, an agreement between the teachers' association and the local board provided that whenever appropriate from the standpoint of the maturation level of the group, controversial issues could be studied in an unprejudiced and dispassionate manner. The agreement delegated to the association what issues were to be considered. A teacher in the district was directed by the superintendent not to conduct a debate on the subject of abortion in his seventh grade class. He appealed to the association which sought to have the issue arbitrated by the American Arbitration Association. The trial court held that a local board of education had the responsibility to decide whether a debate on abortion was proper subject matter, and that that responsibility could not be left to an arbitrator. The contract in that respect was declared *ultra vires* (outside the power) of the board and was therefore unenforceable. *Bd. of Educ. of Rockaway Twp. v. Rockaway Twp. Educ. Ass'n.*, 295 A.2d 380, N.J. 1972.

Similarly, a Colorado case agreement contained the sentence that "the board shall have the right to determine the process, techniques, methods and means of teaching any and all subjects." Acting under the agreement, the board directed that ten books previously used were to be deleted from the program of studies in English. Teachers who taught English courses using the books brought an action to test the board's right to control the curriculum. The federal district court held that normally, although teachers may reasonably be expected to exercise their professional judgment as to what is studied in the classroom, this constitutional protection can be bargained away in the same manner as an editorial writer agrees to write the views of a publisher or an actor contracts to speak the author's script. "One can," said the court, "agree to teach according to direction." *Cary v. Bd. of Education*, 427 F.Supp. 945, Colo. 1977. On appeal, the Tenth Circuit Court reversed the court below on the ground that state statutes gave the board the right to select textbooks, including those used in elective courses, and that since the board had such a right already, it would have no need to bargain such an item with the local teachers' association. *Cary v. Bd. of Education*, 427 F. Supp. 945, Colo. 1977, *Affirmed*, 10 CA July 10, 1979. On that basis, the court found it unnecessary to consider whether teachers' unions can bargain away the rights, if any, of their individual members to choose what textbooks they will use in the classroom.

Professional judgment (or lack of it) among teachers may lead to complications, as illustrated by a case that arose in Illinois. Three non-tenured teachers engaged in team teaching were terminated by the board for introducing into their class "Woodstock" materials that referred to the joys of smoking marijuana and invited children to dismiss the discipline of home and moral environment and enter a new world of freedom. The court upheld their dismissal on the grounds that (1) the materials served no defensible educational purpose; (2) the materials were not suited to the developmental level of the students; (3) no expert was needed to see that the materials were "dirty" (the teachers had introduced expert testimony that the materials were harmless); and (4) the context and manner of presentation were faulty (the materials were merely passed out without comment). The Circuit Court of Appeals affirmed the court below, stating that the language and substance of such materials were inappropriate for students of elementary age. *Brubaker v. Bd. of Educ., Cook Co.,* 496 F.2d 700, Ill 1974.

A teacher in California was faced with the problem of how to teach poor readers to communicate. To arouse class interest, she assigned a composition in which students could write about anything they wished. To motivate them, the teacher told them to disregard spelling and grammar, and concentrate on things that interested them at the moment. Given these freedoms, the students wrote poems and essays containing vulgar references to the genitalia and the sex act. When the teacher received these materials, she had to make a choice between rejecting the lot, or, in the interest of reaching the students, tell them that what they wrote was not evil. She chose the latter course, and had the materials duplicated since the handwriting was almost illegible. She then handed the materials out to the class with instructions to return them all to her at the end of the period. About a month later, a boy in the class who had been disciplined by the teacher turned in a copy of the materials to the principal, who recommended that the teacher be fired. Acting on his advice, the board fired the teacher and she sought reinstatement in court. Her case was successful.

"Under the circumstances," said the court, "the trial court was not warranted in branding the teacher for the rest of her life as displaying 'evident unfitness for service' in her chosen profession. There was no violation of academic freedom involved in an inquiry into whether or not the teacher's conduct is such as to constitute evident unfitness for teaching. A teacher faced with such a problem should be encouraged to experiment in order to reach the students at their own level of development." Said the court:

> We should also consider that in this world there are many cultures and many concepts of what is acceptable sexual conduct, and of what sexual conduct may be the subject of free and open discussion or publication in folklore or literature. It may be impossible to impose one strict moral code on all of society, and we may have to acquaint ourselves with, and accept, without puritanical prudery, as natural to them, the standards of others. *Oakland Unified School Dist. v. Olicker,* 25 CA3rd 1098, 1972.

These cases raise the natural question, "What is the legal definition of obscenity, and what are the limitations placed on the teacher thereby?" Hardly any constraints have been imposed on public school classroom teachers by the *legal* definition of obscenity, which provides that these three components all be present before the state may limit the materials in question:

1) Whether the average person, applying contemporary community standards, would find that the work, taken as a whole, appeals to the prurient (sexual) interest;
2) whether the work depicts or describes, in a patently offensive way, sexual conduct specifically defined by the applicable state law; and
3) whether the work, taken as a whole, lacks serious literary, artistic, political, or scientific value.

Miller v. California, 413 U.S. 15, Cal. 1973.

Under this test, what would be obscene for an elementary school child might not be obscene for a high school student, or what is obscene for a high school student might not be considered so for a junior college student. In California, a junior college instructor of English read to her class a poem of her own composition that was sprinkled with "obscenities, slang references to male and female sexual organs and to sexual activity, and profane references to Jehovah and Christ." She had also shown students photographs of nude couples to illustrate the textbook chapter on censorship, pornography, and obscenity. No one under 18 was in the class, and the teacher had told the students they might skip the class if they wished and later attend a substitute session. When the teacher was dismissed, she brought an action for reinstatement, admitting she might have been wrong in her professional judgment as to the efficacy of the procedure used. The court ruled in her favor on the grounds that the board had failed to show that her conduct had adversely affected the students in any way. *Bd. of Trustees, LA Jr. College v. Metzger*, 501 P.2d 1172, Cal. 1972.

In summary, teachers may safely introduce materials into their classrooms if they select such materials on the basis of these guidelines which courts have laid down: (1) the materials must be directly related to a valid educational purpose acceptable to the course of study; (2) the materials must be suited to the age and relative maturity of the students; and (3) there is no board rule or regulation which specifically

Figure 8-5

ANOTHER CASE IN POINT

A high school English teacher assigned the class outside reading from a novel, *The Thread That Runs So True*, which described how in a one-room rural school the girls sat on one side of the room and the boys on the other. Discussion brought out that the students thought the seating arrangement was ridiculous. The teacher remarked that other things are just as ridiculous—for example, "taboo" words. He wrote the word "goo" on the blackboard and asked the class for a definition. After it was established that no one could define it, the teacher said that this word did not exist in English but that in another culture it might be a taboo word. He then wrote on the blackboard the word "fuck" and asked for a definition. A student defined it as sexual intercourse. "Here we have two words," said the teacher. "One word is acceptable in society, the other is not. It is a taboo word." After some discussion of other taboo words, the teacher went on to other matters. The board heard about the lesson and discharged the teacher, who sought reinstatement in court.

If you were the judge, would you rule in favor of the teacher or the board of education?

The court ruled in the teacher's favor. The use of the word had a legitimate educational purpose, it was fitted to the age and maturity of the students, and was presented in a professional (not erotic or obscene) manner. There was no disturbance from the use of the word, the word was in other books in the school library, and there was no school rule against the introduction of the word into the classroom. *Mailloux v. Kiley*, 323 F.Supp. 1387, Mass. 1971, Affirmed, 448 F.2d 1242, 1971.

outlaws such materials beforehand. Since teachers must be free to experiment with alternative methods of presentation, boards should not penalize them for lack of judgment alone so long as the other points given above are carefully observed in practice.

You and the Affirmative Action Program

WHAT AFFIRMATIVE ACTION IS

When the term first came into use in American law, "affirmative action" referred to the power—even the duty—of the National Labor Relations Board to "effectuate the policies of the National Labor Relations Act." *NLRB v. National Casket Company*, 107 F.2d 992, 998, N.Y. 1939. Today, the term has a much broader meaning, including not only its original NLRB meaning as before, but a civil rights implication as well. Affirmative action places a positive duty on governmental bodies, employers and the like, which is far beyond the negative obligation not to discriminate. It means that there must be a plan to take positive action to eliminate any existing or potential pattern or practice to discriminate, and avoid any discriminatory actions in the future. *So. Ill. Builders Ass'n v. Ogilvie*, 471 F.2d 680, 684, Ill. 1972.

Thus, affirmative action "plans" have come into being. Their purpose was expressed by the court in *City of Minneapolis v. Richardson*, 239 N.W.2d 197, Minn. 1976, "to eliminate existing and continuing discrimination, to remedy lingering effects of past discrimination, and to create systems and procedures to prevent future discrimination." This broader focus is related to the civil rights movement, and illustrates a wide range of coverage—race, sex, employment, access to educational resources, and similar opportunities related to one's civil rights before the law.

In *City of Minneapolis v. Richardson*, a 12-year-old black youth sued the city for damages for his arrest and related alleged discrimination. In the course of his brush with the law, the youth's testimony revealed racial slurs against him by the arresting officers. After a hearing before the Minnesota Human Rights Commission, the Commission ordered the police chief to write a letter of apology to the boy. The question before the court was whether such a measure came within the meaning of "affirmative action." The court held that the Commission's action was improper, since it was "calculated to humiliate and debase its writer, not to remedy the lingering effects of past discrimination." A proper action might have been to issue a cease and desist order against the police department relative to its dealings with minority individuals, or to order the city to draw up an affirmative action program to deal with police discrimination in the future. However, the city was held to be liable for damages for its actions taken under cover of state law, although the individuals involved were not liable. This is an example of a state case proceeding under a state statute. Many of the states have human rights legislation, supplemented by federal legislation and various executive orders. This creates a network of legal problems since plaintiffs must know something of this area of the law in order to seek and gain relief in discrimination matters.

Besides state legislation guaranteeing human rights, the Congress implemented the affirmative action concept in the Civil Rights Act of 1964, notably Titles VI and VII, which forbid employers in both public and private employment from engaging in discriminatory activity. In addition, the various executive orders by Presidents Kennedy, Johnson and Nixon specifically outlawed employment discrimination in the federal governmental service. Armed with these laws and executive tools, the courts have vigorously enunciated criteria to be followed to come into compliance with the requirements. These criteria either outline how compliance can be achieved, or in specific instances where there has been a pattern or practice of past discrimination, how the wayward parties should proceed to respond to claims of lack of fundamental fairness in their actions. This chapter is about affirmative action plans for public schools, how to proceed to develop them, their characteristics, their problems, and how boards can avoid appearances of discriminatory actions in their day-to-day operations.

HOW TO PROCEED

A district board that wishes to draw up either a voluntary or court-ordered affirmative action plan should begin with a positive statement such as the following policy statement developed by the Aurora Public Schools, Aurora, Colorado.

The ————————— School District will provide equal opportunities for employment by recruitment, training and advancement to all people regardless of race, color, creed, national origin, sex or any other factor not directly related to the duties of the job involved. Affirmative actions toward achieving equal employment opportunities within the district will be given a high priority by the Superintendent and administrative staff and shall receive the prompt and full attention of the Board at all times. The Superintendent shall have overall responsibility for the implementation of the District's Affirmative Action Program. The District will measure itself against specific objectives which will continue to move its employment posture toward full and equal participation of all employees in the District.

The Superintendent will determine whether the program is achieving its objectives by periodic surveys. The survey results will be reported to the Board of Education together with appropriate recommendations for action to correct any deficiencies.

The Board believes that the principle of setting employment goals for minorities and women is appropriate and directs the Superintendent to begin immediately to develop and implement those goals and report back to the Board by ————————— 19 ——— with a recommendation for adoption concerning these goals.

The ————————— School District has always had outstanding leadership in the area of education and by providing equal opportunities for all, the Board will continue to exemplify outstanding leadership.

Date of Adoption —————————

Signed: —————————

—————————
—————————   Members of the Board of Education
—————————
—————————

The foregoing policy statement relates to Title VII of the Equal Employment Opportunity Act of 1972. A similar policy statement should be adopted relating to the eradication of all discrimination on the basis of sex in schools (Title IX) and on the basis of race (42 U.S.C. §1983, 1981) taken either intentionally or inadvertently under color of state law.

DEVELOPING THE AFFIRMATIVE ACTION PLAN

The discrepancy model described in Chapter 12, page 172 is the typology to be followed in developing your affirmative action plan. The procedure consists of finding out where the district currently is with respect to compliance or lack of compliance, an establishment of goals and timetables to come into full compliance, and how the district will proceed to come into full compliance given the present status and the perceived needs of the district. (See Figure 9-1.)

The data needed will include the numbers and kinds of job openings available in the district, the population make-up of the district (in metropolitan areas, the district must sometimes approximate the ethnic distribution of the whole area rather than its own ethnic make-up), and the present procedures for hiring and promoting district personnel. What is important is to attain as clear a picture of the district's employment practices as possible in the status stage of the study.

Once the present condition has been established, it then is a simple matter to compare current status with the desired status toward which the district must work in order to come into full compliance. For each discrepancy noted, there must be a plan for removing the discrepancy within a certain time frame. Goals and timetables must be realistic, that is, they must be attainable, measurable, specific enough to be identified, non-rigid in nature, and designed to take care of possible expanding enrollments in the district. Most important is the assignment of responsibility for removing the discrepancy—the superintendent, the personnel director, or other individual should be "written into" the program so that no doubt remains as to who is to do what. Finally, the plan should be adopted officially by the board and the details entered into the minutes. Periodic review of progress should be provided for as well as in-depth reports of remaining deficiencies to be removed. Success of the plan will depend on how clearly the plan is known and understood by those who will have some part in its completion. This implies a period of publicity, a beginning stage, a period of review and re-direction, and an ending period for the project. The plan is doomed to failure if it is ambiguous, lacks realistic goals and timetables, and/or is done for show only.

Figure 9-1

DEVELOPMENT OF AFFIRMATIVE ACTION PLANS, AN OUTLINE

I. Analysis of the Deficiencies
    A.   Work form analysis (listing of each job title)
    B.   Analysis of all major job groups
    C.   Analysis of the minority population of the area and work force

II. Establishment of Goals and Timetables
    A.   Goals and timetables must be
        1. Attainable
        2. Measureable
        3. Specific
        4. Non-rigid
        5. Designed to take care of expansion (and/or contraction)
        6. Designed to correct deficiencies

III. Provisions for Full Dissemination to Staff and Community

IV. Establishment of Responsibility

V. Action-Oriented Program with
    A.   A design to eliminate problems
    B.   A design for implementation
    C.   A design for an internal auditing and reporting program
    D.   A design for active support of community action programs

---

AFFIRMATIVE ACTION PROGRAMS IN EMPLOYMENT

The establishment of hiring goals and quotas pertains to one's right to obtain and remain in a job according to one's merit. Employers in both the private and public sectors are prohibited from discriminating against any person in the hiring, retention and promotion processes. In *Griggs v. Duke Power Co.*, 401 U.S. 424, 1971 the Supreme Court struck down an employment screening plan because it excluded a disproportionate number of minority applicants. Said the Court on that occasion, "If an employment practice which operates to exclude Negroes cannot be shown to be related to job performance, the practice is prohibited." If schooling of a certain kind is required, it must be shown that it is indeed related and applicable to the available job openings before the employer can use such a requirement for hiring purposes. The burden of proof required by the compelling state interest formula will almost always invalidate a discriminatory practice. For example, if the board is to require a certain degree of an applicant, or call for additional college work to qualify for the job, it had better be ready to show that there is a definite relation between its requirement and the job to be done. Discrimination may be said to exist where there are differential rates of applicant rejection for women or for minorities. If the district is unable or unwilling to do the research required to support a hiring practice, you should then adjust employment procedures so as to eliminate the conditions suggestive of employment discrimination.

Sex may be a bona fide occupational qualification, but race may not. A *bona fide* occupational qualification (BFOQ) means that the employer must be ready to show that the job cannot be done at all by a woman (actor, weight lifter) in order to require that only male applicants need apply. Other discriminatory practices might be the following: (1) making selection of employees or rejection depend entirely upon a single test score; (2) using tests without evidence that they are valid predictors of job performance; or (3) using a test that discriminates against any minority group.

Sometimes the courts will direct the board to enact policy to remove a pattern or practice that tends to discriminate in employment. In *Moore v. Board of Education of Chidester School District*, 448 F.2d 709, Ark. 1971, the court ordered the board to "use *objective* nondiscriminatory standards in the employment, assignment and dismissal of teachers." The court allowed the board to continue to use "established and previously announced nondiscriminatory *subjective* factors" in making such decisions. The board had dismissed a teacher who was pregnant and unwed. The court of appeals held that the board had acted arbitrarily in failing to give the teacher, before dismissal, notice of the charges against her and an opportunity to meet such charges. What the court was driving at was that moral judgments are subjective, not objective in nature. "We find it difficult to recognize the validity of the moral standards used to evaluate (the teacher) because the board, prior to integration, had never established and announced that it would use such subjective standards in determining whether to employ or dismiss teachers."

In any event, the board continued to operate the schools without benefit of either written or orally announced employment standards, making policy and applying standards in a subjective, individual and unannounced manner despite the directions and guidelines set forth in *Moore*. In due time, a similar case arose, where a black teacher was dismissed because she was pregnant and unwed. When the teacher also challenged her dismissal, she won back salary, $7,500 in damages due to the stigma caused by the board's action, in addition to attorney's fees and court costs. *Cochran v. Chidester School District*, 456 F.Supp. 390, Ark. 1978. In pointing out that the fact situations were "identical," the court said in part, "The Board cannot simply determine that a teacher offends some personal moral code of its members, or even some 'universal code' of the community. The Board, under the previous ruling in *Moore*, must adopt and announce, preferably in writings delivered to each teacher at the time of employment, the objective criteria which will be utilized in the decisions of the Board as to the hiring, assignment and dismissal or non-renewal of its teachers."

The point is well made here that while courts will sometimes accept subjective standards for employment of personnel, they ordinarily are more impressed by written, previously announced policies that attempt at least to objectify hiring practices. That is the end and purpose of any affirmative action program, and boards should not wait until they are directed by a court to develop such objective criteria, for by that time it may be too late.

The court held that the imposition by the board of an adverse stigma on the teacher might result in a deleterious effect on her future employment opportunities—a professional stigma. Lack of a due process hearing before dismissal would deprive the teacher of her liberty interest under the circumstances. Since this case was decided after the Supreme Court ruled that school districts may be considered "persons," the district in *Cochran* had to pay the costs (see *Monell v. Dept. of Special Services, City of New York*, 98 S.Ct. 2018, 1978, overruling *Monroe v. Pape*, 365 U.S. 167, Ill. 1961).

The court went on to charge the individual board members, however, with the affirmative duty to "notice and have knowledge of the many decisions which have been handed down by the Supreme Court and lower Federal courts in terminating a teacher." The board had been directly informed in *Moore* of the requirements for adoption and communication of policies to teachers (the same requirements as in *Wood v. Strickland*, 420 U.S. 308, Ark. 1975). Thus, the board members, as individuals, could be held personally liable for failure to provide due process procedures, while the superintendent, who was not an employee of the district at the time the action was taken, was spared this liability.

"No standard (for non-discrimination in employment) shall be applied or enforced," said the court, "until the same has been submitted to this court for consideration and has been on file herein for not less than 30 days after filing. A copy of the approved standard must also be given to each teacher 30 days before its effective date, and to each applicant for a teaching job in the district at the time of applying. No such standard shall be deleted, modified, or added to without the filing and posting (for 30 days in a prominent place available to teachers) as provided for in this opinion." Further, the district was enjoined from applying any non-adopted or unannounced standard without the court's consent in future. (If you think you have problems, wait until you're under a court order to come up with an affirmative action plan to eradicate a pattern and practice of discrimination in the treatment of your school's employees. You won't be able to move without first checking back with the judge.)

"This court will retain jurisdiction over the defendant school district and school board until further order of the court, for the purpose of ensuring compliance with its order and judgment," are words that have a certain finality to them. To avoid such finality, it's always better to volunteer the formulation of affirmative action guidelines early on, lest in hesitating you open the door for the judge to take your case "under advisement until further notice."

REVERSE DISCRIMINATION

One obvious conflict in overcoming past discriminatory practices is "reverse discrimination"—whether one who is denied a benefit or favor in order that a minority individual may gain it instead is treated unconstitutionally in the process. Courts at first did not agree. In *Anderson v. San Francisco Unified School District*, 357 F.Supp. 248, Cal. 1972, the federal district court examined the board's personnel policy that favored the employment of applicants of minority racial and ethnic backgrounds over "anglos" and found it "necessarily deprives non-minority individuals of equal opportunity."

After being denied admission to a state-operated law school, DeFunis brought suit asking that the school's minority preference admission policies be declared racially discriminatory. Pending the outcome of his case, DeFunis was allowed to enter the law school and was in his final quarter of study when his case came before the U.S. Supreme Court. The Court held that since DeFunis was about to graduate, the case was moot, and refused to rule on the reverse discrimination issue. "The usual rule is that this Court must decide active controversies only," said the majority of seven justices, "and that active controversy must exist at the time of review as well as at the legal action's beginning." Thus, the issue was not settled then, and continues to puzzle watchers of the Supreme Court, although some light has been shed on the reverse discrimination problem in subsequent cases. *DeFunis v. Odegaard*, 507 P. 2d 1169, Wash. 1973, *dismissed as moot*, 416 U.S. 312, 1974.

In *Regents of U. of Cal. v. Bakke*, 98 S.Ct. 2733, 1978 the Court had before it the issue of whether the regents' admission policy to the medical school at Davis unconstitutionally deprived a white male applicant of his civil rights. The trial court found that the special program operated as a racial quota, because minority applicants in that program were rated only against one another, and 16 places in the class of 100 were reserved for them. Declaring that the school could not take race into account in making admissions decisions, the program was held to violate the Federal and state Constitutions and Title VI. Bakke's admission was not ordered, however, for lack of proof that he would have been admitted but for the program. The California Supreme Court, applying a strict-scrutiny standard, concluded that the special admissions program was not the least intrusive means of achieving the goals of the admittedly compelling state interests of integrating the medical profession and increasing the number of doctors willing to serve minority patients. That court held such a special admissions program violated the equal protection clause of the Fourteenth Amendment. The

United States Supreme Court affirmed the judgment of the California Supreme Court and ordered Bakke admitted, but reversed the court below in its holding that race cannot be a factor in future admission policy decisions.

Both sides claimed victory, the white group claiming that their cause was vindicated because Bakke was ordered admitted, the minority group claiming victory because race can be a factor in formulating admission policy in higher education. The case raised more unsolved questions than it solved, and subsequent rulings of the Court must be forthcoming before a clear path for school authorities is apparent.

Bakke was an admissions case; other cases are grounded in employment. The confusion in time no doubt will be cleared up but it is still unclear what effect *Bakke* and subsequent cases will have on the issue of reverse discrimination. Bakke was ordered admitted only because the regents could not prove that he would not have been admitted even if there had been no special admissions program. The second issue—whether race can be used as a basis for admissions—also is unclear. The Court said that racial classifications "call for strict judicial scrutiny," meaning that the courts will now proceed on the theory that if race is an element in admitting students into graduate schools, there is a presumption that the state is acting illegally in so doing. "Nonetheless," said the Court, "the purpose of overcoming substantial, chronic minority underrepresentation in the medical profession is *sufficiently important* (emphasis supplied) to justify petitioner's remedial use of race. Thus, the judgment below must be reversed in that it prohibits race from being used as a factor in university admissions."

In *DiLeo v. Board of Regents, Univ. of Colorado,* 590 P.2d 486, Colo. 1978, plaintiff, an American of Italian ancestry, unsuccessfully sought to be admitted to a law school graduate program. Claiming that because he was of a minority group he was being discriminated against "in reverse," whereas other minority groups were being admitted, DiLeo charged the admissions plan was unconstitutional. The court held that his claim was without merit, and that he lacked standing to challenge the special admissions program since he was not a member of a minority group identified by the university as having been educationally and culturally deprived, or which was seriously underrepresented in the legal profession.

A reverse discrimination case that will have an impact on employment practices is *United Steelworkers v. Weber* (see Figure 9-2). The U.S. Supreme Court held that "carefully tailored" affirmative action plans do not necessarily result in "reverse discrimination" where they voluntarily seek to rectify past discriminatory employment practices.

GUIDELINES FOR AFFIRMATIVE ACTION PROGRAMS

Despite the confusion surrounding affirmative action programs in public schools, there appear to be these guides to boards of education:

1. Don't wait until a court orders your district to develop an affirmative action plan because then it may be too late. No board wants to report to a court of law to see what it can and cannot do. Voluntary conformity with legal standards looks better and is the preferred way to go.
2. Definite goals and timetables for the hiring, retention and promotion of minority employees should be preceded by a board policy statement, and an open and conscientious involvement of the community in its development. If tests are to be a part of the hiring and employment picture, the board must be ready to bear the burden of proof that there is a relation between the job and the test results.
3. Courts will look at your affirmative action program to determine if it excludes majority members of the population. Such "reverse discrimination" can be justified only when you can prove that you are meeting a "compelling state interest" under the equal protection clause of the Fourteenth Amendment.
4. When the goals and timetables have been met, an affirmative action program must then be adjusted in the light of new data. Affirmative action programs should not be viewed as a permanent educational solution to civil rights problems but rather should be thought of as temporary corrective devices to alleviate conditions that are repugnant to the constitutional guarantee that every individual has the right to life, liberty and property under the Constitution.

In a footrace, such as that between the tortoise and the hare, an unfair start can be inferred from an unfair outcome. If one runner is shackled and the other is not, the one without the shackles will ob-

Figure 9-2

WHAT THE WEBER CASE IS ALL ABOUT

How much special treatment must employers give to employees in order to overcome the negative effects of past discrimination? The Supreme Court held in 1979 that employers could give job preference to blacks to remedy "manifest racial imbalance" in the work force over the more than three hundred years involved in America's struggle with conscience in treatment of blacks.

In 1974, Brian Weber, a white employee of Kaiser Aluminum and Chemical Corp. in Gramercy, La. was excluded from a program to train unskilled workers for higher-paying jobs with the company. Instead, black employees with less seniority were accepted.

The firm's negotiated agreement with the United Steelworkers provided a $50/50$ racial mix in the program. Weber contended that the agreement, which was voluntarily entered into to avoid possible civil rights violations, deprived him of his right to work and that he was a victim of "reverse discrimination." The Supreme Court could not agree.

In a 5-2 decision bound to have major impact on employment practices in the future, the Court held that "properly tailored" affirmative action plans do not constitute reverse discrimination. Narrowly confined to Title VII of the CRA of 1964, which prohibits discrimination in employment, the Court's holding does not forbid private employers and unions from voluntarily rectifying previously disparate treatment of black employees. "No employer," said the Court, "is *required* to grant preferential treatment to any group because of race," although race can be taken into account in arriving at a balanced work force.

"It would be ironic indeed if the law triggered by a Nation's concern over centuries of racial injustice and intended to improve the lot of those who had 'been excluded from the American dream for so long' constituted the first legislative prohibition of all voluntary, private, race-conscious efforts to abolish traditional patterns of racial segregation and hierarchy," said the opinion. Not clear in the opinion is the question of whether the same rules applied by the Court here in the private sector apply equally well in the public sector of the economy. No doubt another case involving reverse discrimination in the public sector must be decided before it can be concluded that the *Weber* decision applies to affirmative action plans in public schools and colleges.

United Steelworkers v. Weber, 46 L.W. 4551, June 27, 1979.

viously go further. The intent of the law is to help the parties start equal and finish equal to each other. But not all runners begin with the same individual traits—personality, motivation, self-discipline, or wealth. The real question of law here is how can the shackled be unshackled without creating a disadvantage to the runner with no shackles to begin with? Must the runner who has had the advantage in prior races be penalized—be awarded a handicap, such as in bowling or golf—in order to make it an even race? The equal status of American citizenship is the basis on which the structure of inequality must be built to take into account the inequality of distribution of talent in the population. In that respect, reverse discrimination may be a betrayal, rather than a fulfillment, of the Great American Dream.

Keeping on the Safe Side When Dismissing Personnel

WORKING A RIGHT OR PRIVILEGE?

By far the most fertile field of litigation on educational matters is that of teacher dismissal or non-renewal. In most states, the competition for jobs is unprecedented. Thousands of teachers have been laid off, and more will be laid off in coming months. It seems reasonable, therefore, to anticipate that school administrators and board members should be informed on this area of the law in order to effectively reduce the work force when it is necessary to do so without fear that your actions will land you or your board in court.

There are generally three reasons for dismissal or non-renewal of a public school teacher: (1) need to reduce your teachers due to falling enrollments; (2) lack of funds to continue certain programs; and (3) need to dismiss or non-renew an individual teacher for cause. Each of these categories will be treated in turn.

Falling enrollments

Declining birthrates in the middle 1970's caused an excess of both capacity and staff. Once it has been established that staff must be laid off, it is crucial that teachers be laid off in strict compliance with the state tenure statutes and within the teachers' federally protected constitutional rights. Due to the shortage of jobs, teachers' associations will be examining every lay-off in minute detail. State tenure laws differ greatly, so the place to begin is with the tenure law in your state. Does it provide specifically for lay-off of teachers when there is a justifiable decrease in the number of teaching positions? (See Figure 10-1.) Some states allow for suspension of teachers' contracts when enrollments decrease. In others, the statutes are silent on dismissals for economic reasons, but do allow dismissals for such causes as immorality, misconduct, or incompetency. The statutes in which "just cause" can form the legal basis for non-renewal will be discussed later in this chapter. At any rate, you should become familiar with your state's tenure law in those cases in which there is to be a lay-off of those on tenure.

Figure 10-1

STATE LAWS GOVERNING DISMISSAL
OF A TENURED TEACHER

- The law lists certain kinds of misconduct as grounds for dismissal not including dismissal for economic reasons or for "good cause." LA, MD & OK.
- The law allows the board to "suspend" a teacher's contract because of falling enrollments. KY, OH, PA and RI.
- The law is silent as to dismissal for economic reasons, but lists incompetency, insubordination, and immorality as well as "for other good and just cause." MS and WY.
- The law specifically provides that in the event of a justifiable decrease in enrollments, teachers may be laid off. AL, CA, CN, DE, HA, KS, ME, MA, MI, MN, NV, NC and VA.
- The law authorizes boards to place teachers on leave because of a decrease in enrollment, reorganization of schools or lack of money. MO.
- The law permits boards to dismiss teachers "for cause" without specifically indicating the types of misconduct that are included in the term. WA.
- The law provides for annual renewal of the contract of employment unless the board gives notice to the teacher before a specified date. MANY STATES.

Sometimes the order in which teachers are to be laid off has been negotiated with the union. Apparently, these clauses are legal so long as they don't deny someone a hearing when one is required. In most instances where teachers are not protected by tenure, they may be laid off without giving reasons, except that if there is an indication that the lay-off may be the result of a teacher's exercise of a constitutional right, the teacher will then be entitled to a hearing on the merits.

No one, no matter how well prepared, has a *right* to work for the government. Working for the public schools is a *privilege*, conditioned on having the right certificate, being employed by a board of education at a legally called meeting, and otherwise being fully qualified. Nor does tenure extend the right to work—it merely assures that if the teacher is to be let off, he or she is entitled to a hearing. Since most tenure laws spell out the way in which a tenured teacher is to be laid off, the statute is controlling and laying off a teacher in any other way is null and void and to no effect.

Teachers' associations sometimes get into arguments with local boards on just how many teachers are to be employed. Generally speaking, the local board is the legal judge of what is adequate staffing, although the association or union can make the board look foolish or niggardly. It is not well settled that boards need to bargain class size with the union, but some do. Courts generally hold that boards have been given the power to hire and fire by the legislature, and they will not interfere in this power unless there is evidence that something is wrong. At any rate, there are no national standards on how many staff members are best, so this is generally a negotiable item when bargaining time comes around.

There are four situations in which a probationary teacher (one not on tenure) whose contract is not renewed has a right to a hearing:

- The first situation is where the non-reappointment will seriously damage the teacher's standing, reputation, or relationships in the community. An example might be where the board has claimed that the teacher is a homosexual, without more.
- The second situation is where adverse publicity given the firing by the board will foreclose the teacher's job opportunities. This "liberty" interest means the board must move carefully in making charges so that a "stigma" will not attach to the teacher due to the board's actions.
- The third occurs when the teacher is non-renewed because he or she exercised a constitutionally protected right, such as growing a beard or being active in the union.
- The fourth occurs when *de facto* tenure exists, as where a teacher has been in a job for many years and has a vested

interest in it even though not technically protected by the tenure laws of the state. *Board of Regents v. Roth*, 408 U.S. 564, Wisc, 1972; *Perry v. Sindermann*, 408 U.S. 593, Tex. 1972.

Lack of funds as just cause

Often the two go together—falling enrollments and lack of funds. The connection is that state per-pupil aid is paid on the basis of how many students the district has. When the number falls, the income from the state falls with it. School districts have raised the defense in some dismissal cases that they no longer have the money with which to pay teachers, so they must let them go. Another cause of lack of revenue is the refusal of the electorate to vote budgetary increases on property in the district. Millage elections are lost for many reasons— inflation, poor communications between the schools and the tax- payers, people's fear of losing their homes, and disenchantment with the job the schools are doing. School costs are going up faster than the costs of other consumer goods, a factor that taxpayers cannot readily understand. Those teachers not on tenure can be invited to a hearing on the actual fiscal condition of the district, or given individual hearings if they so desire. Those on tenure must be treated in the way the state law provides (see Figure 10-2).

Boards can often soften the blow of laying off teachers because of economic ill-health if they will project their needs beyond the one-year budgetary cycle. Also, boards can bargain with teachers on what pro- grams (hence, which teachers) they will lay off in a planned sequence of events. Some states have statutes that do not permit laying off tenured teachers when there are non-tenured teachers still on the payroll. Some even specify that a tenured teacher cannot be dismissed because of declining enrollments if there is a position available in the district for which he or she is qualified.

Most states do not specifically enumerate which order should be followed in laying off teachers. The board should therefore undertake negotiations with the teachers' union on what order is to be followed in the event that large numbers of teachers have to be laid off.

It is not clear whether probationary employees have a right to a hearing when released because of reduction in force or for reasons of economy. The courts have consistently upheld the right of teachers on tenure to such a hearing, but are divided on whether probationary

---

Figure 10-2

MINIMUM ESSENTIALS OF DUE PROCESS OF
LAW IN DISMISSALS

Courts have generally upheld the following minimum requirements of due process of law in dismissal cases:

- Clear and actual notice of the reasons for termination or non-renewal in sufficient detail to enable the person to know the reason for the proposed action and to enable him or her to present evidence relating to those reasons;
- The names of those who have made allegations against the person and the specific nature and factual basis for the charges;
- A reasonable time and opportunity to present testimony in the person's defense;
- The opportunity to cross-examine witnesses and to face those who accuse him;
- A hearing before an impartial board or tribunal; and
- The right to appeal to higher authority.

Provided the board is to be represented by legal counsel, this right should also be accorded the teacher.

---

teachers are so favored. *Kodish v. Spring-Ford Area Sch.Dist.*, 373 A.2d 124, Pa. 1977. The controlling factor seems to be the state statute, and the purpose of a hearing would be to see whether the dismissal falls within the statutory grounds and procedures to be followed. One thing is certain: *the courts will not invent a right for teachers*—if it is not granted by the state, the court will not provide it for them. Courts do protect the rights of teachers where stigma might attach (see four "situations, page 141), where job opportunities may be foreclosed by what the board is doing, where teachers are exercising a constitutionally protected right, or where *de facto* tenure already exists that may give teachers a "vested" interest in their contracts of employment.

Other just cause for dismissal

Ordinarily, the state statute will enumerate the grounds on which the board may dismiss a teacher; these generally are found in the state's teacher tenure law. For example, the tenure act for teachers in

---

Figure 10-3

WHAT IS A "TENURE LAW"?

A teacher tenure act is a law that provides at least these two guarantees after a teacher has gone through a probationary period (usually three years) in the same district:

- *Continuing contract*: the teacher on tenure is entitled to a contract for the ensuing year during good behavior, and

- *Impartial hearing*: if the board deems it necessary to non-renew the teacher's contract, the teacher is entitled to a full evidentiary hearing before an impartial tribunal before the non-renewal is final.

Many laws that are dubbed "tenure" laws are really not tenure laws at all, but only continuing contract laws of the spring variety.

Colorado lists these: physical or mental disability, incompetency, neglect of duty, immorality, conviction of a felony, insubordination, or other good and just cause. The latter clause is construed to mean that it, like the others before it in the act, is to be determined by the board, but the burden of proof rests with the board to prove that the just cause it selects from the available list is pertinent and that the teacher has violated some accepted standard for which he or she may be legally dismissed if the accusation is proved to be true.

A Colorado statute allowing a board to terminate a tenured teacher without a hearing "when there is a justifiable decrease in the number of teaching positions" was declared unconstitutional because the statute did not provide for a due process hearing. *Howell v. Woodlin S. Dist. R-104,* 596 P.2d 56, Colo. 1979. Some of the states use such terms as inefficiency instead of incompetency, and willful and persistent violation of reasonable regulations instead of insubordination, but the thought is there: teachers are expected to perform in a preconceived way, and any deviation from this standard that tends to embarrass the board or result in students not learning may prove grounds on which the teacher's employment may be terminated. Also, local standards can be applied to the teacher's performance—what may be allowed in one community may be grounds for dismissal in another.*

---

*See AASA's *Staff Dismissal: Problems and Solutions,* 1801 N. Moore St., Arlington, Va. 22209, 1978 for good advice on what districts are doing to meet this critical issue.

An example of this kind of thinking occurred in South Dakota. The school was in a rural area, and the teacher, who was unmarried, lived with her boyfriend in a trailer near the school. The board met with the teacher and indicated its embarrassment at the situation, asking her to remedy the situation or it would have to take official action. When she demurred, the board dismissed her on the grounds of immorality and incompetency, believing in good faith that her conduct "would have an adverse effect upon the pupils she was teaching," despite the fact that she was "a good teacher" and there was no proof of disruption or interference in the classroom.

The teacher did not flaunt her relationship. However, the board was mindful of the wishes of local parents, and their contention that the teacher's conduct "violated local mores, that her students were aware of this, and that because of the size of the town, this awareness would continue." The teacher brought suit for recovery of her job, and for damages against the board members. The Eighth Circuit Court of Appeals held that the board was not a "person" under Section 1983 and ruled that the board had met the good-faith requirements "by acting without malice, by balancing the constitutional interests of the teacher against the interests of the school community, and by not depriving the teacher of constitutional rights that were 'settled' and 'undisputed' in law." *Sullivan v. Meade Indep. School Dist.*, 530 F.2d 799, S.D. 1975, rehearing denied, March 24, 1976.

In another community where teachers were not so visible, the situation would perhaps not have been so critical as in a less populated area. This "double standard" seems archaic, but is upheld by the Supreme Court in the matter of local option as to what is "obscene." See *Miller v. California*, 413 U.S. 15, Cal. 1973. The same standards the courts apply to obscenity are therefore, by extrapolation, stretched so as to apply to local mores on which local boards of education may safely operate.

The civil rights movement spawned budding rights for many minorities, among them homosexuals. Despite its incidence in the population since earliest times, homosexuality has escaped serious scientific study, and there is still a considerable lack of provable data on the subject. In 1974, the American Psychiatry Association removed homosexuality from its list of mental illnesses. The public's attitude is also changing somewhat toward homosexuals, although slowly. Schools have been the scene of some predictable confrontations involving homosexual teachers, and there still remains much to be done to define the legal status of homosexuals in the public schools. In 1962, Illinois became the first of a dozen states to decriminalize homosexual activities between consenting adults. In the courts, the case law is divided and often misunderstood. Case law goes back only about 20 years, beginning in the early 1960's. See for example *Odorizzi v. Bloomfield Sch.Dist.*, 54 Cal.Rptr.533, Cal. 1966. The absence of cases before that time does not, however, mean that no homosexuals were employed by the public schools. Given the ten percent of the population that supposedly are homosexuals, it is likely that homosexuals were employed in teaching as in other professions. It took the civil rights movement to make them come out of the closet. If teachers were dismissed before the 1960's for homosexuality, the fact of their homosexuality was not discussed in court. Given the autonomy of school boards before that time, it is likely that homosexual teachers were forced to resign or face exposure of their status. Encouraged by civil rights people to assert their rights, homosexual teachers and other employees now are organized and are fighting discrimination directed toward them.

The Supreme Court has never accepted for review a case involving a homosexual public school teacher, although many state supreme courts have handled homosexuality as a factor in employment. Since education is a state function, and most states have requirements that teachers be "of good moral character," the Court has decided that each state should be the judge of its own teaching personnel. In federal employment, the Supreme Court has ruled that homosexuals are more susceptible to blackmail than heterosexuals, making them poor risks as spies. The lack of Supreme Court guidance on the issue of homosexual teachers has led to a dozen cases in which the state and federal courts have held that inasmuch as teachers are supposed to be "exemplars" to their students, public knowledge that a teacher is a homosexual, although not *per se* sufficient grounds for teacher dismissal, can be used by the board to build a case that such knowledge casts doubts on the teacher's effectiveness in the classroom. This generally occurs where criminal conduct on the part of the teacher results in a conviction for homosexual behavior, mainly solicitation to perform a homosexual act. In one case, a teacher's dismissal was upheld for "fraud" where he knowingly denied he was a homosexual in filling out an applicaton blank. The court held he could not be denied employment merely because he was a homosexual, but he could be dismissed for "deception" where he purposely misled school officials in his application for a job. *Acanfora v. Bd. of Educ. of Montgomery Co.,* 491 F.2d 498, Md. 1974; cert. den; 419 U.S. 836.

Two cases involving oral copulation, which in California is a criminal charge, came up in 1974. The court upheld dismissal of both male teachers on the grounds that their behavior was immoral. The court held that the board had the right and the duty to shield "children of tender years" from the possible detrimental influence "of teachers who commit acts beyond a reasonable doubt." Nor does one who stands trial on a criminal charge undergo double jeopardy when he must submit later to a civil hearing before the board of education. The constitutional bar against forcing one to stand trial more than once applies only to criminal cases, said the court in refusing to hold that the teacher had been unjustly treated. *Governing Bd. of Mountain View Sch. Dist. v. Metcalf,* 111 Cal. Rptr. 724, 1974 and *Bd. of Educ. of El Monte Sch. Dist. v. Calderon,* 110 Cal. Rptr. 916, 1974.

The Supreme Court ruled that even though a teacher's remarks to the principal in private were considered by that individual to be "petty and unreasonable, hostile, insulting, loud and arrogant," and made to one "who was an unwilling recipient," they are nonetheless protected by the First Amendment, and insufficient to warrant her dismissal. Whether remarks are made in public or in private makes no difference in the outcome—a teacher has a legitimate right to criticize the board's policies on desegregation without fear of retaliatory reprisal. Nor did a unanimous Supreme Court believe the "captive audience" claim. "The principal, having opened the office door to the teacher, was hardly in a position to argue that he was the 'unwilling recipient' of her views," said the Court in striking down the teacher's dismissal. *Givhan v. Western Line Consol. Sch. Dist.,* 99 S.Ct. 693, Miss. 1979.

In Ohio, a school board defended itself against a claim that it had acted unconstitutionally in terminating a non-tenured teacher. The board, in fighting the case all the way to the U.S. Supreme Court, survived the litigation and got its district on the map in a landmark case that will bear the name of the district as the point of law that boards must use their power or lose their power. The evidence established that the teacher had been involved in a physical altercation with another teacher, an argument with school cafeteria employees, an incident in which he swore at students, and another in which he made obscene gestures to female students. He had also telephoned a radio station in a nearby city to report that his school principal had unilaterally issued a teacher dress code to the school's teaching staff, a news item that was widely publicized. Claiming he had a right to freedom of speech, the teacher, upon being non-renewed, sought to be reinstated to his job. The superintendent's recommendation to the board had been that the teacher not be rehired because of "a notable lack of tact in handling professional matters which leaves some doubt as to your sincerity in establishing good school relationships." The teacher claimed his First Amendment rights had been denied him and that he was being punished because he spoke out against the principal. His case was unsuccessful.

The question before the Supreme Court was whether the teacher's constitutionally protected right to speak out had been a "substantial" factor in the decision not to renew his contract. The teacher claimed that it had been the "motivating factor" in his dismissal; therefore, it was null and void. The board countered by saying that while it used the radio station incident as "part" of the evidence against the teacher, it had other factors which it felt would have led to a firing *without* the radio station incident. The Supreme Court then put forward this rule in holding for the board and against the teacher: if the board can show, by a preponderance of the evidence, that it would have reached the same decision to fire the teacher even without the protected conduct, it acts within its sphere of authority. In remanding the case for further action based on this new rule, the Supreme Court set in motion a whole new era of teacher dismissal law to this effect. Initially, the teacher must bear the burden of proof that his protected conduct was a substantial factor in the board's decision to fire him; having carried that burden, however, the court will then go on to determine whether the board had shown by a preponderance of the evidence that it would have reached the same decision (to fire him) even in the absence of the protected conduct. This "Mt. Healthy" rule has become ruling case law in teacher dismissal cases since that time. *Mt. Healthy City School Dist. v. Doyle*, 429 U.S. 274, Ohio 1977.

Figure 10-4

WHICH TEACHER SHOULD YOU KEEP, WHICH SHOULD YOU LAY OFF?

Terminating the unproductive teacher is becoming easier all the time. Courts are listening to boards that do their homework and prepare their cases carefully with the thought of children's well-being uppermost in their minds. But which teachers do you keep, which let go? In modern schools, those who are most worthy of their high calling as teachers are those who are the "three-F teachers."

What's a "three-F" teacher? Well, it's one who's Firm, Friendly, and Fair.

Firm? Yes, one whose students know their limits as to discipline, and when they can depend on the teacher to set his/her foot down. At one time, it was enough just to be firm, because discipline was a first priority. But to firmness, today's teacher must add...

Friendly. Not every teacher thinks of himself or herself as a foster parent, a child advocate, a legal surrogate. Keep those that feel they should be counselors as well as teachers, and you've added a very significant dimension to your staff. But every teacher must also be...

Fair. Fair? Yes, because children in school are "persons" under our Constitution, and they must be given due process and equal protection of the laws, not only because they are citizens, but also because it is in this way that they learn to exercise their freedom within a framework of law and order.

How many three-F teachers have you been able to retain on the staff?

DEFAMATION OF CHARACTER

It is not at all unusual for teachers to claim they have been defamed in the dismissal procedure. In Kansas, a principal claimed he was libeled when the board wrote him a letter of reprimand. The Supreme Court of Kansas held that such a letter, if written within the scope of the board's powers, would be protected by absolute privilege. *Schulze v. Bd. of Educ.,* 559 P.2d 367, Kan. 1977.

Libel is written defamation; slander is oral defamation. Most communications by the board in the line of duty are protected by "privilege," which must be based "upon a proper occasion, from a proper motive, in a proper manner, and based upon resonable or probable cause." The most important aspect of privileged communications is the animus of the person who is the alleged defamer. If he acts in good faith, and in the line of duty, even though the allegations may be false, the privilege will protect him. But the speaker or writer is responsible for both falsehood and malice if such animus is proved. In the Kansas case above, the Kansas Supreme Court ruled that the board, sitting in its judicial capacity, had *absolute* privilege, where it voted a reprimand and placed it in the principal's file. Acting within its scope of authority and motivated by the prospect of better education for children, a local board would receive the same treatment in most of the states of the union.

In Wyoming, a teacher was dismissed for lack of discipline and for untidiness in her classroom, but a jury concluded that these were not the actual reasons for her dismissal. The jury felt the teacher had been dismissed because of her size, lack of church attendance, the location of her trailer, and the conduct of her personal life. Damages were assessed against the board members and the superintendent and the teacher was ordered reinstated and awarded back pay and fringe benefits. *Stoddard v. School Dist. No. 1, Lincoln Co.,* 429 F.Supp. 890, Wyo, 1977. However, a federal district court in Delaware was unconvinced by the discharged assistant superintendent's argument that the charges against him were so trivial as to constitute violation of his substantive rights. In the court's view, the evidence convincingly established that the employee's involvement in an extramarital affair caused him to neglect his duties and that certain of these acts were immoral. *Sedule v. Capital School Dist.,* 425 F. Supp. 552, Del. 1976.

Reinstatement and back pay are not always ordered in cases where there is a finding of violation of procedural due process. The courts will leave to the school board the question of whether it wishes to rehire the teacher or pay his or her back pay and fringe benefits. If embarrassment is involved, as in a case in which a homosexual teacher was not ordered reinstated, the board is left to judge whether it wishes to continue the teacher's employment. *Burton v. Cascade School Dist.,* 512 F.2d 850, Ore. 1975.

As a general rule, damages for pain and/or humiliation are not recoverable. In Oregon, a non-tenured teacher was required under a board regulation to resign rather than take maternity leave for the remainder of the year. The court held that she had been wrongfully dismissed, but that inasmuch as any anxiety and worry she may have suffered was not due to the board's action, in the eyes of the court, she could not recover damages for humiliation. *School Dist. No. 1, Multnomah Co. v. Nilsen,* 534 P.2d 1135, Ore. 1975.

Failure to promote employees on the basis of race is rewardable by back pay and either promotion or comparable salary as long as the employee is retained. *Cross v. Bd. of Educ. of Dollarway,* 395 F. Supp. 531, Ark. 1975. But it's clear that an employee may not ignore a direct order of a superintendent to come into his office and communicate with him while employed in the district. *Hastings v. Bonner,* 578 F.2d 136, Fla. 1978.

The remedy available to teachers dismissed because of their political beliefs is reinstatement and back pay. In West Virginia, it was shown that the board did not rehire and often in fact demoted employees who had not supported successful candidates for the school board. The court held that such a practice would raise a suspicion of political discrimination and would constitute a pattern and practice of discriminatory action by the board and the superintendent. *Miller v. Bd. of Educ.,* 450 F.Supp. 106, W. Va. 1978.

Finally, where the board's heavy hand may subject a teacher "to a badge of infamy" in the course of non-renewing his contract, the teacher is entitled to a hearing. At a meeting in which the board discussed a teacher's dismissal, the teacher had no written charges against him, and the only reason given by the board was "the best interest of the school." Individual board members stated that the teacher "neglected his duties," and had "a drinking problem." Later, at a full hearing on the question, the board stood by its former decision and dismissed the teacher. The court found that allegations of "a badge of infamy" (drinking) subjected the teacher to a deprivation of a civil right (his liberty interests) and held that the teacher was entitled to an opportunity to "clear his name" although not entitled to retention on the payroll or to back pay since his right to due process did not encompass the right to continued employment. *Dennis v. S & S Consol. Rural High School Dist.,* 577 F.2d 338, Tex. 1978.

11

How to Avoid Stigmatizing Children in Grouping

THE PROBLEM IS SORTING

Robert Benchley once noted that there are two kinds of people—those that divide people into two classes, and those that don't. The remark is significant for schools because schools are "sorters" —they separate kids into the "Bluebirds," the "Robins," and the "Turtles," from Day One. And the sorting never stops. Kids are screened, diagnosed, tracked, labeled, grouped, classified, compared, categorized, and identified *ad infinitum*. Ordinarily, these sorting techniques would not reach a constitutional barrier, but since *Brown v. Board of Education* (1954) the courts have held that segregating children into groups gives rise to "suspect" classifications that may have a lasting psychological effect on them throughout their lives. "Separate but equal facilities for the races," said the Court, "are inherently unequal." The reason given was that dividing children on the basis of their race was a "badge of servitude," and is therefore a denial of equal protection of the laws. Now any grouping of children must be justified in the light of what the district is trying to do, as well as on a showing that what is being done is necessary from the standpoint of the state's valid legal interest. This chapter is about grouping problems that may arise in which the board must come to the forefront and prove its need to group in such a way that individual constitutional rights are not violated or denied while the state is busily engaged in meeting its valid educational purpose at the same time.

Any grouping pattern that results in groups having only one religion, sex, nationality, ethnic group, age, language, or economic standing is like a red flag to a bull—it is immediately *suspect*. In the landmark case of *West Virginia State Board of Education v. Barnette*, 319 U.S. 624, 1943 a child was excluded from school for refusal to salute the flag. In striking down the board's action as a denial of freedom of religion, the Court said in part:

> If there is any fixed star in our constitutional constellation, it is that no official, high or petty, can prescribe what shall be orthodox in politics, nationalism, religion, or other matters of opinion or force citizens to confess by word or act their faith therein. Boards of education have important, delicate, and highly discretionary functions, but none that they may not perform within the limits of the Bill of Rights. One's right to life, liberty, and property, to free speech, a free press, freedom of worship and assembly may not be submitted to vote; they depend on the outcomes of no elections.

In holding that grouping may force upon those grouped a feeling of "inferiority," the Court in *Brown* said that when a state decides to offer a free education to its children, such an opportunity is a right which must be made available to all on equal terms. Grouping in public schools, therefore, must withstand the strictures of both the equal protection and the due process clauses of the Fourteenth Amendment in order to be legally acceptable to the courts.

In *San Antonio School Dist. v. Rodriguez*, 411 U.S. 1, Tex. 1973 the Supreme Court in a divided vote held there is no such thing as equal educational opportunity guaranteed in the Federal Constitution. The state, however, in offering a free education to its children, may not be allowed to discriminate against any one or group of them. The dangers of grouping are many, and may involve a denial of a state constitutional right. Upon the state is the burden of proof that what it is doing is not discriminatory. (See Figure 11-1.) While the Federal Constitution does not provide equal educational opportunity, many state constitutions provide for a "thorough and uniform" system of education wherein the children are to be educated. Since grouping patterns may deny this right, it is imperative that the board be made aware of any pattern or practice that may result in denial of educational rights within the borders of the state.

Figure 11-1

ILLEGAL GROUPING OF CHILDREN
MAY HAVE THESE EFFECTS

- The grouping system may cast a child into a training program and predestine him or her to schooling at odds with his or her native talents or career plans.
- The grouping system may cast a child into a career for which he or she is not particularly suited.
- The grouping system may create a stigma—retarded child, ineducable—which may create a psychological injury that will never be overcome.
- The grouping pattern may lock a child into a group—e.g., into a track—from which that child is never able to extricate himself.
- The grouping system may keep a child from enjoying a specially constructed program of studies tailored to his own particular needs.
- The grouping system may deny the child a chance to become familiar with heterogeneous groups throughout the school.
- The grouping system may deny a child contact with the power structure within the community, and foreclose later chances for gainful employment.
- The grouping system may treat intelligence as determined by heredity alone—a politically dangerous precedent.
- The grouping system may not place the child in the least restrictive environment within the school, thus denying him or her the resources of the district most apt to develop all his or her talents.
- The grouping system may "functionally exclude" children who are in school physically but in reality out of it insofar as their participation in a meaningful program of studies is concerned.

TRACKING

Tracking is one form of grouping that may have deleterious effects on children for two reasons: (1) it assigns children to a track for lengthy periods of time unless there is provision for periodic review; and (2) it casts a stigma on students because it is obvious to which track they belong. There is also the possibility of misclassification—assigning a student to a track that he clearly does not belong in. A state appellate court in New York awarded $500,000 to a young man who demonstrated that the board had negligently diagnosed and educated him as mentally retarded when in fact he was not. He alleged that his opportunities in life were severely curtailed as a result. The error was apparently made by a school psychologist who misinterpreted a severe speech defect as a mental problem. The situation was complicated by a failure to correct the placement even after the error was discovered. The court stressed that the case was one of "negligence" but not one of "malpractice" because the fault of the district was not a mere failure to educate according to some vaguely defined standard, but rather was due to "specific affirmative acts which imposed additional and crippling burdens on the student." *Hoffman v. Bd. of Educ. of Cty. of N.Y.,* 410 N.Y.S. 2d. 99, N.Y., 1978.

The classic tracking case is *Hobson v. Hansen,* 408 F.2d 175, D.C. 1969. In the District of Columbia schools, children were placed in one of three tracks according to the school's assessment of each student's ability to learn. The court held such a system was a denial of equal educational opportunity since it militated against poor Negro children living in the district. Children, said the court, are "locked in," and there is too little "cross tracking" to allow them to break out of a track once they are assigned to it. In effect, then, the system of tracking has become "a system of discrimination founded on socioeconomic and racial status rather than ability, resulting in the undereducation of many District students."

The system, which was devised to help integrate the schools, has survived "to stigmatize the disadvantaged child of whatever race relegated to its lower tracks—from which tracks the possibility of switching upward, because of the absence of compensatory education, is remote."

Observing that even on paper the tracking system was discriminatory (it is founded on the idea that some children will go into white-collar and others into blue-collar work), the court pointed out that "the risk of a child wearing the wrong collar is far too great for this demoncracy to tolerate." The system fails to bring the great majority of children "into the mainstream" of public education, and thereby denies the child equal protection of the laws. The court permanently enjoined the District Board from operating a track system in the District of Columbia schools.

One should not assume, however, that all tracking is *per se* unconstitutional. In order to meet the constitutional standard required, the board must make sure that two conditions are met: (1) original placement in a track or curriculum should meet due process standards, i.e., be fundamentally fair and deliberate, and (2) there must be provision for periodic review of the child's progress or lack of progress in a track or curriculum, so that appropriate changes can be made. Where a child is not making progress, he or she is entitled to remedial services so that success can be made possible. As the court said in *Hobson*, "The simple decree enjoining the track system does not interpose any realistic barrier to flexible school administration by a school board genuinely committed to attainment of more quality and equality of educational opportunity." 408 F.2d at 189-90.

ABILITY GROUPING

Most studies of ability grouping show that school classifications have marginal and sometimes adverse impact on both student achievement and psychological development of the child. The science of testing is not so open and shut that one can unequivocally say that this or that placement is the best for the child. Even if one could succeed in grouping children on one ability, they would still be misclassified on another. The courts have said that discriminatory *intent* does not have to be proved; it is enough to show discriminatory *outcomes* from testing to prove that the schools are engaging in an illegal and unconstitutional testing practice.

Some companies give prospective workers a test in deciding which ones to hire, promote, or let go. The Fifth Circuit Court of Appeals ruled that a test is not valid or invalid *per se*, "but must be evaluated in the setting in which it is used." The case has become a guideline for schools in administering tests that may discriminate against children, and sets up a four-hurdle course for them to follow. *U.S. v. Georgia Power Co.*, 474 F.2d 906, Ga. 1973.

First, the school must demonstrate that the test has *differential validity*, that is, it has separate validation scores for each minority on which it is to be used. Differential validity is to be distinguished from content validity, which is simply the question of whether the test measures characteristics found among persons in the particular group. Some tests also have *predictive* validity, which means that scores on the test are highly related to success on the job or in a curriculum. For many teachers and administrators, such sophisticated statistical computations are out of the question without expert advice and counsel; hence, their case flounders immediately because they are unable to prove the test's *differential validity* on different groups on which it is to be used.

The second hurdle requires the board to demonstrate that the level of confidence of the test is at least at the 0.5 level. This is the same as saying that the probability of obtaining the same test results through mere chance is no greater than one in twenty. School personnel often lose on this basis, provided of course that they have survived the first hurdle at the outset.

To clear the third hurdle, the school must show that the testing procedure contains an adequate sample to be statistically significant. Small samples tend to be ruled out or suspect as not being truly representative of a wider universe of the population. Finally, to survive the fourth hurdle, the school must show that the test was administered to all testees under substantially the same circumstances as those used in standardizing the test itself. Under this rubric, the courts will not accept results where the testing sample, the purposes of the test, and the test conditions are not on all fours with those used in making up the tests in the first place.

Courts also prohibit testing in recently desegregated schools regardless of test bias or validity. The reason is to protect against further continuance of the effects of past segregation practices, and applies to intraschool tracking as well as to dual schools testing. The duration of this ban seems to be "until the district has established a unitary school system." Schools are on thin ice in testing because the burden of proof is with the district to show that its testing program is non-discriminatory and meets a valid state purpose.

Most judges now take the position that there is no such thing as a "culture-free" test; those who claim such perfection must bear the burden of proof that at last they have constructed a test that does not distinguish between black and white, Spanish-speaking and English-speaking, rich or poor children in its administration. So far, it seems fair to say that no one has met this difficult standard. Even if they were to do so, a nation as diverse and pluralistic as ours defies educational standardization and it is undemocratic and discriminatory in the extreme, as one judge put it, to assume that "all should be cut from the same mold."

The fact remains that the school does not have resources to place one child with one teacher: grouping must be done in self-defense. So long as you can show that your system *does not discriminate*—that placement is fair and there is provision for periodic review—you can withstand challenges to your testing and grouping system before the law.

MINIMUM COMPETENCY PROBLEMS

Thirty-six states have legislation or state board requirements on competency testing. The legal problems surrounding this concept are potentially enormous. In Florida, ten black students filed suit in federal court against the state, charging unconstitutionality of the state literacy testing law. A second suit was filed in North Carolina. Essentially, these challenges turn on the fairness of the tests being administered, since the evidence tends to show that the tests cause proportionately more minority children than whites to fail. The outcomes of these suits will be watched with much interest by school personnel because of the legal issues involved.

Minimum competency standards raise four kinds of legal issues: (1) adequacy of the phase-in period; (2) adequacy of the match between the content of the minimum competency test and the instruction provided students; (3) possible discriminatory effects on minority students; and (4) questions related to handicapped students.

Phase-in period

Since those being tested have not been taught the minimum competencies they are expected to know, the question here is how long the phase-in period ought to be. Some plaintiffs claim that even 12 years might be considered inadequate notice where a student is denied a high school diploma based on the results of a recently instituted competency test. The board should refrain from requiring too much of the students until an adequate time has passed in which to teach the competencies that the board has picked as minimal for awarding a high school diploma. It appears that the board, charged with the responsibility for teaching minimum amounts of knowledge and skill, must at the same time assume responsibility for doing what it has to do in a fair and reflective manner lest it find itself in court.

Match between tests and instruction

First, you agree to include certain information in the curriculum, you actually do include it, and then you actually *teach it*. This may open the door to certain "malpractice" suits such as that instituted by a high school graduate in San Francisco, who was graduated from high school with only a fifth grade reading competency. He sued the board for educational "malpractice" in the amount of one million dollars, claiming the district failed to provide him with the basic academic skills. His suit failed. He based his case on *negligence* and *misrepresentation*, the latter because the district personnel had told his mother that her son was achieving at or near the normal grade level in basic skills. Both grounds were rejected by the court. If the district is to be liable in tort, it must first owe the plaintiff a duty. The court concluded that the school district owed no duty of care to the boy within the meaning of the existing tort law of negligence.

To win on intentional misrepresentation, the plaintiff must include allegations that he relied on the misrepresentation, which was not shown here. Since the Doe's had not alleged they had relied on the school's assurances, the court held that they could not collect on either grounds. *Peter W. Doe v. S.F. Unified Sch.Dist.*, 131 Cal. Rptr. 854, 1976.

Discriminatory treatment

Districts in which there has been a history of discrimination are especially susceptible to claims that they are also discriminating in their minimum competency testing program. There is the possibility that the results of tests given now reflect discrimination in the past. Students should be tested only in their native language. If tracking results from the tests, there is the possibility that this could be considered a "pattern or practice" sufficient to nullify the program entirely. Should those who fail consist mainly of minority students, the tests are not fair and another route must be found to effectuate the competency concept in your district.

Since the district must defend its choice of the cut-off scores above and below which students are either graduated or denied graduation, considerable work will have to be done to validate those scores before a defense can be made. Although minimum competency was an idea whose time may have come, it will be some time before it can be legally implemented to the satisfaction of the courts.

Handicapped students

Students with special needs are included under the Congressional Act known as P.L. 92-142, the Education for All Handicapped Children Act. More will be said in Chapter 12 on this subject. Suffice it here to say that machinery should be available in each district by which to determine placement, periodic review, and remediation for all handicapped children on a due process basis. These children must be handled on a case-by-case basis to determine what their minimum competencies may be. These papers should be included in each student's file required by the act.

If there is ever an area in which you should not be without legal counsel at all times, it is in this area of grouping, testing, assigning, reviewing, and "sorting" school children. The potential for litigation is great, but the potential for landmark progress in helping children is worth it. If competency testing is to succeed, it will take the best efforts of all including school attorneys, boards, teachers, administrators, parents and others. Not to try would only be to delay the day when better schooling will be available to kids, and to deny those same children their rightful birthright—to learn, to know, to be informed, to be free.

TESTING, GROUPING AND PRIVACY

The right of privacy is not specifically stated in the Constitution but is implied—the right to be let alone. Some of the states enacted laws proscribing the administration of "brain-probing" tests without parental consent. Also, the Congress enacted the Family Educational Rights and Privacy Act (the Buckley Amendment) in 1974, which provides for more open records than before. Chapter 12 will contain more on this famous act. The net effect has been that school personnel must now be more open and aboveboard with parents and students not only in counseling them but also in stigmatizing them through the records that are kept. An example of this type of problem came up in Pennsylvania in 1973 and illustrates the kinds of "groups" that are prohibited.

A school district undertook a program to identify as early as possible those children who were thought to be potential drug abusers. A letter was sent home to parents mentioning, in cosmetic terms, the desire to teach the ill effects of drugs and alcohol. The parents, however, were not aware of the extent of the district's probes into the inner lives of the children. Nevertheless, they gave their consent to the project and all went well until some parents brought suit to discover what was going on. Despite the good intent of the program (to provide special counseling for those decided to be potential drug abusers), the court ordered the district to discontinue its program. The letter, said the court, had lacked the necessary "substance" to provide a parent the opportunity to give knowing, intelligent, and aware consent to the plan. "The interests of the individual to privacy and good reputation must be balanced against the interests of the state in avoiding the dangers and effects of drug abuse. This court must balance these rights. In so doing, we strike the balance in favor of the individual in circumstances such as are shown here. The interests of individual privacy and the right to a good reputation far outweigh the state's interest in abating drug abuse. The label of 'potential drug abuser' may become in time a self-fulfilling prophecy, and test results or the refusal to take the test could result in scape-goating." *Merriken v. Cressman*, 364 F.Supp. 913, Pa. 1973.

A school that gives a test must be prepared to show that the test does not stigmatize a person both now and in the future. When testing or grouping results in someone being labeled, and such a label could remain with that person for the remainder of his or her life, the margin of error must be nil.

The classic stigmatization case occurred in Wisconsin, which had a statute requiring the posting of the names of problem drinkers in taverns and package stores without first holding a hearing on the merits. One Constantineau challenged the statute on the grounds it denied her due process of law. Her challenge was successful. "The Due Process Clause forbids arbitrary deprivation of liberty," said the U.S. Supreme Court in holding the statute unconstitutional. "Where a person's good name, reputation, honor, or integrity is at stake because of what the government is doing to him (sic), the minimal requirements of the Clause must be satisfied." *Wisconsin v. Constantineau,* 400 U.S. 433, 437, 1971.

12

Managing Children Who Need Special Help

THE CHILD'S RIGHT TO LEARN

The Supreme Court has consistently ruled that children have the right to learn. (See Figure 12-1.) This right, when exercised, is far greater than the teacher's right to teach, inasmuch as teachers work under the conditions laid down for them by the board of education, whereas students have virtually no legal limit on their curiosity and desire to learn. This often creates problems for school boards where parents urge censorship of library books and other learning materials, the abolition of sex education classes, and elimination of controversial subjects from the curriculum. This chapter explores the legal ramifications of this problem, especially as it relates to the education of children with special learning difficulties. For it is clear that the more handicapped the child, the more entitled he is to special handling at the hands of the state.

CIVIL RIGHTS FOR THE HANDICAPPED

Throughout history, handicapped children have received less than their fair share of educational benefits. However, with the passage of the Rehabilitation Act of 1973 by the Congress and the intervention of the courts (see Figure 12-1), a new era in the civil rights of the

Figure 12-1

THE CHILD'S RIGHT TO LEARN IS VIRTUALLY
WITHOUT LEGAL LIMITATION

- No clear danger to the state stems from young children studying a foreign language such as German, and a state law to the contrary is unconstitutional. *Meyer v. Nebraska*, 262 U.S. 390, 1923.
- Children cannot be standardized by the state. *Pierce v. Society of Sisters*, 268 U.S. 510, Ore. 1925.
- Children may not be required to salute the flag as a condition of attending the public schools. *W.Va.St.Bd. of Educ. v. Barnette*, 319 U.S. 624, 1943.
- Separate but equal facilities for the races are inherently unequal because of the potential psychological harm to the children so separated by race. *Brown v. Bd. of Education, City of Topeka*, 347 U.S. 483, Ks. 1954.
- Due process of law is not for adults alone. There must be no double standard, one for children, another for adults. *In re Gault*, 387 U.S. 1, Ariz. 1967.
- Tracking is illegal if it locks children into an inflexible system from which they cannot escape. *Hobson v. Hansen*, 408 F.2d 175, D.C. 1969.
- State-operated schools may not be enclaves of totalitarianism. Children are "persons" under our Constitution and do not shed their rights at the schoolhouse gate. *Tinker v. Des Moines Ind. Comm. Sch. Dist.*, 393 U.S. 503, Iowa 1969.
- Gifted children can be held back but only under reasonable rules which take into account the physical, social and emotional maturity of each student. *Ackerman v. Rubin*, 231 N.Y.S.2d 112, 1962.
- Girls cannot be barred from boys' sports if the school district does not provide a similar program for girls, and the girls can participate on an equal basis with boys. *Brenden v. Ind. Sch. Dist.*, 477 F.2d 1292, Minn. 1973.
- Married students may not be excluded from school merely because they are married. *Romans v. Crenshaw*, 354 F.Supp. 868, Tex. 1972.
- It is within the power of the state to require sex education of all children despite the objections of the parents. *Hobolth v. Greenway*, 218 N.W.2d 98, Mich. 1974.
- Limiting theories of man's origin to only that contained in the Book of Genesis amounts to an establishment of religion. *Epperson v. Arkansas*, 393 U.S. 97, 1968.

Figure 12-1 (continued)

- Pregnant students cannot be excluded from the public schools merely because they are pregnant. *Ordway v. Hargraves*, 323 F.Supp. 1155, Mass. 1971.
- Children who do not know English are entitled to assistance from the district in order that they may learn without obstruction. *Lau v. Nichols*, 414 U.S. 563, Cal. 1974.
- Children facing suspension for more than three days are entitled to minimal due process of law, since going to school is a property right protected by the U.S. Constitution. *Goss v. Lopez*, 419 U.S. 565, Ohio 1975.
- Illegal expulsion of children from public schools may impose damages upon those who perpetrated the deprivation complained of. *Wood v. Strickland*, 420 U.S. 308, Ark. 1975.
- Educational advantages may not be denied a child who is an alien. *Hosier v. Evans*, 314 F.Supp. 316, V.I. 1970.

---

handicapped began. Title V of that Act reads, "No otherwise qualified handicapped individual in the United States ... shall, solely by reason of his handicap, be excluded from participation in, be denied the benefits of, or be subjected to discrimination under any program or activity receiving Federal financial assistance." The section is significant because it is the first major statutory civil rights law that protects handicapped individuals from discrimination in employment and educational opportunities, as well as accessibility to federally supported programs and activities.

The intent of the Congress in enacting the Rehabilitation Act of 1973 was the same as Title VI of the Civil Rights Act of 1964 (outlaws discrimination based on race) and Title IX of the Education Amendments of 1972 (outlaws discrimination based upon sex). The penalty for violation of Section 504 is withholding of all federal financial assistance until full compliance is achieved.

There is one additional "plus" for those who are covered under Section 504 of the Act, and that is that since they are handicapped, they are not considered "equal" to other children because they begin with a handicap. "Handicapped persons may require different treatment in order to be afforded equal access to federally assisted programs and activities," reads a HEW guideline, "and identical treatment

Figure 12-2

A SAMPLER OF LEGAL RIGHTS OF THE HANDICAPPED CHILD

- All mentally retarded persons are entitled to admission to the public schools and placement in the least restrictive environment. *Pennsylvania Assoc. for Retarded Children v. Commonwealth*, 334 F.Supp. 1257, Pa. 1971 (consent decree).
- The local board has a legal duty to provide special education for handicapped children. *Mills V. Board of Educ.*, 348 F.Supp. 866, D.C. 1972.
- Where one racial group is over-represented in EMR classes through the testing program, the district must defend its grouping pattern under the Constitution. *Larry P. v. Riles*, 343 F.Supp. 1306, Cal. 1972.
- A child's handicap is the sort of "immutable characteristic determined solely by the accident of birth" to which the "inherently suspect" classification can be applied. *In the Interest of G.H.*, 218 N.W.2d 441, N.Dak. 1974.
- A school district may be made to pay for a handicapped child's education in a private institution even though the schools have a program that is otherwise suitable for a child with those handicaps. *In re Kirkpatrick*, 354 N.Y.S.2d 499, N.Y.1972.
- A plan which picks up 75% of the cost for educating a handicapped youngster, leaving 25% to the parents, discriminates against poor parents. *Kruse v. Campbell*, 431 F.Supp. 180, Va. 1977.
- Gifted and talented children are in fact deprived and can suffer psychological damage ... equal to or greater than the similar deprivation suffered by any other population with special needs. *Hart v. Community Sch.Bd. of Brooklyn*, 383 F.Supp. 769, N.Y. 1974.

may, in fact, constitute discrimination. The problem of establishing general rules as to when different treatment is prohibited or required is compounded by the diversity of existing handicaps and the differing degree to which particular persons may be affected." Thus, all children do not begin with the same rights, since, by extrapolation, those with more severe handicaps are entitled to *more* assistance from the schools than are normal children or those with less severe handicaps. This leaves much ground for subjective interpretive of how much is enough, and of course, to more litigation until such time as the guidelines can be clarified. In general, one can say that each case must rest on its own special facts, and one cannot say unequivocally when different treatment of handicapped persons should be considered improper and when it should be required.

Hampering the administration of Section 504 in most districts is the entire lack of interpretive guidelines, such as cases, statutes, or administrative guidelines. This can prove both frustrating and costly. The interlocking problems associated with this area will continue to hamper full realization of the idea of equity for the handicapped for some time to come. At any rate, now that "handicapped" is a "suspect" classification, it rates alongside race, ethnicity, sex, age, and native language. Unless there is clearly a discriminatory intent, the courts have been reluctant to employ the strict scrutiny test to these cases, preferring to employ the rational basis test instead. This requires that the board must defend its action with some "demonstrable" and "rational" proof that it was acting to fulfill a valid state purpose in what it did. This is particularly significant in the placement of students in "mainstreaming" routes, or into "segregated" groupings where students may challenge the board's actions. Subpart B applies to employment practices while Subpart C of Section 504 requires recipients of federal financial assistance to ensure that no qualified handicapped individual is denied or excluded from participating in or benefiting from any program or activity because a recipient's facilities are inaccessible to handicapped individuals. This means that your buildings and rooms in those buildings must be accessible to handicapped persons. In concert with the Education for All Handicapped Children Act (P.L. 92-142), the federal government herewith requires that to the maximum extent appropriate, handicapped children are educated with children who are not handicapped, and that special classes, separate schooling or other removal of handicapped children from the regular educational environment occurs only when the nature or severity of the handicap is such that education in regular classes with the use of supplementary aids and services cannot be achieved satisfactorily. The agency must guarantee that "alternative placements" are available for handicapped children. The needs of the handicapped child should determine what direct and support services are to be provided, and in which educational setting (the *least restrictive* is mandated). Furthermore, the district may not plead physical facility inaccessibility as a legal or ethical exemption from providing educational services to a handicapped child in a specific educational setting.

Parents of a child suffering from spina bifida, which left the child with minor physical impairments including incontinence of the bowels and a noticeable limp, brought an action to have their daughter admitted to the public school. The board had not had the child examined by a physician nor did it give the parents an opportunity to come to a hearing on pupil placement. Under the circumstances, the court held that the child could not be excluded from the public schools. *Hairston v. Drosick*, 423 F.Supp. 180, W.Va. 1976.

In another case, this one on Section 504, a federal district court ruled that the school is not required to provide catheterizing services to a handicapped child on pain of loss of its financial funding from the federal level. *Sherer v. Waier*, 457 F.Supp. 1039, Mo. 1978. As these cases arise, the picture concerning what is required from the school staff and what is not will become clearer, but each case must be tried on its own merits, and the time consumed in their clarification will continue to be an administrative problem in the public schools.*

LITIGATION ON SPECIAL EDUCATION

Colorado law required that children applying for special education funds and services should undergo physical and psychological examination "by state accredited personnel." The parents of a 15-year-old girl had her examined by a chiropractor, but the State Board of Education refused her admission to the special services on the grounds that the examining individual was not a "licensed physician" within the meaning of the law. The Colorado Supreme Court eventually held that "state accredited personnel" included chiropractors because they were licensed in Colorado to practice the healing arts. *Flemming v. Adams*, 377 F.2d 975, Colo. 1968.

The cases in which special education funds are at stake are quite numerous. In New Jersey, where local school systems bear financial

---

*See for example Richard Clelland, Section 504: *Civil Rights of the Handicapped*, Arlington, Va.: AASA, 1801 N. Moore St., 1978, 128 pages.

responsibility for the private school tuition of children not served in the public schools, a dispute arose as to the residence of an emotionally handicapped child for whom tuition was owing. The child had lived with foster parents in a town away from her natural parents, but she had run away from the foster home while maintaining a continuing relationship with her natural father, who contributed to her support. The court held that the residence of the father was the residence of the child for tuition purposes. *Bd. of Educ., Little Egg Harbor v. Bd. of Educ., Galloway,* 366 A.2d 977, N.J. 1976.

New Hampshire's plan for allocating funds for the private education of the handicapped was challenged. The statute required the state to pay any part of the tuition cost not paid by the local district. There were not enough funds available to the state board to fund all the programs, so it set up a priority list and proceeded to fund the categories in order. There were no funds for the fourth category, emotionally handicapped, and a student from that group challenged the state's plan as a denial of equal protection. A federal district judge found no merit in the argument. The state is fulfilling a vaild state purpose, said the court, and it need not consider financial need when meting out the state's benefits, nor is its failure to hold a hearing on the merits a denial of due process of law. *Doe v. Laconia Supv. Union No. 30,* 396 F.Supp. 1291, N.H. 1975.

New York law requires parents who are financially able to contribute to the child's maintenance costs to do so, except for the parents of blind and deaf children. Thus, the state paid tuition and transportation for all handicapped students but paid all costs only for the blind and deaf children. Parents challenged the plan on the grounds it denied them equal protection of the laws. Their challenge was unsuccessful. The court held that the handicapped do not constitute a suspect classification, education is not a fundamental right, and there is a rational relationship between the statute and an allowable state purpose. *In re Levy,* 382 N.Y.S.2d 13, 1976. In another case, the parents who failed to file promptly for reimbursement for tuition costs had lost their right to complain through *laches* (failure to file a complaint seasonally). The court held that the claims for tuition must be filed promptly after tuition is paid and always within the school year for which the tuition was paid. *L. v. New York St.Dept. of Educ.,* 348 N.E.2d 867, N.Y. 1976.

Some litigation concerns the definition of a handicapped child. Is a child who is physically handicapped the only one eligible to receive special assistance from the state, or is the child who is "mentally or emotionally disadvantaged" also legally eligible for relief? In New York, the courts had been denying special educational assistance to emotionally and mentally disadvantaged children on the grounds that the state's definition of a handicapped child as one who is "afflicted with a physical defect" did not include the mentally disadvantaged. However, in 1976 the courts began to recognize that the intent of the legislature had been to interpret "handicapped" as being much wider than the narrow confines of the physically afflicted category. *In re Patrick*, 380 N.Y.S.2d 877, N.Y. 1976. In that year, the legislature divided the responsibility, with the local school district having it for the regular school year, while the courts were to decide how each child should be educated during the summer school term.

The federal government, under the terms of the Education for All Handicapped Children Act of 1975, makes funds available to the states to be used for special education. The states in turn funnel these funds to local school districts by means of a state plan approved by the federal government. Thus, local control and responsibility are maintained while federal standards and aid are available. The law lists the rights of parents to participate in the diagnosis, placement, education, and periodic re-evaluation of their children (see Figure 12-3), and lists similar rights for the children (see Figure 12-4). The aim is to preserve local control, use federal funds, and provide the least restrictive environment for the child. Such an approach has been hailed by parents and educators alike as a major new breakthrough in the education of the handicapped. The future will reveal what effect the program will have on the increased rights of both children and parents to provide appropriate schooling for handicapped children.

DISCREPANCY MODEL

The district is responsible for its own planning to come into line with the requirements of Section 504. Three types of organizational action are required to do this: (a) remedial action, (b) voluntary action, and (c) self-evaluation. If the district has discriminated against individuals either in its buildings or program accessibility, in violation of Sec-

Figure 12-3

PARENTS' RIGHTS

According to the Education for All Handicapped Children Act parents of handicapped children have the right to:

- participate in the annual planning meeting for your child's Individual Educational Program (IEP) of the affected school year.
- agree to a time and place for those meetings (always held before the beginning of the affected school year).
- instruct the local school agency to hold those meetings in your primary language (or make special arrangements for your handicap, if any, including deafness) so that you can understand the proceedings.
- give your consent before an evaluation is conducted.
- give voluntary written consent to any activities proposed for the child.
- seek an independent evaluation of your child at public expense if you find the school's evaluation inappropriate. (The school may request a hearing to decide the appropriateness of its evaluation. If the ruling is in the school's favor, you still have the right to submit an independent evaluation which must be considered but which is then conducted at your expense.)
- have written notice of any proposed change in identification, evaluation or placement of your child or the school's refusal to change any of these.
- attend and comment at the annual public hearings held prior to adoption of state program plans. (Hearings must be publicized in advance.)
- receive a full explanation of procedural safeguards and a description of any proposed actions regarding your child and their basis.
- see, review, and if necessary, challenge your child's record in accordance with the Family Educational Rights and Privacy Act of 1974 (the Buckley Amendment).
- request a hearing on any proposal to initiate or change the identification, evaluation or placement of your child, or the agency's refusal to do so within 45 days of your request.
- request a copy of information from your child's record before it is destroyed in compliance with the law, 5 years after its usefulness ends.

From NETWORK, Feb. 1977, a publication of the National Committee for Citizens in Education (NCCE), 410 Wilde Lake Village Green, Columbia, Maryland 21044. Used with permission of the Committee.

Figure 12-4

HANDICAPPED CHILDREN'S RIGHTS

According to the Education for All Handicapped Children Act, handicapped children have the following right to:

- a free and appropriate public education (FAPE) if they are between the ages of 3 and 18 by September 1, 1978 and if 3-21 by September, 1980.
- the same variety of programs and services that children without handicaps enjoy, including nonacademic subjects and extracurricular activities.
- placement in the least restrictive learning environment as much as possible with non-handicapped children and whenever possible at the same school they would go to if not handicapped.
- the availability of a number of alternative learning settings if attending a local public school is not possible.
- priority use of supplemental federal funds for those not now being served at all.
- appointment of a person to act as parent, to be the child advocate and to participate in evaluation and program meetings with the school if natural parents are unavailable or if the child is a ward of the state.
- participation in the writing of their own Individual Educational Program (IEP) "where appropriate."
- placement outside the local school district in another public or private school at the state's expense if local schools do not have an appropriate program.
- testing for purposes of evaluation and placement that is free of racial or cultural discrimination.
- annual review of placement based on IEP and at least an annual review of that program before each school year begins.
- remain in present placement during any administrative or judicial proceedings or the right to attend a public school if the complaint involves an application for admission to public school.
- privacy and confidentiality of all personal records.

From NETWORK, Feb. 1977, a publication of the National Committee for Citizens in Education (NCCE), 410 Wilde Lake Village Green, Columbia, Maryland 21044. Used with permission of the Committee.

---

tion 504, it must take such *remedial* action as directed by the appropriate federal agency. In addition, the district must take *voluntary* action to eradicate lack of accessibility to local programs by the handicapped. Finally, the district must set up a program for planning, conducting and analyzing a *self-evaluation* design.

Discrepancy analysis is the comparison of what is with what ought to be and what has to be done to meet the discrepancy (see Figure 12-5). There are three components to the discrepancy model: (1) the status study, which provides information on the *actual* state or condition; (2) the normative study, which provides information on the *desired* state or condition; and (3) the plan to remove what *discrepancy* has been found. Discrepancies can be positive, where performance exceeds the standard, or negative, where performance is less than the standard. Where there are negative discrepancies, they may be resolved in three ways: (1) an unrealistic normative standard may be reevaluated and redesigned; (2) performance may be brought into line with current conditions; or (3) if the discrepancy cannot be removed, a program may be altered or terminated.

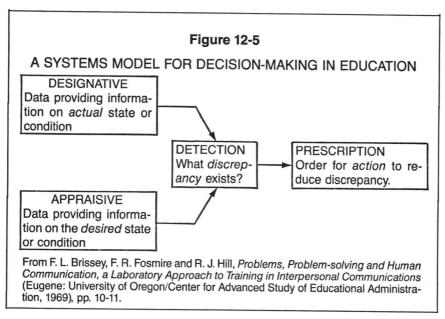

Figure 12-5

A SYSTEMS MODEL FOR DECISION-MAKING IN EDUCATION

From F. L. Brissey, F. R. Fosmire and R. J. Hill, *Problems, Problem-solving and Human Communication, a Laboratory Approach to Training in Interpersonal Communications* (Eugene: University of Oregon/Center for Advanced Study of Educational Administration, 1969), pp. 10-11.

Removal of a discrepancy normally falls into eight steps: (a) determination of the need; (b) definition of objectives; (c) identification of constraints; (d) generation of alternatives; (e) analysis and selection of alternatives; (f) development of pilot implementation; (g) evaluation; and (h) feedback and modification of the plan. In general, these eight steps follow the five steps of the scientific method well known to science: (1) statement of the problem; (2) collection of the data needed; (3) hypothesize; (4) test the hypothesis; and (5) evaluate. These decision-making tools are not fully developed in education, although there have been valiant attempts to adapt them to the field. If people were to react in a similar vein in any and all situations, the effects might be more predictable.

MAINSTREAMING

Section 504 requires that districts place handicapped individuals "in the least restrictive environment possible." The ideal would of course be to place the handicapped child in a regular classroom without special help, but this plan does not take into account the child's need for such aid as will overcome his handicap. The Pennsylvania Right to Education consent decree (*PARC v. Commonwealth*, 334 F.Supp. 1257, 1971) states that placement of mentally retarded children is preferable in regular public school classrooms rather than in special public school classes since there is less possibility of discrimination in such a setting. If hetereogeneity is to be the ideal, then it follows that delivery systems for the handicapped should be ranked in the following order, with the most desirable first and the least desirable last: (1) regular classes full-time with no special help; (2) regular classes with consultant or helping teacher available to the regular teacher and/or students; (3) special classes with part-time spent in regular classes for selected academic work (4) regular classes with itinerant teacher assistance; (5) regular classes with part-time resource room aid; and (6) special classes with regular class time for non-academic work such as physical education, art, music and the like. The best motto for educating the handicapped is "to each child, in his own way, in his own time." Since each child is a unique entity, the district must take the time and effort to insure that placement is according to due process of law in every respect.

Due process in placement and periodic review of the handicapped calls for at least these minimum essentials: notice to the parents clearly indicating specific and complete reasons for the action to be taken; a description of any alternative educational opportunities available on a permanent or temporary basis; and the family's other rights, which might include:

- free independent medical, psychological and educational evaluation by a government-funded diagnostic center
- right to be represented by legal counsel at the staffing hearing
- right to free legal assistance if the family is unable to pay
- right to examine the child's school records including results of tests
- right to present evidence and testimony, including expert medical, psychological or educational testimony
- right to have an employee of the school present with evidence upon which the proposed action may be based
- right to confront and cross-examine any witness testifying for the schools.

These principles of law emerge from the cases, statutes and public laws dealing with the handicapped child in today's public schools:

1. Children may not be excluded from the public schools merely on the grounds that they have a handicap and the school district has no program at the time.

2. Children must be given a "meaningful opportunity to participate in the educational program" of the schools in the least restrictive environment possible in the light of the handicapped person's particular handicap.

3. The burden of proof that the district is not discriminating against the handicapped child rests with the school district.

4. The state must show a rational relationship between what it is doing and the state's interests in seeing that every citizen receives all the schooling he or she can profit from.

5. The object of the handicapped children's act is not to eradicate all inequality among and between children, but to compensate those who have handicaps in such a way as to bring them reasonable opportunity for success in school and in later life.

6. Children are "persons" under our Constitution, and do not shed their rights to due process and equal protection at the schoolhouse gate.

7. Although the district may classify its children for instructional

purposes, this right is not unlimited. Only those placements that accrue to the benefit of each child can be defended.

8. Children are entitled to full access to the educational program. Any structural barriers, such as stairs, must be removed. Any impediments to the learning process, such as speaking a foreign language, must be compensated for in placing the handicapped in the least restrictive environment possible.

CHAPTER

13

Legal Aspects of Dealing with Unruly Students

A RECURRING PROBLEM

The sixties were years of academic turmoil and upheaval. College students by the thousands forsook their classrooms to protest their lack of civil rights. Now some of them as public school teachers are learning to live with the unrest they spawned, and many are finding it difficult to reconcile their classrooms with their upbringing. For nine out of the last ten years, the Gallup Poll has revealed that "discipline" is America's Number One educational problem. Until teachers and administrators learn to live with the new rules governing pupil discipline and control—and that's a big order—unrest and litigation will continue. The truth is, managing students in today's more liberal environment is "a whole new ball game," and woe unto him who does not understand what is going on, and govern himself—and his classroom—accordingly.

First high schools, then junior highs, and eventually elementary schools took on the same militancy shown by the college students of the sixties—an unwillingness to delay gratification, demands for immediate rights of confrontation, and far more asked for than was given up. In the spirit of the times, these pre-college students rode in on the coattails of the civil rights movement. Like other minorities, they were at the right place at the right time to gain rights they never had before. The Supreme Court backed them, holding in *Tinker v. Des Moines Ind. Comm. School Dist.,* 393 U.S. 503, Iowa 1969 that children both in and out of school are "persons" under the Constitution and do not shed their constitutional rights at the schoolhouse gate. Other subsequent cases were to the same effect, so that today's teacher and administrator must think twice before handling a discipline problem lest they become liable for deprivation of a civil right.

Many "old-timers" who could not adjust to the new rules left teaching, while those who remained were diligently trying to work something out. Those younger teachers—the ones who were in college when the academic revolution hit—are no better off. They sowed the wind, and are unsure just how to proceed to reap the whirlwind. The answer lies in the twin concepts of equal protection and due process of law contained in the Fourteenth Amendment. Before that point is reached, however, it is good to look at the concept of discipline as it was originally conceived in public schools in order to build a foundation on which to construct a new and emerging philosophy of discipline for tomorrow.

THE SCHOOL *IN LOCO PARENTIS*

Colonial parents were charged with full responsibility for their children's upbringing. When the states gradually took over the education of the young in tax-supported schools, and compulsory attendance laws were enacted, the law had to change to meet the new circumstances. Since the child was absent from his natural parents, someone must be found to look after his interests—his physical safety, his conduct while away from home, and his need to learn. All this could be accomplished through the concept of *in loco parentis*—in place of the parent. Simply stated, the doctrine is that some adult— usually the teacher—is to stand in place of the parent, with the right of discipline and control over the child accompanied at the same time by the responsibility for the child's safety. (See Chapter 4, "How to Deal with Tort Liability.") This chapter deals with the right of the teacher or other school employee to discipline and control student conduct under the rubric of *in loco parentis*.

But Americans are divided on how the young should be brought up. (See Figure 13-1.) On the one hand, many people believe that the schools should be more severe with children, more traditional, using

Figure 13-1

FOR CHILDREN: WHICH APPROACH?

A serious polarization is occurring between the two camps on the means by which children are to be disciplined in school. The ends are the same: "Better education for all children." However, the camps differ on the means by which these ends can be accomplished. One says "More Repression," the other, "More Freedom for Children." Ideally, the circles below would overlap—there would be opportunity given for a child in school to be a person within a framework of law and order. How that can be done remains the challenge of the future.

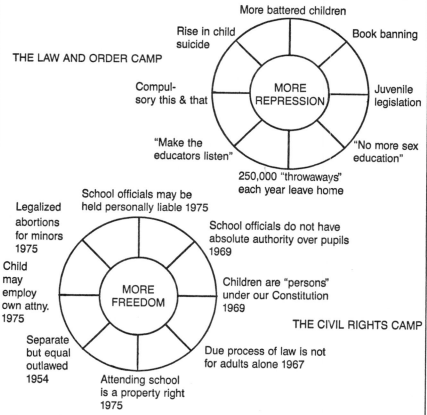

"Law enforcement is forever at odds with civil liberty. Law, by definition, imposes limitations on individual conduct. ... Boundaries must be set between ... the attainment of justice and the containment of power." A. Barth, *The Price of Liberty*, pp. 19-26.

corporal punishment and other sanctions to attain complete conformity. The other camp, with the support of the Supreme Court, has taken the position that children should be given more freedom to participate in the decisions that affect their lives in school. The clarification movement to shed light on the problems of discipline in school reached a high point in 1975, when the Supreme Court held that children facing suspension or expulsion were entitled to minimal measures of due process of law. Attending school, said the Court, is both a property and a liberty right protected by the Fourteenth Amendment, and this right cannot be arbitrarily denied without observance of the fundamental rules of fair play. In 1975, also, the Supreme Court held that within certain limits the administration of reasonable corporal punishment to a child in school is not a denial of his constitutional rights (see Figure 13-2). The Court followed this case in 1977 with another ruling, declaring that corporal punishment is not a violation of the Eighth Amendment prohibiting cruel and unusual punishment, even though the corporal punishment may be excessive. Relief for those who complain about corporal punishment is not through a civil rights action in a federal court, but is to be found rather in a state court case for assault and battery. Thus, reasonable corporal punishment is still legal in public schools, even though it has been eliminated from all other institutions in the American legal system.

SUSPENSION

Students who did not do well in public schools were often summarily suspended for long periods of time in the expectation that they would become discouraged and drop out of school. Beginning in the early 1970's, however, the courts began to rule that students who were suspended for up to 30 days without an expulsion hearing were being denied due process of law. *Graham v. Knutzen,* 351 F.Supp. 642, Nebr. 1972. The Supreme Court affirmed this concept when in 1975 it had before it a case arising in Ohio. A student who is suspended for more than three to five days, said the Court, is entitled to at least these minimal due process guarantees: (1) to know the reasons for his suspension; (2) to know the kinds and sources of evidence against him; and (3) to tell his side of the story. Also, if suspended for more than three to five days, he is entitled to a hearing on the merits. *Goss v. Lopez,* 419 U.S. 565, Ohio 1975.

Lopez, who with about 75 other students was suspended when a fight broke out in the lunchroom, was an innocent bystander. Lopez never had a hearing. He was suspended under an Ohio law that allowed the principal to suspend a student for up to ten days without a hearing. The Supreme Court was asked to determine whether that particular law was unconstitutional. It held that the law was indeed unconstitutional since it deprived a student of a valuable right (a property right) without due process of law, and ordered references to his suspension to be removed from his permanent file.

"Education is perhaps the most important function of state and local government," said the Court, quoting from an earlier case (*Brown v. Bd. of Educ.,* 347 U.S. 483, Kans. 1954). Total exclusion from the educational process for more than a trivial period is a serious event in the life of the suspended child. Neither the property interest in educational benefits temporarily denied nor the liberty interest in reputation, which is also implicated, is so insubstantial that suspensions may constitutionally be imposed by any procedure the school chooses, no matter how arbitrary."

At the very minimum, therefore, students facing suspension must be given some kind of notice and afforded some kind of hearing. "Once it is determined that due process applies," said the Court, "the question remains what process is due." Since too much due process would take too much time in relation to its effectiveness, any punishment must be followed by these three minimal requirements: (1) that the student be told why he is being suspended; (2) he must be told what evidence you have against him; and (3) he is entitled to tell his side of the story, "all within minutes after the incident complained of."

EXPULSION

The Supreme Court has ruled that "in these days, it is doubtful that any child can reasonably be expected to succeed in life if he is denied the opportunity of an education." *Brown, supra.,* 1954. "That boards are educating the young for citizenship is reason for scrupulous protection of constitutional freedoms of the individual." *W.Va.St.Bd. of*

Figure 13-2

THE CORPORAL PUNISHMENT CASES

- Administering corporal punishment without due process of law is not inherently unconstitutional because if the punishment is unreasonable and excessive, it is no longer lawful and the perpetrator of it may be criminally or civilly liable. The law and policy do not sanction child abuse. *Ware v. Estes*, 328 F. Supp. 657, affirmed, 458 F.2d 1360, Tex. 1971, cert. den., 409 U.S. 1027, 1973.

- A parent may veto corporal punishment for his own child but he must be prepared to discipline his errant child himself. The parent must actively, promptly and effectively assert his authority so that the other children will not be hampered in their educational pursuits and school activities will not be disorganized. As always, with rights goes responsibility. *Glaser v. Marietta*, 351 F.Supp. 555, Pa. 1972.

- So long as the child knows beforehand what misconduct will result in physical punishment, and is told why he or she is being punished, school officials may corporally punish pupils in the absence of a state law to the contrary. In addition, corporal punishment should never be employed as the first line of punishment for misbehavior. There must be an adult witness present, and if the parents request it, a written explanation of the reasons for the punishment and the name of the second official present. The parent may not veto corporal punishment for his own child. *Baker v. Owen*, 395 F.Supp. 294, U.S. Supreme Court affirmed, 44 L.W. 3235, N.C. 1975.

- The Eighth Amendment's prohibition of cruel and unusual punishment applies to criminals only and does not apply to children in school. Even though there may be a charge that the corporal punishment administered to a child in school is excessive, the proper relief is to be found in a state court for assault and battery. The rights of the individual against invasion of privacy are to be balanced against the state's interest in a peaceful, ongoing school system. So long as the rules are not arbitrary or capricious, and are aimed at attaining a valid state purpose, corporal punishment is not illegal. *Ingraham v. Wright*, 97 S.Ct. 1401, Fla. 1977.

The foregoing would suggest that individual teachers and/or administrators may be held personally liable for negligence in the administration of corporal punishment if they go beyond the "reasonable" stage in corporal punishment. There need be no due process accompaniment of corporal punishment, but a child may be awarded nominal damages for violation of his due process rights in cases where a student is illegally suspended without a full hearing on the merits. *Carey v. Piphus*, 98 S.Ct. 1042, 1978.

Educ. v. Barnette, 319 U.S. 624, 1943. Nor are constitutional protections for the favored few— "Due process (of law) is not for adults alone." *In re Gault,* 387 U.S. 1. Ariz. 1967. "Children are persons under our Constitution, and do not shed their rights at the school-house gate." *Tinker v. Des Moines Ind.Comm. Sch. Dist.,* 393 U.S. 503, Iowa 1969. Finally, the Supreme Court held that students facing the loss of a considerable length of time from school are entitled to the full panoply of due process procedures, and that if the board knew, or reasonably should have known, that they were depriving an individual of a civil right, they could be held personally liable in damages for their lack of care.

Two sophomore girls in the Mena, Arkansas schools brought suit against the board and the school district, including the superintendent, because they were expelled for spiking the punch at a school function, in contravention of a board rule forbidding the use "of any intoxicating beverage" in such affairs. Although the board never established that the students possessed or used an "intoxicating" beverage, it nevertheless expelled the girls for three months. The Court held that such a lack of evidence, and such precipitous action by the board in expelling the girls, amounted to a denial of their rights to due process of law. At the very least, the student who is faced with expulsion is entitled to these minimal guarantees: (1) written notice given with sufficient time to prepare a defense; (2) right to an impartial hearing on the evidence; (3) right to appear with counsel and cross examine opposing witnesses and present witnesses in his own defense; (4) right to a transcript of the proceedings; and (5) the right to appeal to higher authority. Where such a heavy penalty as loss of valuable and irreplaceable school time is involved, these are the bare essentials of due process before the law. *Wood v. Strickland,* 420 U.S. 308, Ark. 1975.

EXCLUSION FROM ACTIVITIES

Board exclusion of students for being pregnant or married have long since been overthrown. In Ohio, a high school senior who was a good baseball player but who was married was barred from participating in spring baseball, although he was allowed to go to classes. The board had a rule excluding married students from participation in extra-curricular activities. The evidence showed that several colleges were interested in giving the boy a scholarship, and big league scouts were competing to offer him a contract. The federal district court to which he applied for relief held that the board's action might wreck the boy's marriage, as well as deny him considerable economic advantage. "What greater invasion of marital privacy can there be than one which could totally destroy his marriage?" asked the court. Nor was the fact that he was barred from an extra-curricular activity an inconsequential denial of a guaranteed right, where it was shown that he could make more money playing baseball than he could ever earn in an academic setting. *Davis v. Meek,* 344 F.Supp. 298, Ohio 1972.

Unless a board can show that a girl's presence in school when she is unmarried and pregnant would invade the rights of others, or cause a clear and present danger or disruption to the program, it cannot deny that student the right to attend school. *Ordway v. Hargraves,* 323 F.Supp. 1155, Mass. 1971. And where a girl can show that she can compete on an even footing with boys in contact sports and there is no comparable program for girls in her high school, the board cannot bar her bid for a place on the boys' team. *Gilpin v. Kansas High School Act. Ass'n.,* 377 F.Supp. 1233, Kans. 1973.

No child may be excluded from school because he or she is mentally retarded, unless that child is provided with an adequate alternative educational program or services to meet his needs and a constitutionally adequate prior hearing and periodic review of the child's status and progress are accorded him. *Mills v. Bd. of Educ., D.C.,* 348 F.Supp. 866, D.C. 1972.

Exclusion can be either *absolute,* in which there is no education being given, or *partial,* in which the student is being excluded from certain parts of the program. Lately, the legal term "functional exclusion" has come into the language, meaning that a student may be present in body but not really benefiting from his placement in the school's educational environment. While absolute and complete exclusion is outlawed, the disposition of cases in which functional or partial exclusion is alleged must be decided in each case on the merits of the facts presented in evidence. Courts of law will still deal with the educational rights of each individual child on the grounds that the state owes that child the least restrictive environment possible under the circumstances.

MISCELLANEOUS PUNISHMENTS

Various types of punishments have been sanctioned by the courts, others denied. For example, the courts have held that no cause of action derives from the teacher's verbal chastisement of a student, even though such punishment was given in front of the class. *Wexell v. Schott,* 276 N.E.2d 735, Ill. 1971. Of course, there must be a complete absence of malice or wantonness in such punishment. A teacher who is "out to get a student" may be held liable in damages for assault and battery, or for deprivation of a civil right, just as any other school official.

Many schools knock down grades as a means of punishment for skipping school or for tardiness. "The use of grades as a means of punishment is improper," said the New Jersey Commissioner of Education. "Hence, a student's rights are prejudiced where he is given a zero for truancy and then given a make-up test, but the zero is weighed against the result." *Minorics v. Bd.of Educ.,* N.J. Comm'r. of Educ. Dec., 1972.

A Colorado school district adopted a policy that denied academic credit if students failed to meet the attendance requirement established by the policy. The board denied credit in any semester in which there were more than seven "absences," which included personal illnesses, professional appointments, serious personal or family problems, and other reasons. The board policy did not provide for a review panel to examine cases on a case by case basis. A state statute required students to be in school 172 days but made allowances for days missed due to temporary illness or injury. The court held that the board's policy was contrary to the School Attendance Law, since it did not provide for any exceptions, was automatic, and did not meet due process standards. *Gutierrez v. School Dist. R-1, Otero County,* 585 P.2d 935, Colo. 1978.

Guilt by association is illegal. In Iowa, a high school student who knowingly rode in an automobile where beer was being consumed, and who was denied a year's eligibility in his sport, outside the season, and while school was not in session, was denied due process of law; this amounted to guilt by association. *Bunger v. Ia.H.S.Ath.Ass'n.,* 197

N.W.2d 555, Iowa 1972. And where a student's athletic letter was revoked after he had won it because he had been caught drinking beer outside the season, the board was ordered to restore his award. *O'Connor v. Bd. of Educ.,* 316 N.Y.S.2d 799, 1970.

Sometimes a teacher goes too far in punishing his students. This occurred in Louisiana, where a fifth grade teacher overheard two of his students say a famous four-letter Anglo-Saxon word. For punishment, he made them write that word 1,000 times each. He was dismissed by the board and sought reinstatement in court. His suit was unsuccessful. The court held that no academic or educational purpose was served by the punishment and that the board did not act arbitrarily in ordering his dismissal. *Celestine v. Lafayette Parish School Board,* 284 So. 2d 650, La. 1973.

SEARCH OF STUDENTS

"Given the responsibility of school teachers in the control of the school precincts and grave threat, even lethal threat, of drug abuse among school children, the basis for finding sufficient cause for a school search will be less than required outside the school," said one judge in holding that a search of a student had been legal. *People v. D.,* 358 N.Y.S.2d 403, 1974. Teachers, who stand *in loco parentis,* are further protected by that status in searching students for suspected contraband. Thus, where a dime was missing and the teacher went through a kid's pockets, the search was upheld "to clear the child's name." *Marlar v. Bill,* 178 S.W.2d 634, Tenn. 1944.

The Fourth Amendment provides that the people shall be secure in their persons, houses, papers and effects against unreasonable searches and seizures. Nowhere, however, does the Constitution state what constitutes *unreasonable* search or how *probable cause* is to be determined. What constitutes unreasonableness or probable cause has been the subject of an endless number of court actions. There is no ready test for determining reasonableness other than by balancing the need to search or seize against the invasion which the search or seizure entails. *Terry v. Ohio,* 392 U.S. 1, 1968. Where a prior violation has occurred, police have "reasonable cause" to stop and search. Thus, where a motorist ran a stop sign, and his car was searched as a result, the Supreme Court held that contraband obtained in the search could be admitted into evidence.

School officials may play one or more of three roles: (1) *in loco parentis,* where the right to search is implied in the interests of the child; (2) private citizen status, where a warrant must issue or (3) state agent, which requires a warrant before seizure is legal. So long as the teacher or principal can support the argument that he or she acted in the interests of safety of children, or to protect the good name of a student, the courts will not interfere. Whether a search is in the best interest of a student or students is not always clear.

In *Phillips v. Johns,* 12 Tenn. App. 354, 1930, a student charged that she was forcibly searched by a teacher for $21 that was actually stolen by another student. The court held that the teacher stands *in loco parentis,* and has the same rights as a parent under the circumstances. On appeal, the appellate court reversed and held that even though the search was in good faith and without force or violence, it was made for the teacher's benefit, and not for the benefit of the student. More recent rulings are to the effect that where school officials act in good faith and not in ignorance or disregard of settled indisputable principles of law, they have an immunity much as a parent would have in those situations. *Bellnier v. Lund,* 438 F.Supp. 47, N.Y. 1977; *State v. McKinnon,* 558 P.2d 781 Wash. 1977.

Personal searches

Students are sometimes asked to empty their pockets on suspicion that they contain contraband. For example, a New York teacher noticed bulges in a boy's pants' pocket so he took the boy down to the office. On the way, the boy broke and ran. He was caught three blocks from the school and turned over to a policeman when an eyedropper and hypodermic needle were found on him. The court held that *in loco parentis* doctrine is so compelling in the light of public necessity that any action, including a search taken thereunder upon reasonable suspicion, should be accepted as necessary and reasonable. *People v. Jackson,* 30 N.Y.S.2d 734, 1972. Similarly, a "reasonable cause to believe" was the basis for a principal's search of a student where marijuana was found. Another student had reported by telephone to the principal that a large amount of money and something thought to be drugs were in plaintiff's possession. When plaintiff arrived at school, the principal called him into his office and asked him to empty his pockets. When he refused, the principal said he would call the police unless he complied, whereupon the student obeyed the demand. The court held that the search was legal, that there was no police involvement, and that the principal had reasonable cause to believe that a violation had occurred. *M. v. Bd. of Educ.,* 429 F. Supp. 288, Ill. 1977.

Where, however, the principal collaborates with the police, he may be included with them in the category of "state agents." A ring was missing from a classroom, and the principal sealed off the room and instituted a search. When no ring appeared, he called the police, who sent a woman cop to the classroom. She required the girls to strip down to their bras and panties, but still no ring was found. In a suit against the principal and vice-principal, the girls were successful. Where an individual's right to privacy is involved, said the court, the plaintiffs can recover if there is collusion with the police or conspiracy on the part of the school employees. *Potts v. Wright,* 357 F.Supp. 215 Pa., 1973. "It is the nature of the act taken by the school official," said the court, "and not the status of the person as a state official which provides the element of 'under color of state law.'" The principal and vice-principal could be held liable only if "they participated with the police in making statements or taking actions, the natural consequences of which could be said to have caused the plaintiffs to succumb to the searches, or if the evidence established an understanding or agreement between the school officials and the police to deny plaintiffs their constitutional rights."

Locker searches

School lockers, as one might surmise, may be searched more readily than a student's person or effects. The courts are in agreement that a student has privacy in his locker as against other students, but not as against school officials. A principal has the right, even the duty, to search lockers for contraband in order to protect the safety of the students. It is doubtful that the school could discharge its duty of supervision over students if it failed to retain control over its lockers. The right becomes a duty when there is suspicion that contraband may be present.

Figure 13-3

SOME SEARCH AND SEIZURE CASES

- A California judge ruled that evidence of a dog's high level of performance and great degree of accuracy in detecting marijuana odors justified reliance on the dog's reactions as corroboration of a reliable informant's tip that there might be possible narcotics in defendant's possession, so as to justify warrantless search of his baggage at an airport. *People v. Furman*, 106 Cal. Rptr. 366, 1973.

- Teacher violated the constitutional rights of fifth graders by conducting a strip search for stolen money. The court held it was not necessary to show probable cause for the search but reasonable grounds for suspecting certain students must be provided, and only those students could be searched. Because they acted in good faith, school officials were immune from liability. *Bellnier v. Lund*, 438 F.Supp. 47, NY. 1977.

- School authorities acted properly in a situation involving a gun and the evidence was admissible in a juvenile court hearing. The student had made a suspicious movement and school authorities grabbed his hand, thereby finding the gun. *In re Ronald B.*, 401 N.Y.S.2d 544, 1978.

- An after-hours search of a counselor's desk by a school board member in hopes of identifying the author of a cartoon ridiculing the financial policies of the board was held to constitute a violation of the Fourth Amendment committed under color of state law. The case was remanded for a hearing on the damages to be assessed. *Gillard v. Schmidt*, 579 F.2d 825, N.J. 1978.

On the day following a burglary at a coin shop, two police officers came to the school and requested the principal to open the locker of a certain boy, a student at the high school. With the boy's consent, the principal opened the locker and found a key which led to a locker at the bus depot. With a warrant this time, the police searched the bus depot locker and found some of the stolen coins. The boy was found guilty of burglary. Not only could the principal search the locker, but also he did not have to give a *Miranda* type warning to the student before doing so, said the court in upholding the conviction. *State v. Stein*, 456 P.2d 1, Kans. 1969, *cert. denied*, 90 U.S. 966, 1970.

Although a school does not own or control student automobiles, the presence of cars on school grounds may bring them under the authority of the school officials. When articles of a dangerous nature are suspected of being concealed in a car on school property, the principal would seem to have the obligation to notify the police. It is doubtful he could search the car absent a warrant, unless contraband was in plain sight, or he had probable cause to suspect that the vehicle was being used for illegal purposes.

14

The Problem of Students'
Constitutional Rights

STUDENTS AS PERSONS

Sweeping changes in the concept of the legal rights of children both in and out of school have occurred since 1954. In other chapters, the discipline and control of school students under these new freedoms has been explored. In this chapter, the emphasis will be on the possible implications of the Supreme Court's holding in *Tinker* that children are "persons" under our Constitution and do not shed their rights at the schoolhouse gate.

What that clause means—that children are "persons" —is only recently coming in for serious study. Do children have the *same* rights as adults? Must one take into account the age of the child in determining legal rights? How much freedom are children entitled to in school? Do they have the right to participate meaningfully in the making of decisions that affect their lives in school? No doubt these and other similar questions of a legal nature will occupy the attention of the courts for some time to come. In the meantime, the schools must deal with the new freedoms and develop new strategies to harness them. Just what changes will be needed is still obscure, but there are some insights available, and much is being written on the subject. In effect, the schools have been called on to invent entirely new structural arrangements in order to implement the Court's decisions and to experiment with what will and will not work. Clearly, this is an age of transition—we know only that old strategies will no longer work and that we must have the foresight to live with changes that we will not fully understand. This chapter will deal with the fundamentals necessary to develop such strategies and form the foundation for later arrangements more in line with the Court's holdings.

WHO ARE THE DISADVANTAGED?

When is a class of people discriminated against? In *San Antonio School District v. Rodriguez,* 411 U.S. 1, Texas 1973, the Supreme Court had before it the question of whether the Texas scheme for financing public schools discriminated against the "poor." Rodriguez, a resident of a poor district, maintained that since less money per child per year was spent in his district than in more affluent districts in the state, he and others like him were being discriminated against. He asked the Court to rule that the state of Texas was denying the class of poorer citizens equal protection of the laws. A majority of the Court held that the "poor" are not a suspect class, since there were poor people living in rich districts as well as in less favored districts. The Court then went on to define the traditional bases on which it will determine whether a particular class of persons is "suspect."

First, to be a suspect class, the group of persons must be relegated to a position of political *powerlessness* so as to demand extraordinary protection from the majoritarian political process. In many respects, children as a class might come under this category, but not always: they do not vote, nor do they know groups powerful enough to cast votes in their favor. Perhaps handicapped children come under this "suspect" classification, but recently there have been some powerful groups coming out in favor of legal help for the handicapped, so that the classification may come in for some changes due to circumstances. Second, the class must be saddled with *disabilities* that work against their full realization of civil rights due them under the Constitution. This might refer to the indigent, who have no means by which to fight their legal battles. Children might qualify here also, since they ordinarily do not have ready access to sums of money with which to fight legal battles in the courts. Third, a class is suspect if it has been subjected to such *a history of purposeful unequal treatment* as to warrant compensatory treatment under the law. Under this definition, blacks might be considered a "suspect" classification by virtue of their servitude. It also applies to women, Indians, homosexuals and other minorities who have been subjected to unequal treatment historically. Thus, children under these classification definitions may be discriminated against if it can be shown in court that (1) they are politically powerless and this suit is the only way they can be accorded justice, (2), they are saddled with lack of funds or experience in gaining their civil rights, or (3) they have been historically discriminated against so as to warrant the rating of a "suspect" classification before the law.

In *Rodriguez,* the Court majority would not say that the "poor" are a suspect class for purposes of obtaining equal educational opportunity. "We must conclude that the Texas system does not operate to the peculiar advantage of any suspect class," wrote Justice White for the majority. "Education is not among the rights afforded explicit protection under the Federal Constitution. Nor do we find any basis for saying it is implicitly so protected. So long as the poor child is receiving the same minimal quantum of education as the rich, there is no denial of equal protection of the laws. In such a complex arena in which no perfect alternatives exist, the Court does well not to impose too rigorous a standard of scrutiny lest all local fiscal schemes become subjects of criticism under the Equal Protection Clause."

In refusing to hold the State of Texas to the high standard of strict scrutiny, the majority strengthened a principle of law that had been in existence for many years: the Supreme Court will not create a right out of thin air, but will only support the rights that have already been established by the state itself. Here, the right was entitlement to a free education. The Court held that what that means will differ from state to state depending on each state's educational guarantee in its state constitution. While the state is not required to set up a system of public education, when it does choose to do so, it must make the benefits of that system "available to all on an equal (non-discriminatory) basis." Thus, education at public expense is not a "fundamental" right on a par with the right to vote or be represented by counsel. A child's constitutional right is his *state's* constitutional mandate subject to legislative discretion. It means that the child is entitled to equal access to the state's school resources as his birthright, and no more. He cannot look to the Federal Constitution to create a right that is not his granted by the state in the first place. This distinction, while facially a distinction without a difference, is nonetheless the foundation of the child's edu- cational rights in our system of public/private education today.

The grandfather of the school finance cases was *Serrano v. Priest,* 487 P.2d 1241, Cal. 1971. It spawned more than 50 cases of a similar nature in the states, among which was *San Antonio v. Rodriguez.* The evil that plaintiffs set out to cure was the allegation that the quality of a child's education is a function of the wealth of his district of residency— a violation of the equal protection clause. The investigation revealed wide-ranging discrepancies in the availability of educational oppor- tunities within and among the states. However, there was a general lack of demonstrably strong correlation between low property wealth school districts and the incidence of poor families. Apparently, the poor are where you find them, which may or may not be in a property-poor school district.

Education is a unique and important commodity, however, and the Supreme Court has ruled that denial of education at public ex- pense is a violation of the Fourteenth Amendment unless constitu- tional safeguards are observed. Going to school is both a "property" and a "liberty" right protected by that amendment. If the state is to deny it to any qualified individual, it must do so only after due process and equal protection have been fully vindicated. *Goss v. Lopez,* 419 U.S. 565, Ohio 1975; *Wood v. Strickland,* 420 U.S. 308, Ark. 1975.

STANDING TO SUE: THE CLASS ACTION SUIT

An individual's rights depend on his or her standing to sue, that is, to the right of relief. Class action suits have become the engine by which social changes have been realized under the civil rights aegis. The class action suit is not novel, since it was used as early as the Reconstruction Period following the War Between the States. What is novel today is its frequency of use. A person might benefit from a class action suit without knowing that he has been included as a member of that action, since one does not have to be a party to a suit to be bound thereby. Members may be either "known" (names and addresses on file somewhere) or "unknown" (these latter must step forward on sufficient publicity of their possible inclusion in the class). Too, a person may opt out of a pending action in a class action suit if he does not wish to be included.

Class action suits are governed by Rule 23(a) of the Federal Rules of Civil Procedure as amended in 1966, which requires that all of the following criteria be met in order to qualify as a classification suit:

1) The class must be so numerous that joinder of all members is impracticable;
2) There must be questions of law or fact common to the class;
3) The claims or defenses of the representative parties must be typical of the claims or defenses of the entire class; and
4) The representative parties must fairly and adequately protect the interests of the class.

One of the threshold questions in court cases is whether the plaintiffs are suing for "other individuals so situated" as well as for themselves. This is a point of law to be determined by the judge. For example, two female high school students challenged a ruling of their state high school league prohibiting females from participating in boys' interscholastic athletic programs. The girls had demonstrated that (a) they could compete on an equal footing with boys, and (b) their high schools did not have programs comparable to those offered to boys. The judge pointed out, however, that the case was not a class action suit—that every girl who later challenged a similar rule must show that she could compete equally with boys and that her high school did not provide an equal program for girls. *Brenden v. Ind. Sch. Dist.*, 477 F.2d 1292, Minn. 1973. Thus, not all girls who were excluded from boys' interscholastic athletics were to be considered in future as having been discriminated against merely because of such exclusion.

The essence of the class action suit is that an individual is a member of a class that is being treated differently from other classes of people. The reasoning is self-evident, the right unalienable. Because of its obvious economy, the class action suit will doubtless be with us for many more years to come.

Most of the school desegregation cases, including *Brown v. Bd. of Education*, have been class action suits, involving millions of children and hundreds of defendant school boards. It works this way: first, the class demonstrates to the satisfaction of the court that there may be grounds for saying that a class of persons is being discriminated against; second, the burden of proof then shifts to the defendants (here the school board) to show that it has acted within the appropriate constitutional constraints in doing what it has done. An example will serve to illustrate how it works.

In Des Moines, students wore black armbands to school to protest the war in Vietnam. They were told they must take off the armbands or go home. They challenged the rule in court, and won. When they showed that their right to free speech was involved (black armbands are "akin" to pure speech), the burden of proof then shifted to the board to show cause why it had enacted the rule under color of state law. The board, being unable to show that it had to do so in order to escape disruption of the academic program, lost. *Tinker v. Des Moines Ind.Comm. School Dist.,* 393 U.S. 503, Iowa 1969. The rule of law was expressed by the Court in this manner:

> In order for the State, in the person of school officials, to justify prohibition of a particular expression of opinion, it must be able to show that its action is caused by something more than a mere desire to avoid the discomfort and unpleasant that always accompany an unpopular viewpoint. ... In the absence of a specific showing of constitutionally valid reasons to regulate speech, students are entitled to freedom of expression of their views.

Many classes are determined by whether an individual member of that class can break out of it or not. Thus, classes based on race, ethnicity, country of origin, sex, age, religion, or native language, are "suspect" at the outset. In *Lau v. Nichols,* 414 U.S. 563, Cal. 1974, for example, 1,800 Chinese-speaking pupils sued the San Francisco School Board for remedial English language instruction, claiming violation of the equal protection clause. The Court did not have to go as far as the Fourteenth Amendment to find that the district must provide such assistance. An HEW guideline stated: "Where inability to speak and understand the English language excludes national-origin minority group children from effective participation in the educational program offered by a school district, the district must take affirmative steps to rectify the language deficiency in order to open its instructional program to these students." Thus, any district that gets federal funds must agree to abide by this guideline, or suffer possible loss of its federal funds. Since this proved to be a sufficient incentive to the San

Francisco board, it was not necessary for the Court to go to the question of whether its state action amounted to a denial of equal protection of the laws.

Most of the rights that children have gained in the first 20 years of the civil rights movement were obtained by the use of class action suits. More recently, the emphasis has been on the due process clause, but even there considerable class action litigation has resulted. Busing, "the issue that will not go away," is based on *Brown II (Brown v. Bd. of Education,* 349 U.S. 294, 1955), which provided that all cases involving school desegregation issues should be retained under the jurisdiction of federal district courts in the states in which the cases arose. "Separate but equal schools for the races are inherently unequal," hence unconstitutional. Local school authorities have the primary responsibility for implementing the *Brown I* decision. The function of the federal courts is to decide whether a school board is complying in good faith and to reconcile the public interest in orderly and effective transition to constitutional school (unitary) systems in line with the constitutional requirements themselves. The courts ordinarily will not construct a plan for the local district, but in the event that the local board cannot find such a solution, the court will issue guidelines to be followed, and even in some instances go so far as to construct some of the guidelines themselves. A prompt and reasonable start must be made by the board ("with all deliberate speed") to come into compliance as ordered by the court.

Busing has not been universally accepted as a means of desegregating the schools, although most federal courts support this solution. See Richard Kluger's *Simple Justice,* Knopf 1976 for an exhaustive discussion of the *Brown* decisions. "Seldom in its history has the Supreme Court taken a position on an issue with so little support from either elected representatives or the public," says Gary Orfield (*Must We Bus? Segregated Schools and National Policy,* Brookings Institute, 1977).

The benefits of the class action suit are as follows:

1) to give an individual his/her day in court (the pacification benefit);
2) to provide a means of compensating individuals for their losses (the compensatory benefit); and

3) to discourage would-be wrongdoers from proceeding to take unfair and unbridled advantage of others (the deterrent benefit).

Whatever their advantages and disadvantages, class action suits seem here to stay. They are mighty engines for social change, casting at a single stroke the future of many groups of persons within the society. They are efficient, far reaching, and capable of vast amounts of social progress in one fell swoop. Although the charge is made that attorneys may be getting rich where they win vindication for a certain group, there is insufficient evidence to conclude that they are using the class action suit as a device to reap big profits while individual members of the class recover a mere pittance.

SUBSTANTIVE V. PROCEDURAL DUE PROCESS

Certain rights that children enjoy are based on content—the substantive rights, while others are based on required procedure—the procedural rights. It is clear that being in school is a property right protected by the Fourteenth Amendment, and that if the school is to deny this right to an individual pupil, it must do so only after certain recognized fair-play procedures have been observed. This distinction can be illustrated by a three-way test regarding a school rule which comes into question. Suppose that a board had a rule that boys could wear slacks to school, but that girls could wear slacks made only of some material other than blue denim. The board bases its rule on a belief that "girls in overalls look masculine." The rule is challenged by a group of girls who claim that they are being discriminated against since all boys may wear slacks made of any material including denim.

The first question involving student rights is this: "Is this a reasonable rule under the circumstances?" Since the board cannot justify its rule—that girls look masculine in blue denim slacks—the rule would be unreasonable. It is based on an opinion, not a fact. A rule is reasonable only when the board can show that it has a valid relationship to its carrying out a valid state purpose, and that the public benefit outweighs the individual inconvenience. The second question, "Does the rule apply equally and equitably to all to whom it is applied?" also shows that the rule is indefensible since it applies to girls but not to boys. Even here, though the board might be able to show that its rule, although applying more to one sex than another, is justified (not in this case, however). The third question, a procedural one (the first two apply to substantive rights of students), is this: "Is the punishment to be applied for violation of the rule fundamentally fair?" If there are no exceptions, the procedural aspects of rule enforcement are missing, and the rule must fall because of lack of constitutional safeguards.

In Denver, Chicano students asked the principal if they might wear black berets in school to demonstrate their ethnicity. The principal talked it over with them, then decided to let them try it. After the students threatened to take over the school, the principal told them they could stay but the black berets must go. They challenged the rule on the grounds that it violated the "symbolic speech" ruling in *Tinker.* Pending outcome of the trial, the students were allowed to attend school *sans* the black berets. The principal won. *Hernandez v. School Dist. No. 1,* 315 F.Supp. 289, Colo. 1970.

Said the court, in upholding the rule, and ruling against the students:

> The plaintiffs (students) were becoming arrogant, and they were boisterous. They were trying to take over the school. This created an atmosphere of tension and apprehension throughout the whole school. In an attempt to avoid necessary suspension of the plaintiffs, the principal talked with the parents; in some cases he got support, in others he did not. But in any event, he received no cooperation whatsoever from the plaintiffs. When he told the plaintiffs they must take off the berets or leave school, we must assume that he did it because of the impending disruption of the program of studies. The court concludes that the statutory procedures for temporary suspension are not a denial of procedural due process and that they did not deprive the plaintiffs of any requirement under the Federal Constitution.

Similarly, a rule that students could not wear the Confederate flag as a shoulder patch or on their clothing was reasonable because *every time some student wore the patch, a riot broke out. Melton v. Young,* 465 F.2d 1332, Tenn. 1972, *cert. den.,* 93 S.Ct. 1926, 1973. Figure 14-1 illustrates the application of this three-way test to a grievance procedure for students in the public schools.

Figure 14-1

STUDENT GRIEVANCE FORM

To the Student: A grievance is defined as a complaint in writing presented by a student to the school staff/authorities alleging one or more of the following:

A. That a rule is unfair; and/or

B. That a rule in practice discriminates against or between students; and/or

C. That school personnel used an unfair procedure in assessing a form of punishment or penalty against the student.

COMPLAINT

Date_____

Check one blank: Counselor, Level 1 _____; Asst. Principal, Level 2 _____; Principal, Level 3 _____.

I, _____, hereby file a grievance complaint to
     (Student's Name)

_____

     (Counselor's Name)

My grievance is based on A._____ B._____ C. above. (More than one blank may be checked.)

Specifically, my grievance is that _____

_____

I hereby petition for a hearing on my grievance at the convenience of the school personnel, but in no event later than five school days from the date of this petition.

_____
     (Student's signature)

The student may be represented at the conference by an adult, but the student must be present to elaborate on his/her grievance at the given time and place for the conference. Failure to appear at the appointed time and place effectively waives the student's right to the conference provided for by the school, unless extenuating circumstances make it impossible for the student to appear.

Figure 14-1 (continued)

SCHOOL'S RECORD

Date Complaint Received_____Date of Conference_____
Place of Conference_____Time of Conference_____
Comments:_____
_____
_____
Resolution of the Case:_____
_____

_____
Signature of
School Representative

See M. Chester Nolte, "Why You Need a Student Grievance Procedure," *American School Board Journal*, Aug., 1975, pp. 38-40.

Suppose that ninth grade students in a junior high school containing grades seventh through ninth wish to protest the fact that they are excluded from electioneering in student elections held each spring because they will not be back the following year. They would fill out a grievance complaint, specifying that the rule is unfair, that it discriminates against ninth graders as a class, and that they are disenfranchised without due process of law. They would then file the complaint with a counselor on the staff, who would set up a hearing on the merits within five days of the receipt of the complaint. If the hearing does not result in a finding acceptable to the students, they could then appeal, again within five days, to the assistant principal, who would set a time and place for the hearing and sit on appeal. If the students still were not satisfied, they could appeal to the principal, who would settle the controversy. In this particular instance, students were allowed to participate in electioneering, but could not be candidates for election since they would not be around the following semester.

CONSTITUTIONAL LIMITS OF STUDENTS' RIGHTS

It is clear that students do not have quite the same rights as adults, since the courts will take into account the limitations of the school

Figure 14-2

STUDENTS' RIGHTS AND RESPONSIBILITIES

It is the student's right to	It is the student's responsibility to
Attend school in the district where his parents/guardian reside.	Attend school daily, except when ill, and to be on time at all classes.
Attend school until graduation from high school at public expense.	Attend school until age 16 or completion of the eighth grade.*
Obtain free textbooks and supplies* in the course of study.	Pay admission to activities if attendance therein is voluntary.
Attend school at no expense even though married.	Obey reasonable restrictions on married students where board rules exist on the subject.
Assist in making decisions affecting his/her life in school.	Pursue and attempt to complete the course of study.
Express his/her opinions verbally or in writing.	Express his/her opinions and ideas in a respectful manner so as not to slander others.
Expect that the school will be a safe place for students to gain an education.	Be aware of all rules and regulations for student behavior and obey them.
Dress in such a way as to express his/her own personality.	Dress and appear so as to meet fair standards of propriety, safety, health and good taste.
File a grievance with the appropriate school official when accused of misconduct.	Be willing to volunteer information in disciplinary cases should he/she have knowledge of importance.
Be afforded a fair hearing with the opportunity to call witnesses in his/her own behalf, and to appeal his/her case in event of disciplinary action.	Be willing to volunteer information and cooperate with school staffs in disciplinary cases.

*May vary from state to state according to state law.

Figure 14-2 (continued)

Expect that where he/she bears witness in a disciplinary case, his/her own anonymity will be honored by the school.	Assist the school staff in running a safe school for all students enrolled therein.
Be represented by an active student government selected by free school elections.	Take an active part in school student government by running for office, or voting for the best candidates, making his/her problems known to the staff or his/her representatives.
Assist in the making of school rules and regulations.	Assume that until a rule is waived, altered or repealed, it is in full force and effect.
Be represented by an adult at any disciplinary hearing before an impartial tribunal.	Bear true witness in any disciplinary hearing on the facts of the case at hand.

---

setting in deciding whether students have been denied any rights in school. The art of school management has changed considerably from the days when anything went, to consist of at least the following accommodations to the rights of students:

- A willingness to go along with students' wishes even though there may be honest doubts about the wisdom of the request. This is the willingness that the principal showed with respect to the wearing of black berets in the case above.
- A sympathy with students' needs to forge an identity of their own, and a willingness to protect their right to do so.
- A courage to risk unpleasantness and possible disruption in the interests of "seeing if it will work."
- A genuine attempt to include students in the decision-making processes not because they will be helpful in making decisions but because they are more likely to abide by decisions they make rather than those that are made for them.
- A fairness of principle that says even the least of these is entitled to be heard; and
- An interest in students in the hope they can learn independence and good citizenship not by living in a dictatorship but by actually practicing in a system shaped after the one that they will experience once they leave school.

The ultimate solution to the problem of whether students are "persons" in school is to conclude that they are—and take them in as junior partners. In this way, they learn not only how the system works, but also how they can live harmoniously on a day-to-day basis with it.

Students may exceed their constitutional limitations when they do one or more of the following:

- They substantially disrupt the on-going program of the schools for any length of time;
- They become a clear and present danger to the peace and good order of the community, such as during a riot when they may destroy property or harm others bodily;
- They invade the rights of others;
- They pose a real threat to the governance of the schools, such as where they exhibit take-over tendencies as in the case of the black berets.

CHAPTER

15

How to Cater to the Open Mind

...and you will know the truth and the truth will make you free.
(John 8:32.)

Does the United States Constitution create the student's right to learn, to know, to be informed, and to hear the truth? An emerging series of cases deals with this very interesting idea. In analyzing the "right to know" one must be aware that two opposing and quite opposite philosophies of the law are involved. First, education is a state function and state legislatures have plenary (complete) power over how the young shall be educated, within the limits of the Bill of Rights. The power encompasses, among other things, broad control over each curriculum and student by the local board of education acting for the legislative body of the respective state. This authority is not unlimited, however—it cannot infringe on rights protected by the First Amendment which is applicable to the states via the due process clause of the Fourteenth Amendment. The question becomes important where boards of education remove books from school libraries, or place constraints on the students' right to explore knowledge and publish it in official and unofficial school newspapers. This chapter is about some cases that have come up related to this area of the law, an area only now becoming the focus of litigation.

The Supreme Court has said that it will not *create* a right within a state where that right is not already guaranteed by the state itself. *San Antonio Ind. School Dist. v. Rodriguez,* 411 U.S. 1, Tex. 1973. In holding that the Constitution does not guarantee equal educational opportunity, the Court's majority (5-4) pointed to the fact that the Rodriguez child was receiving the same minimal schooling enjoyed by every other Texas child and that the fact that richer districts were spending more per pupil per year did not deprive the child of equal protection of the laws. This casts some doubt as to whether the Court would rule that a child has the right to know, to learn, to be informed, inasmuch as the majority held in *Rodriguez* that if there is a right to free education it must be found in that child's respective state constitution. In effect, the Court was merely saying that no child shall be discriminated against in receiving educational benefits: if the state decides to offer free public education, it must be made available to all on a non-discriminatory basis. To determine whether there is a constitutional right to learn, we must approach the question from a different angle, that of removing books from school libraries. First, a look at the historical foundation of the problem is in order.

EVOLUTION OF THE RIGHT TO LEARN

The foundation of the right to know and to learn was laid down by the Supreme Court in *Meyer v. Nebraska,* 262 U.S. 390, 1923. As a result of WWI, both Nebraska and Iowa had statutes prohibiting the teaching of foreign languages to children below the ninth grade level. The Court held that the statutes violated the due process clause of the Fourteenth Amendment, stating that they were arbitrary and intended impermissibly to "interfere with the calling of modern language teachers, *and with the opportunities of pupils to acquire knowledge.*" (Emphasis added.) Thus, at the early part of the 20th century, the concept of the right to learn was established, and the idea laid down that state legislation on public education was not absolute and must not conflict with the Constitution. *Bartels v. Iowa,* 262 U.S. 404, 1923.

Two years later, the Court upheld the right of parents to educate their children in non-public schools if they chose to do so. "The child is not the mere creature of the state," said the majority. "The fundamental theory upon which all governments repose excludes any general power of the state to standardize its children by forcing them to accept instruction from public school teachers only." *Pierce v. Society of Sisters,* 268 U.S. 510, Ore. 1925. In 1943, the Court ruled that boards of education "have important, delicate and highly discretionary functions which they must perform, but none they may not perform within the limits of the Bill of Rights." *West Va. State Bd. of Educ. v. Barnette,* 319 U.S. 624, 1943.

Children have the right to study alongside children of other races, said the Court in ruling that separate but equal school facilities for the races are inherently unequal. *Brown v. Bd. of Education,* 347 U.S. 483, Kans. 1954. "Neither the Bill of Rights nor the Fourteenth Amendment is for adults alone," said the Court in "equalizing" the rights of youth with those adults. Yet in matters involving the curriculum, and the tools of instruction, such as textbooks, the courts continued to uphold the right of the local board to select such materials as a part of the state's interest in an enlightened citizenry.

Grouping children so as to lock them into a "track" may be unconstitutional, since it tends to sort them according to race, ethnic and economic factors rather than on their ability to learn or their need for instruction. *Hobson v. Hansen,* 408 F.2d 175, D.C. 1969. Children are "persons" under our Constitution, said the Court, "and do not shed their constitutional rights at the schoolhouse gate. In our system, state-operated schools may not be enclaves of totalitarianism. School officials do not possess absolute authority over their students. Students in school and out are 'persons'. .... *They may not be confined to the expression of those sentiments which are officially approved.*" (Emphasis added.) *Tinker v. Des Moines Ind. Comm. School District,* 393 U.S. 503, Iowa 1969.

The year before, the Court had decided that textbooks containing Darwin's theory of evolution of the species could not be barred from the public schools of Arkansas. Its decision was based not so much on the right to teach (academic freedom) as on the theory that where a state limits knowledge of man's origins to only that version contained in Genesis, such limitation amounts to an establishment of religion. *Epperson v. Arkansas,* 393 U.S. 97, 1968. Other decisions provided that "gifted" children could be held back but only under reasonable rules that take into account the physical, social, and emotional maturity of each student (*Ackerman v. Rubin*, 231 N.Y.S.2d 112, 1962), and that pregnant (*Ordway v. Hargraves*, 323 F.Supp. 1155, Mass. 1971) or married (*Davis v. Meek*, 344 F.Supp. 298, Ohio 1972) students could not be excluded from public schools because of the fact that they were either pregnant or married or both.

It is within the power of the state to require a teaching curriculum that includes instruction on sex for the non-pregnant (and, incidentally, for the non-impregnating) students who, because of lack of information on the subject, have become pregnant, or who have caused pregnancy. *Cornwell v. St.Bd. of Education*, 314 F.Supp. 340, Md. 1969, aff'd. 428 F.2d 471, *cert. den.*, 400 U.S. 942, 1971. Nor may the state confine its services in family planning to only those citizens who are over age 16, since it cannot demonstrate the connection between promiscuity, the evil it seeks to control, and the availability of birth control devices. "The right to privacy in connection with decisions affecting procreation extends to minors as well as to adults," said the Court. *Carey v. Population Services International*, 431 U.S. 678, N.Y. 1977.

Figure 15-1

STUDENT RIGHT TO FREE EXERCISE

One's education is not complete without a study of comparative religion or the history of religion and its relationship to the advancement of civilization. When presented objectively, the Bible and religions may be presented as a part of a secular program of education.

The place of religion in our society is an exalted one, achieved through a long tradition of reliance on the home, the church and the inviolable citadel of the individual heart and mind. We have come to recognize through bitter experience that it is not within the power of government to invade that citadel, whether its purpose or effect be to aid or oppose, to advance or retard. In the relationship between man and religion, the State is firmly committed to a position of neutrality.

Mr. Justice Clark for the majority in
Murray v. Curlett, 374 U.S. 203, Md. 1963

A statute that requires a girl of 16, unmarried and pregnant, to first obtain the consent of her parents for an abortion, since she wishes to continue her education, is unconstitutional. *Foe v. Vanderhoof,* 389 F.Supp. 947, Colo. 1975. And a girl of 14 whose interests are contrary to those of her parents, and where the stigma of delinquency might attach by what her parents are doing to her, has the right to obtain counsel in her own behalf. *Wagstaff v. Superior Court,* 535 F.2d 1220, Alaska 1975.

Educational advantages cannot be withheld from a child merely because that child is an alien. *Hosier v. Evans,* 314 F.Supp. 316, V.I. 1970. And children who cannot profit from instruction in the public schools in English because their primary language is not English are entitled to assistance from the district so that they can learn the English language. *Lau v. Nichols,* 414 U.S. 563, Cal. 1974. Children who are handicapped cannot be excluded from the public schools, but must be taken as they are and a program of studies provided for them in "the least restrictive environment" and in accordance with their individual needs. *Pennsylvania Association for Retarded Children v. Commonwealth of Pa.,* 334 F.Supp. 1257, 1971, amended consent decree, 343 F.Supp. 279, 1972. A long line of similar cases attests to the fact that even though handicapped, a child has the right to learn, to know, to be informed, and to succeed.

Said the Supreme Court in emphasizing the importance of education to the individual in today's world:

> Today, education is perhaps the most important function of state and local governments. ... In these days it is doubtful that any child may reasonably be expected to succeed in life if he is denied the opportunity of an education. Such an opportunity, where the state has undertaken to provide it, is a right which must be made available to all on equal terms. *Brown v. Bd. of Education,* 347 U.S. 483, 485, Kans. 1954.

In the light of the foregoing long line of cases to the effect that the child has the right to learn, to know, to succeed in school, and to be informed, we turn now to those cases where boards have removed books from the school library and have been challenged for their acts of alleged censorship over the student's right to learn.

REMOVING BOOKS FROM STUDENTS

The courts are not in agreement on issues related to removal of books from school libraries and approved reading lists. The Second Circuit Court of Appeals acknowledged such a right in *Presidents Council, Dist. 25 v. Community School Board, Dist. 25,* 457 F.2d 289, N.Y. 1972. Plaintiffs were the organization of presidents and past presidents of various parent and parent-teacher associations, some junior high school students and parents. The litigation commenced when the board voted to remove from all junior high school libraries in the district all copies of *Down These Mean Streets,* a novel by Piri Thomas. The parties stipulated that the board had the right to select suitable textbooks and other instructional materials, but plaintiffs claimed a denial of the students' right to read. The Second Circuit Court of Appeals, however, ruled that the First Amendment is not violated by a school board's making a book about a youth's life in Spanish Harlem available to junior high school students only on request of their parents. The U.S. Supreme Court refused to review the case. 409 U.S. 998, 1972.

To the opposite effect was an Ohio case in which five public high school students brought a class action against the Strongsville City School District, its board members and superintendent claiming a denial of constitutional rights when the board refused to approve textbooks recommended by the teachers. The board denied approval to Kurt Vonnegut's *God Bless You, Mr. Rosewater,* and refused to consider *Cat's Cradle,* another Vonnegut novel. The board also recommended that these books be removed from the high school libraries. The federal district court dismissed the case on the grounds that no constitutional rights were involved. On appeal, the Sixth Circuit Court of Appeals reversed, finding the removal of the books from the school library violated the students' First Amendment rights. *Minarcini v. Strongsville City School District,* 541 F.2d 577, Ohio 1976. The Sixth Circuit Court of Appeals ruled that although the state is under no constitutional compulsion to establish a library, once having created such a "privilege for the benefit of its students," neither the state nor the school board can place conditions on its use which relate "solely to social or political tastes of school board members." The court directed the school board to replace the books which had been removed.

Relying substantially on *Virginia State Board of Pharmacy v. Virginia Citizens Consumer Council, Inc.,* 425 U.S. 748, 1976, a consumer information case, the *Minarcini* court held there is a right to know embodied in the First Amendment. Students could not be denied the right to receive information which they and their teachers wished them to have, once the materials providing that information had been placed in the school library. The availability of the books from other sources would not minimize the burden placed on the students by the removal of the books. Accordingly, the *Minarcini* court held that the school board's removal of the library books because of their content violated the student's First Amendment right to receive information.

Virginia Pharmacy invalidated a state statute that made the practice of licensed pharmacists of advertising the price of prescription drugs equivalent to "unprofessional conduct." At issue was whether a state may completely suppress the dissemination of concededly truthful information about entirely lawful activity, "being fearful of that information's effect upon its disseminators and its recipients." Mr. Justice Blackman, writing for the majority, held that freedom of speech protected the recipient of the communication as well as the source, and concluded that the state could not suppress this information. Based on *Virginia Pharmacy,* the *Minarcini* court agreed with Mr. Justice Marshall, "It is now well established that the Constitution protects the right to receive information and ideas. ... This right to receive information and ideas, regardless of their social worth, is fundamental to our free society." *Stanley v. Georgia,* 394 U.S. 557, 564, 1969. The Supreme Court declined a request to review the case, thus letting stand the decision of the Sixth Circuit Court of Appeals.

Virginia Pharmacy pertained to the rights of adults to receive information and it seems settled that the state has an interest in preventing materials of a pornographic or obscene nature from falling into the hands of youth. *Ginsberg v. N.Y.,* 390 U.S. 629, 1968. Unless, however, a film or publication has a prurient interest to minors, is patently offensive when distributed to minors, and lacks serious literary, artistic, scientific or political value to minors, it is still protected by the First Amendment. Thus, *Ginsberg* does not allow the definition of obscenity, even for minors, to include standard art objects, great literature, or mere nudity in any context. Similarly, *Ginsberg* does not allow the suppression of brutality, violence or murder since they are outside the concept of prurient interest. The Supreme Court has ruled (5-4) that the FCC can issue an order banning certain words from airways during hours when children are most likely to hear them. *FCC v. Pacifica Foundation,* 98 S.Ct. 3026, 1978. "Pacifica's broadcast could have enlarged in an instant the vocabulary of a child who might have found 'incomprehensible' a four-letter word in print," wrote Mr. Justice Stevens for the majority. The four dissenting justices said that since the language was clearly not legally "obscene"—it did not appeal to a prurient interest—it was protected by the First Amendment and could not be banned. No doubt the Court would have had second thoughts if the monologue had not contained *repeated* use of offensive language. One can speculate as to whether the Court would have ruled differently had the offensive language been used in passing. "We have not decided that an occasional expletive," said the majority, "would justify any sanction...."

The foregoing cases illustrate the possibility that a constitutional right to know, to learn, to succeed in school, and to be informed rests within the protection of the First Amendment. We live in an age when following Watergate the states have enacted "sunshine," "sunset," and "open records" laws to make sure that the public's right to know is not curtailed in any way. It seems only one step to the conclusion that students have the right to know what is going on, even though that information may be distasteful to the boards of education. Does this create a risk? The answer must of course be in the affirmative. But the Supreme Court held in *Tinker* that this is a risk we must take "in this enigmatic, often disputatious society." The price of libery is eternal vigilance, as always.

THE BOARD AND THE RIGHT TO KNOW

In West Virginia, parents were distressed by the board's choice of certain textbooks and supplemental materials adopted in due course by a panel of teachers and parents, claiming violation of religious freedom and privacy. The offensive books were alleged to discourage Christian morals as well as good citizenship, hence were an invasion of a family's right to inculcate those values the parents thought worthwhile in their children. To avoid such influence, the parents had placed their children in private schools. The federal district court admitted that some of the books were indeed offensive to the religious beliefs of some of the parents. The court could not, however, find any infringement of religious freedom. The First Amendment, while guaranteeing free exercise of religion, "does not guarantee that nothing about religion will be taught in the schools nor that nothing offensive to any religion will be taught in the schools." On the issue of privacy, the court again could find no constitutional invasion of family integrity or privacy. In dismissing the case, the court noted that federal district courts should not infringe upon the board's right to make choices as it saw fit. "Courts are vitally concerned that no constitutional violations shall occur in an educational setting," said the court, "but [we are loath] to intervene in the resolution of conflicts which arise in the daily operation of school systems." In other words, the board is the proper authority to decide matters concerning the curriculum, and if you do not like what the board does, you can vote the rascals out at the next school election. *Williams v. Bd. of Educ. of Cy. of Kanawha,* 388 F. Supp. 93, 1975, *aff'd.,* 530 F.2d 972, W.Va. 1975.

In earlier chapters of this book, we have noted how a board may bargain for and obtain the right from the teachers' representative organization to choose which texts and materials it will use and the manner in which the materials shall be used in the classroom. Where the teacher's organization had agreed in a collective bargaining contract to permit the board to choose curricular materials, it could not later be heard to complain that its rights to academic freedom and the students' right to learn had been compromised. *Cary v. Bd. of Educ. of Adams-Arapahoe School Dist. 28-J,* 427 F.Supp. 945, Colo. 1977, *aff'd.* 10 CA July 10, 1979.

The final case on board censorship arose in Massachusetts. Action was instituted to obtain an injunctive order requiring the school committee of the City of Chelsea to return a banned book to the high school library. The book, an anthology of writings by adolescents, bore the title *Male and Female Under 18,* and was one of a reading collection of 1,000 books purchased by librarian Coleman, who thought it would be useful to students taking adolescent literature and creative writing. When the books arrived, Coleman reviewed them, although she was unable to read every page of all 1,000 books. She was unaware of a poem by a 15-year-old Brooklyn girl under the title "The City to a Young Girl." When she received a telephone call from the Committee chairman, she read the poem, but found nothing objectionable in the book other than the poem itself, which she found did not meet the test of obscenity under *Miller.* (The reader is referred to footnote 1, page 705, of legal opinion *Right to Read Defense Committee of Chelsea v. School Committee of the City of Chelsea,* 454 F.Supp. 703, Mass. 1978.)

Coleman was called to a special meeting of the board and defended the work which Chairman Quigley assessed as "low down dirty rotten filth, garbage, fit only for the sewer." At a subsequent meeting the committee voted 6-0 with one abstention to remove the book in its entirety from the library.

After a hearing, the federal district court issued a temporary restraining order barring Coleman's transfer *inter alia,* and ordering that the book be returned immediately to the library without deletion and that pending outcome of the trial the librarian should have access to the book, but might check it out only to those students who have written permission from their parents or guardians. *Right to Read Defense Committee, supra.* The school committee defended against the suit by claiming an unconstrained authority to remove books from the shelves of the school library. The court would not support the committee's argument, declaring there are boundaries to the committee's authority to remove a book from a library.

In upholding the plaintiffs and ruling against the committee, the court said in part:

> There is ample evidence to support the plaintiffs' assertion that the work is relevant to a number of courses taught at Chelsea High School. No contention was made that the book was improperly selected, insofar as Chelsea procurement regulations were concerned. The work, taken as a whole, is not obscene, despite some

objectionable language. Neither limitations of shelf space nor money are factors here. The book has already been purchased and paid for. It is a small paperback approximately one inch thick. There has been no suggestion that its presence in the library has contributed to any shelf space problem.

The court then concluded that the reason the board members banned the book was that it was "filthy," "obscene," and "disgusting," and that it might have a damaging impact on high school students. Their concern does not serve a substantial governmental interest and their removal constituted an infringement of First Amendment rights of the students and faculty.

The court went on to point out that not every removal of a book from a school library implicates First Amendment values. But, when, as here, "A book is removed because its theme and language are offensive to a school committee, those aggrieved are entitled to seek court intervention. The reasons underlying the actions of school officials may determine their constitutionality." *Mt. Healthy Cty. S. Dist. v. Doyle,* 429 U.S. 274, Ohio 1977. The committee was under no obligation to purchase the book in question, but it did. A state, though having acted when not compelled to do so, may consequentially create a constitutionally protected interest (citing cases). Where the board, not being compelled to set up a library, nevertheless does so, and stocks it with books, it cannot place conditions on the use of the library which are related solely to the social or political tastes of school board members. *Minarcini v. Strongsville City School District,* 541 F.2d 577, Ohio 1976. No substantial governmental interest was served by cutting off the students' access to the book in question. The committee acted because they felt *City's* language and theme might have a damaging impact on the high school students. But at trial expert testimony brought out that *City* is a work of at least some value that would have no harmful effect on the students. As one judge said earlier: "With the greatest of respect to such parents (those who object to curriculum materials), *their sensibilities are not the full measure of what is proper education.*" (Emphasis added.) *Keefe v. Geanakos,* 418 F.2d 359, Mass. 1969.

Judge Tauro expressed the right of the student in these terms:

The library is "a mighty resource in the marketplace of ideas."
... There a student can literally explore the unknown, and discover
areas of interest and thought not covered by the prescribed curriculum. The student who discovers the magic of the library is on the
way to a life-long experience of self-education and enrichment.
That student learns that a library is a place to test or expand upon
ideas presented to him, in and out of the classroom.

The most effective antidote to the poison of mindless
orthodoxy is ready access to a broad sweep of ideas and philosophies. There is no danger in such exposure. The danger is in mind
control....*Right to Read Def. Comm. v. Sch. Comm.*, at 715.

Board members are elected to their sensitive posts with the full
consent of the majority of the population in the school district. Those
who stop to ponder what their election means will soon come to realize
that they are one in a long and distinguished line of school board
members who have fought the good fight to protect the right to read,
the right to be exposed to controversial thoughts and language—a
valuable right subject to First Amendment protection. Those who do
not compromise this principle of law may be removed at the next
school election, but they will have had the good feeling that comes
with knowing they were advocates on the side of the students' right to
read.

As the Court commented in *Red Lion Broadcasting Co. v. FCC*,
395 U.S. 367, D.C. 1969:

It is the purpose of the First Amendment to preserve an unin-
hibited marketplace of ideas in which truth will ultimately prevail.
... It is the right of the public to receive suitable access to social,
political, esthetic, moral and other ideas and experiences which is
crucial here.

In *Tinker*, the Court held that:

In our system, students may not be regarded as closed-circuit
recipients of only that which the state chooses to communicate.
They may not be confined to expressions of those sentiments that
are officially approved. State-operated schools may not be enclaves of totalitarianism. *Tinker v. Des Moines School Dist.*, 393
U.S. 511, Iowa 1969.

To be so soundly grounded in principle that you can stand up for the student's right to read, to know, to be informed is the mark of a truly great school board member. The wonder is that so many of you are so endowed.

Table of Cases

Equal Employment Opportunity Table

EQUAL EMPLOYMENT OPPORTUNITY

FEDERAL

1. CONSTITUTION, STATUTES, EXECUTIVE ORDERS OR OTHER BASIS OF AUTHORITY	2. TYPES OF DISCRIMINATION PROHIBITED GENERALLY	3. INVESTIGATING AGENCY, IF ANY	4. CONCILIATION. FORMAL	5. PLAINTIFF OR EQUIVALENT IN ADJUDICATION PROCEEDINGS	6. LEGAL FORUM FOR EVIDENTIARY HEARING IN ADJUDICATION PROCEEDINGS	7. REVIEW FORUM	8. REMEDY FOR DISCRIMINATION	9. AFFIRMATIVE ACTION REQUIREMENTS	10. ADDITIONAL COMMENTS INCLUDING RELATIONSHIPS WITH OTHER AGENCIES
A. U.S. Constitution-Fourteenth Amendment. No state shall deny to any person the equal protection of the laws.	Any discrimination under color of state law not reasonably related to a legitimate state purpose [1]	The Fourteenth Amendment is implemented by 42 U.S.C. §§1981, 1983 and 1985 set forth below.							42 U.S.C. §1988 allows attorneys' fees to prevailing party (other than U.S.) as part of costs.
B. Title VII, Civil Rights Act of 1964, as amended, 42 U.S.C. §§2000e-2000e-7	Any discrimination in the employment relationship made on the basis of race, color, religion, sex, national origin by any employer, employment agency, or union organization	Equal Employment Opportunity Commission (EEOC)	X	EEOC, Individual Victim(s) [2] Justice Department in actions against state and local governments	Federal District Court	Federal Court of Appeals	Injunction; Declaratory Judgment, incl. compensatory relief	Following adjudication	Must defer to state agency for at least 60 days. Effective July 1, 1979 EEOC will also enforce Equal Pay Act and Age Discrimination Act. Prevailing party may recover attorneys' fees if action is frivolous, unreasonable or without foundation [3]
C. Title VI, Civil Rights Act of 1964, 42 U.S.C. §§2000d-2000d-4	Any discrimination on the basis of race, color, national origin by any recipient under any federally assisted program	Justice Department [4] Government Agency or Dept.	X	HEW, other governmental agencies or any person in the United States	Agency hearing	Whatever is provided to each agency f/similar action on other grounds [5]; federal courts	Termination of assistance; refusal to grant assistance	No	Compliance reports may be required. 28 C.F.R. Part 42. Prevailing party may recover attorneys' fees 42 U.S.C. §1988
D. Title IX, Education Amendments of 1972 20 U.S.C. §§1681 et seq., as implemented by HEW regulations 415 C.F.R. §86.51 et seq.	Any discrimination on the basis of sex in any education program or activity receiving federal financial aid	Department of Health, Education and Welfare (HEW)	X	U.S. and HEW or possibly any person who believes herself or any specific class to be subjected to discrimination prohibited by these regs. [6]	HEW hearing procedures same as those for Title IV [7]	Federal Court of Appeals [8]	Contract termination on suspension in whole or in part [9]	No	Compliance reports may be required. Several federal courts have held that HEW's regulations which purport to regulate employment practices of federal aid recipients are invalid [10]

230

1. CONSTITUTION, STATUTES, EXECUTIVE ORDERS OR OTHER BASIS OF AUTHORITY	2. TYPES OF DISCRIMINATION PROHIBITED GENERALLY	3. INVESTIGATING AGENCY, IF ANY	4. CONCIL-IATION, FORMAL	5. PLAINTIFF OR EQUIVALENT IN ADJUDICATION PROCEEDINGS	6. LEGAL FORUM FOR EVIDENTIARY HEARING IN ADJUDICATION PROCEEDINGS	7. REVIEW FORUM	8. REMEDY FOR DISCRIMINATION	9. AFFIRMATIVE ACTION REQUIREMENTS	10. ADDITIONAL COMMENTS INCLUDING RELATIONSHIPS WITH OTHER AGENCIES
E. Executive Order 11246, as amended	Any discrimination in employment on the basis of race, color, religion, sex or national origin by any federal contractor or subcontractor	Office of Federal Contract Compliance Programs (OFCCP), Dept. of Labor [11]	X	OFCCP, Justice Department	Agency hearing, federal district court	Secretary of Labor, Federal Court of Appeals	Loss of Contract and ineligibility for future contracts, affected class and back pay relief; injunctive relief [12]	Written if 50 employees and $50,000 contract or subcontract	Possible source of reverse discrimination charges under Title VII [13]
F. Equal Pay Act of 1963, as amended, 29 U.S.C. §206	Any sex-based discrimination in pay by any employer, including public bodies [14]	Wage and Hour Div., Dept. of Labor. Effective July 1, 1979, by EEOC		Secretary of Labor or individual employee [15]	Federal District Court	Federal Court of Appeals	Injunction; Declaratory Judgment and/or compensatory relief; liquidated damages	No	
G. Civil Rights Act of 1866, 42 U.S.C. §1981	Discrimination by any person within the U.S. on the basis of race, color or alienage with regard to making contracts, suing and obtaining the full protection of the law	None		Any person within the jurisdiction of the U.S.	Federal District Court	Federal Court of Appeals	Injunction; Declaratory Judgment, including compensatory relief and punitive damages	Following adjudication	Independent remedy, *Johnson v. Railway Express Agency*, 421 U.S. 454 (1975)
H. Civil Rights Act of 1871, 42 U.S.C. §1983	Any discrimination on the basis of race, color or sex under color of state law [16]	None		Individual [2]	Federal District Court	Federal Court of Appeals	Injunction; Declaratory Judgment, including compensatory relief	Following adjudication	School Boards not immune from suit for monetary, declaratory and injunctive relief. *Monell v. Dept. of Social Services of the City of New York*, 98 S.Ct. 2018 (1978)

EQUAL EMPLOYMENT OPPORTUNITY (continued)

1. CONSTITUTION, STATUTES, EXECUTIVE ORDERS OR OTHER BASIS OF AUTHORITY	2. TYPES OF DISCRIMINATION PROHIBITED GENERALLY	3. INVESTIGATING AGENCY, IF ANY	4. CONCILIATION, FORMAL	5. PLAINTIFF OR EQUIVALENT IN ADJUDICATION PROCEEDINGS	6. LEGAL FORUM FOR EVIDENTIARY HEARING IN ADJUDICATION PROCEEDINGS	7. REVIEW FORUM	8. REMEDY FOR DISCRIMINATION	9. AFFIRMATIVE ACTION REQUIREMENTS	10. ADDITIONAL COMMENTS INCLUDING RELATIONSHIPS WITH OTHER AGENCIES
I. Civil Rights Act of 1861 and 1871, 42 U.S.C. §1985	Race, Class (conspiracy only) [17]	None		Individual [2]	Federal District Court	Federal Court of Appeals	Injunction; Declaratory judgment, including compensatory relief	Following adjudication	
J. Age Discrimination in Employment Act of 1967, as amended, 29 U.S.C. §621, et seq.	Any discrimination in employment on the basis of age (40-70) by any employer, employment agency or labor organization	W&H Div. of Dept. of Labor. Effective July 1, 1979, by EEOC	X	Secretary of Labor or individual employee, applicant or union member [15]	Federal District Court	Federal Court of Appeals	Injunction; Declaratory Judgment, including compensatory relief and liquidated damages	No	Jury Trials
K. Labor Management Relations Act, 29 U.S.C. §141, et seq.	[18]	National Labor Relations Board (NLRB)		NLRB, individual employee, employer or union	NLRB, Federal District Court	Federal Court of Appeals	Injunction, compensary relief	No	
L. Industry Regulation	Race, color, religion, sex, national origin, age (see applicable federal statutes)	See agency regulations		Individual	Applicable Agency Procedures	Applicable Agency Procedures	Injunction; declaratory judgment, including compensatory relief		[19]

EQUAL EMPLOYMENT OPPORTUNITY (continued)

1. CONSTITUTION, STATUTES, EXECUTIVE ORDERS OR OTHER BASIS OF AUTHORITY	2. TYPES OF DISCRIMINATION PROHIBITED GENERALLY	3. INVESTIGATING AGENCY, IF ANY	4. CONCILIATION. FORMAL	5. PLAINTIFF OR EQUIVALENT IN ADJUDICATION PROCEEDINGS	6. LEGAL FORUM FOR EVIDENTIARY HEARING IN ADJUDICATION PROCEEDINGS	7. REVIEW FORUM	8. REMEDY FOR DISCRIMINATION	9. AFFIRMATIVE ACTION REQUIREMENTS	10. ADDITIONAL COMMENTS INCLUDING RELATIONSHIPS WITH OTHER AGENCIES
M. Rehabilitation Act of 1973, as amended, 29 U.S.C. §793	Any failure by anyone who enters a contract with the U.S. Gov't in excess of $2,500 for the procurement of personal property and nonpersonal services to employ and advance in employment handicapped individuals.	OFCCP, Department of Labor		OFCCP, and possible individual action [20] and [21]	Agency hearings, federal court	Federal Court of Appeals	Contract termination or suspension in whole or in part, affected class and back pay relief, injunctive relief	Contractor must promise to affirmatively advance and treat handicapped workers without discrimination in all phases of employment; those with contracts exceeding $50,000 and have over 50 employees must prepare and maintain an Affirmation Action Program (APP) within 120 days of commencement of contract	All federal contracts and subcontracts greater than $2,500 must include the Affirmative Action for Handicapped Workers clause
N. Rehabilitation Act of 1973, as amended 29 U.S.C. §794	No qualified handicapped individual shall be denied the benefits of, or be subjected to discrimination under program or activity receiving federal aid.	HEW, other governmental agencies [22]		HEW, other governmental agencies and individuals [23]	Applicable Agency hearing, federal courts	Federal Court of Appeals	Suspension, termination or refund to award federal assistance	No	

FEDERAL

EQUAL EMPLOYMENT OPPORTUNITY (continued)

1. CONSTITUTION, STATUTES, EXECUTIVE ORDERS OR OTHER BASIS OF AUTHORITY	2. TYPES OF DISCRIMINATION PROHIBITED GENERALLY	3. INVESTIGATING AGENCY, IF ANY	4. CONCILIATION, FORMAL	5. PLAINTIFF OR EQUIVALENT IN ADJUDICATION PROCEEDINGS	6. LEGAL FORUM FOR EVIDENTIARY HEARING IN ADJUDICATION PROCEEDINGS	7. REVIEW FORUM	8. REMEDY FOR DISCRIMINATION	9. AFFIRMATIVE ACTION REQUIREMENTS	10. ADDITIONAL COMMENTS INCLUDING RELATIONSHIPS WITH OTHER AGENCIES
O. Vietnam Era Veterans Readjustment Assistance Act of 1974, 38 U.S.C. §§2011, 2012 and 2014	*Any discrimination against disabled veterans and Vietnam veteran in employment by any federal contractor or subcontractor thereof*	OFCCP, Dept. of Labor	X	OFCCP, Justice Department [24]	Agency hearing, federal district court	Secretary, Federal Court of Appeals	Loss of contract and ineligibility for future contracts, affected class and back pay relief and injunctive relief	Written (if 50 employees and $50,000 contractor. or subcontractor)	All federal contracts and subcontracts greater than $10,000 must include affirmative action for Disabled Veterans and Veterans of the Vietnam era
P. State and local Final Assistance Act of 1972, as amended 31 U.S.C. 1221	Any discrimination on the basis of race, color, national origin, sex, religion, age or handicap in program or activity receiving certain federal funds	Treasury Department		Treasury Dept. Attorney General, person aggrieved	Agency hearing	Federal courts	Payments suspension, injunctive relief	No	Attorneys' fees recoverable by prevailing party
Q. Internal Revenue Code	The Internal Revenue Service has released proposed guidelines that it will apply in determining whether certain private schools have racially discriminatory policies as to students which would preclude them from obtaining tax exempt status under §501(c)(3) of the Internal Revenue Code. IRS News Release IR-2-27 (1978).								

NOTES

[1] Discrimination based on a suspect classification, *i.e.*, race, national origin, alienage, illegitimacy, indigency, is prohibited unless the state proves it necessary to promote a compelling state interest. In recent decisions, the United States Supreme Court has declined to expand the list of suspect classifications, rejecting sex and age. *See, Frontiero v. Richardson,* 411 U.S. 677 (1973); and *Commonwealth of Massachusetts Bd. of Retirement v. Murgia,* 427 U.S. 307 (1976).

[2] Class action may be brought pursuant to Rule 23 of the Federal Rules of Civil Procedure.

[3] *See* 42 U.S.C. §2000e-5(k); *Christiansburg Garment Co. v. EEOC,* 434 U.S. 412 (1978).

[4] No remedial action may be taken until the department or agency involved has advised the recipient of federal assistance of failure to comply with Title VI requirements and has determined that compliance cannot be effected voluntarily. If the federal assistance is terminated or refused, the head of the agency or department must file a full written report of circumstances and grounds for action with the committees of the House and Senate having legislative jurisdiction over the program. No action may become effective until 30 days after such report has been filed. 42 U.S.C. §2000d-1.

Under Executive Order 11764 of 1974, the United States Attorney General coordinates the enforcement of Title VI by federal departments and agencies. The attorney general is in charge of prescribing standards and procedures regarding the implementation of Title VI and assisting the departments and agencies in accomplishing effective implementation. The regulations contained in 28 C.F.R. Part 42, Subpart F, §42.401 to 42.415 (1977), set out the minimum requirements for the implementation of Title VI by federal agencies. Implementing regulations for programs receiving aid through HEW are codified in 45 C.F.R. Part 80. Other appropriate agency regulations must be consulted for programs administered by other federal agencies or departments.

[5] 42 U.S.C. §2000d-2 provides that after otherwise unreviewable action terminating or refusing to grant or continue financial assistance upon finding of a failure to comply with this sub-chapter, any aggrieved person (including a state or political subdivision or agency of either) may obtain judicial review under the Administrative Procedure Act, 5 U.S.C. §§701 to 706, in federal district court.

[6] One federal court has held that there is no private cause of action under Title IX, *Cannon v. University of Chicago*, 406 F.Supp. 1257 (D.C.Ill. 1976), *aff'd* 559 F.2d 1063 (7th Cir. 1977); *cert. granted* (1978). *Contra, Piascik v. Cleveland Museum of Art*, 426 F.Supp. 779 at footnote 1 (N.D. Ohio 1976).

[7] *See* 45 C.F.R. §86.71; 45 C.F.R. §§80.6 to 80.11; and 45 C.F.R. Part 81.

[8] Under 20 U.S.C. §1683, any department or agency action taken pursuant to §§1681 *et seq.* is subject to judicial review as may otherwise be provided by law for similar action taken by such department or agency on other grounds. If the action is not otherwise subject to judicial review, any person aggrieved may seek such review under the provisions of the Administrative Procedure Act, 5 U.S.C. §§701 to 706.

[9] Title IX provides that the remedy for non-compliance may be (1) termination or refusal of the federal assistance to any recipient as to whom there has been an express finding on the record, after opportunity for a hearing, of a failure to comply, or (2) any other means authorized by law; provided that no such action shall be taken until the agency has advised the appropriate person of his failure to comply and has determined that compliance cannot be secured by voluntary means. In the case of any action terminating, or refusing to grant or continue, assistance, the head of the federal department or agency must file with the committees of the House and Senate having legislative jurisdiction over the program a full written report of the circumstances and the grounds for such action. No such action shall become effective until 30 days after the filing of such report. 20 U.S.C. §1683.

[10] *See, i.e., Romeo Community Schools v. HEW*, 438 F. Supp. 1021 (E.D. Mich. 1977), *appeal pending; Seattle University v. HEW*, 16 FEP Cases 719 (W.D. Wash. 1978), *appeal pending; Brunswick School Board v. Califano*, 16 EPD ¶8242 (D. Me. 1978).

[11] Prior to October 1, 1978, contract compliance under Executive Order 11246 was scattered among 11 federal agencies. On October 1, 1978, as a result of President Carter's Equal Employment Opportunity Programs Reorganization Plan, the OFCCP, in the Labor Department's Employment Standards Administration, assumed total responsibility for all federal contract compliance activity under Executive Order 11246.

[12] *See United States v. Duquesne Light Co.*, 423 F. Supp. 507 (D.C. Pa. 1976).

[13] *See Weber v. Kaiser Aluminum,* 563 F.2d 216 (5th Cir. 1977), *rehearing denied* 571 F.2d 337 (1978); *cert. granted* (1978).

[14] *See Marshall v. City of Sheboygan,* 16 E.P.D. ¶8334 (7th Cir. 1978); and *Marshall v. Owensboro-Daviess County Hospital,* No. 77-3069 (6th Cir. 1978).

[15] Statutory class action available under 29 U.S.C. §216(b).

[16] State action only.

[17] Covers deprivation of equal protection of the law, denial of constitutional right, privilege or immunity. It is not limited to state action.

[18] Nothing in the Labor Management Relation Act relates directly to discrimination because of race, creed, color or national origin. The National Labor Relations Board, however, has held that complaints or charges lodged by employees with federal or state fair employment agencies and protests pertaining to equal employment opportunity matters are protected concerted activity under the Act. *See, i.e., King Soopers, Inc.,* 222 NLRB No. 80 (1976). In addition, in *Westinghouse Electric Corp.,* 239 NLRB No.19 (1978), the Board held that a union is entitled to a breakdown of employees by race, sex, and Spanish surnames with respect to seniority, hiring, promotions, labor grade, classification and wage rate and day work and incentive basis. Such information was held to be presumptively relevant to the union's duty to enforce the nondiscrimination clause of a collective bargaining agreement. The union was also held entitled to a list of all complaints and charges filed against the employer under the Equal Pay Act, Title VII and Executive Order 11246.

The Board, however, has refused to consider allegations of racism or sexism prior to certifying a union as the bargaining unit agent for a unit of employees; *Handy Andy, 228* NLRB 447 (1977) and *Bell & Howell Co., 230 NLRB 420 (1977).* At least one federal court has upheld such refusal on the grounds that neither the Constitution nor the Labor Management Relations Act requires the Board to investigate allegations of "invidious discrimination" prior to certification. *See Bell & Howell Co. v. NLRB* No. 75-2002 (D.C. Cir. January 8, 1979).

[19] The Fifth Amendment to the United States Constitution, in its Due Process Clause, generally protects "life, liberty or property" from governmental infringement. It applies both to the United States Government and to its regulatory agencies (*e.g.,* Interstate Commerce Commission, Federal Power Commission, Securities & Exchange Commission, Federal Communications Commission) and through the Equal Protection Clause of the

Fourteenth Amendment, to comparable state agencies. The Fifth Amendment does not apply to a private entity *unless* there exists a sufficient degree of involvement of that entity with a governmental body. The Supreme Court found a close enough involvement between the Public Utilities Commission (District of Columbia) and the privately owned Capital Transit Company to inquire into whether the Fifth Amendment had been violated in *Public Utilities Comm'n v. Pollak,* 343 U.S. 451 (1952). When authority derived from the Federal Government is exercised by private persons, it is likened to exercise by the Government itself. *Id.* at 462.

In addition, some Acts authorizing regulatory agencies contain general language prohibiting discrimination. *See, e.g.,* Federal Communications Act, 47 U.S.C. §202(a); Interstate Commerce Act, 49 U.S.C. §2(i).

[20] Complainant has 180 days from date of violation to file a complaint with the Department of Labor. Contractors (including subcontractors) are given the opportunity to investigate any complaint filed with the Director of OFCCP by a handicapped worker referred to it by the Director. Actions must be processed to completion within 60 days of filing of complaint. If no resolution satisfactory to complainant is reached within 60 days, then Department of Labor proceeds with investigation. An opportunity for a hearing is afforded to contractors and subcontractors. 20 C.F.R. Part 60-741.

[21] Several courts have held that there is no individual cause of action under §793 of the Act; *see, e.g., Roger v. Frito-Lay, Inc.,* 433 F. Supp. 200 (D.C. Tex. 1977). *Contra, Drennon v. Philadelphia General Hospital,* 428 F. Supp., 809 (E.D. Pa. 1977).

[22] *See* C.F.R. Part 85 (1978).

[23] A private cause of action may be maintained. *See, e.g., Lloyd v. Regional Transp. Authority,* 548 F.2d 1277 (7th Cir. 1977); and *Kampmeier v. Nyquist,* 553 F.2d 296 (2nd Cir. 1977).

[24] Regulations contained in 41 C.F.R. Chapter 60, part 250.

APPENDIX C

Constitutional Standards for Student Publication Guidelines*

by Michael D. Simpson

Responding to student demands for press freedom, many school administrators are attempting to define the rights and responsibilities of student journalists through student publication guidelines. So far, no court has actually approved a specific set of student publication guidelines. In fact, the courts have struck down as overbroad, vague, or too restrictive virtually every set of student guidelines submitted to them. However, in striking down the challenged regulations, the courts have explained what types of guidelines would pass constitutional muster.

---

*These guidelines are from Student Press Law Report, Vol. II, No. 1, Winter, 1978-79, a publication of the Student Press Law Center, Suite 1112, 1750 Pennsylvania Avenue, N.W., Washington, D.C. 20006. SPLC is published three times per year and is researched and written by journalism and law student interns. The Center is the only national organization devoted exclusively to protecting the First Amendment rights of high school and college journalists. Subscriptions to the SPLC magazine are one year for $5.00 (student newspapers) and one year for $7.00 (individual subscribers). Please address the Center for other publications at the above address.

The first section of this article collects the "suggestions" of judges from the leading student press cases. Taken together, these suggestions form almost a "do and don't" list that may aid school authorities when drafting rules governing student expression. Each statement of law is followed by the first name of the case(s) which announced that particular proposition. The full legal citation for each case can be found in the appendix at the end of the section.

One should note that since many of the cases cited were decided by lower courts, the principles announced are not legally binding on the courts of other jurisdictions. However, these principles should be persuasive for purposes of legal argument or debate. United States Supreme Court decisions are, of course, binding everywhere in the country.

Also, while most of the principles cited are taken from cases involving college and high school students, there is no reason why these principles should not also apply to 7th, 8th, and 9th grade students. At least two courts have already extended First Amendment rights to junior high school students. *Riseman, Cintron.*

The second section of this article presents a set of guidelines formulated by the Student Press Law Center (SPLC) based on the legal principles listed in the first section.

I. *Tinker v. Des Moines*

The basic principle which underlies all student press cases was first announced in the landmark Supreme Court decision of *Tinker v. Des Moines:* public school students have the constitutional right of free expression unless such expression causes a "substantial disruption of or material interference with school activities," or invades the rights of others. As indicated below, this constitutional standard has been refined and clarified by the lower federal courts during the past decade. (See legal analysis in this issue for a detailed discussion of disruption).

One fundamental proposition must be established at the outset. The fact that a student newspaper is totally funded by the school, is printed with school facilities, and is written during school hours under the supervision of an adviser, does not mean that the school (or principal) is the "publisher" of the paper with the attendant power of editorial control. *Gambino, Bazaar, Antonelli, Dickey, Joyner, Schiff,*

Trujillo, ACLU. Indeed, as one court has succinctly put it, "The state is not necessarily the unrestrained master of what it creates and fosters." *Antonelli.*

Even though the school board may fund a student publication, the courts have said that, within certain limits, the students have the final word as to what material is published. Ideally, student publication guidelines should clearly and specifically define what those limits are.

II. Unprotected Speech

Speech may be divided into two broad categories—that which is protected by the First Amendment and that which is not. Student publication guidelines may lawfully prohibit only the publication or distribution of literature which qualifies as "unprotected speech."

1. School officials may lawfully suppress "obscene" literature. *Shanley, Jacobs.* However, one should note that "obscenity" refers to the Supreme Court's definition, not just to literature that might be "offensive" or in "poor taste." *Papish, Bazaar, Sullivan, Jacobs.* The Supreme Court's definition of obscenity appears in the SPLC model publication guidelines in the next section.

2. School officials may lawfully suppress libel. *Shanley, Fujishima.* That a school system may be potentially liable for defamatory statements appearing in the official student newspaper offers a possible justification for censoring libel. This issue has not been decided by the courts. However, this reasoning would not apply to school officials who seek to ban an underground newspaper as no court has found a school system responsible for the content of an underground newspaper. (For a legal definition of libel, see the model publication guidelines.)

3. School officials may lawfully ban speech which is "directed to inciting or producing imminent lawless action and is likely to incite or produce such action." *Brandenburg.*

4. Because of the special circumstances in a school, the Supreme Court has carved out a fourth exception unique to student expression. The court has said that school officials may lawfully ban speech which causes a "substantial disruption of or material interference with school activities" or "invades the rights of others." *Tinker, Trachtman.*

If school officials do not act to suppress student expression on the ground that it is "unprotected speech," they, and not the students, have the burden of justifying that suppression. *Tinker, Eisner, Scoville, Shanley.*

III. Protected Speech

Student publication guidelines cannot provide for the censorship of speech "protected" by the First Amendment. Those allowing such censorship are unconstitutional. However, the court has said that school officials can regulate the time, place, and manner of distribution. *Fujishima.*

Listed below are some of the leading student press cases in which the courts have upheld the right of students to publish or distribute material which school officials sought to suppress.

1. School officials cannot censor criticism or punish those critical of school officials, the government or state legislatures. *Baughman, Dickey.* Officials may not "under the guise of vague labels choke off criticism either of themselves, or of school policies, which they find disrespectful, tasteless, or offensive." *Baughman.*

2. "The mere dissemination of ideas—no matter how offensive to good taste—may not be shut off in the name alone of 'conventions of decency'." *Papish.*

3. School officials cannot prohibit the dissemination of birth control information (even in the official student newspaper). *Gambino, Bayer, Shanley.*

4. School officials cannot cut off funds to the official student newspaper because it editorializes in favor of segregation. *Joyner.*

5. School officials cannot remove an editor because the student newspaper has such poor grammar, poor spelling and poor use of lanaguage that it could "embarrass and bring disrepute on the school." *Schiff.*

6. School officials cannot prohibit the distribution of a "racist" newspaper. *Leibner, Joyner.*

7. School officials cannot ban language which merely advocates

illegal conduct without showing that such advocacy incites imminent lawless action. *Brandenburg, Baughman, Brooks, Joyner, Quarterman.* In *Quarterman* it was held that a student could not be disciplined for distributing a paper which contained the following language: IF WE HAVE TO—WE'LL BURN THE BUILDINGS OF OUR SCHOOLS DOWN TO SHOW THESE PIGS THAT WE WANT AN EDUCATION THAT WON'T BRAINWASH US INTO BEING RACIST.

8. School officials cannot ban a student publication which urges disobedience of school rules without proving that the publication will cause a substantial and material disruption of school activities. *Scoville.*

9. School officials cannot prohibit the use of vulgar or profane words. *Bazaar, Sullivan, Fujishima, Jacobs, Kopell, Papish, Thonen.*

10. School officials cannot ban literature because it advocates the reform of marijuana laws or advertises the services of the National Organization for the Reform of Marijuana Laws (NORML). *Shanley.*

11. School officials cannot ban literature because it was written by a nonstudent or a nonschool employee. *Jacobs, Antonelli.*

12. School officials cannot ban literature because it was not school-sponsored written material, e.g. underground newspapers. *Vail.*

13. School officials cannot prohibit the school paper from accepting "editorial" advertising—ads which advocate a particular point of view on an issue of public concern. *Lee, Zucker.*

14. School officials cannot ban the distribution of literature because it contains advertising or because contributions are solicited in connection with the distribution. Neither may school officials impose an outright ban on the sale of literature. *Jacobs, Peterson, Pliscou.*

15. School officials cannot ban the distribution of anonymous literature; they cannot require that the literature bear the name of the sponsoring organization or author. *Talley, Jacobs.*

16. Although school officials may prohibit speech which causes a substantial and material disruption of school activities, it is insufficient to show merely that "a few students made hostile remarks." *Tinker.* "[T]hose students who would reasonably exercise their freedom of expression should not be restrained or punishable at the threshold of their attempts at expression merely because a small, perhaps vocal or violent group of students with differing views might or does create a disturbance." *Shanley.*

IV. Minimum Constitutional Requirements for Student Publication Guidelines

As noted earlier no reported court decision has ever approved a specific set of student publication guidelines. In striking down challenged guidelines the courts have endeavored to aid school authorities by setting forth certain minimum requirements. These requirements are set forth below.

1. The term "substantial disruption of or material interference with school activities" must be defined. *Nitzberg.*
2. The guidelines must "detail the criteria by which an administrator might reasonably predict the occurrence of such a disruption." *Nitzberg.*
3. The term "libel" must be fully defined and the definition must take into account the rule announced in *New York Times v. Sullivan* and its progeny. *Nitzberg.* (The *New York Times* rule states that before a "public official" can recover in a suit for libel he must prove that the statement was false and published with "actual malice," i.e., with knowledge that the statement was false or with reckless disregard for the truth.)
4. The term "distribution" must be defined. *Baughman.*
5. The term "obscenity" must be defined. *Baughman.*
6. Any publication guidelines must be included in the official publications of the school or circulated to students in the same manner as other official material. *Nitzberg.*

V. Unconstitutional Prior Restraint Provisions

Many school officials have attempted to adopt publication policies incorporating systems of prior review or prior restraint whereby a school administrator is able to read and censor both official and non-school-sponsored publications prior to distribution. Such systems have been justified as an effort to protect students from "unprotected" speech and to prevent a substantial disruption of school activities.

The courts have made a distinction between school rules which empower administrators to read copy prior to publication (prior review) or halt distribution (prior restraint), and rules which merely permit punishment of students after distribution has taken place. If publication guidelines only allow post-publication punishment for un-protected speech, then they need not be very specific. However, guidelines setting up a system of prior review or prior restraint must be specific and narrowly drawn with all important terms fully defined.

The rules in the cases listed below appeared in systems of prior review or prior restraint and were declared unconstitutional by the courts.

1. The dictate that student publications must conform to "the journalistic standards of accuracy, taste, and decency maintained by the newspapers of general circulation in the city" is too vague. *Leibner.*

2. A rule banning literature which is "alien to school purposes" was struck down in *Cintron.*

3. The court in *Baughman* declared unconstitutional a prohibition on literature which "advocates illegal actions, or is grossly insulting to any group or individual."

4. A ban on literature which "incites students to disrupt the orderly operation of the school" is too vague and overbroad. *Peterson.*

5. The court in *Jacobs* struck down a rule banning distribution of literature "while classes are being conducted..."

6. This rule is vague and overbroad: "No student shall distribute in any school any literature that is ... either by its content or by the manner of distribution itself, productive of, or likely to produce a significant disruption of the normal educational processes, functions or purposes in any of the Indianapolis schools or injury to others." *Jacobs.*

7. The court in *Baughman* invalidated a prohibition against "libelous" and "obscene" material noting that the terms "are not sufficiently precise and understandable by high school students and administrators untutored in the law to be acceptable criteria. Indeed, such terms are troublesome to lawyers and judges. None other than a justice of the Supreme Court has confessed that obscenity 'may be indefinable'."

As might be expected systems of prior review have been attacked by students who wish to publish free of censorship. Some courts ruling on the constitutionality of such systems have approved them; other courts have not. The federal courts for the 2nd, 4th and 5th Circuits have ruled that, in theory at least, it is possible to construct a constitutional system of prior review. However, no specific set of guidelines has ever been approved. *Baughman, Shanley, Eisner.* These rulings are binding in the following states: Vermont, New York, West Virginia, Connecticut, Maryland, Virginia, North Carolina, South Carolina, Florida, Georgia, Alabama, Mississippi, Louisiana, and Texas. The federal courts for the 7th circuit (Indiana, Illinois and Wisconsin), Massachusetts and California have ruled that any system of prior review violates the First Amendment rights of students. *Fujishima, Antonelli, Poxon.*

The Student Press Law Center takes the position that student publication guidelines should *not* provide for prior review of literature by school officials. Such a system merely provides an excuse for illegal censorship by high school principals and stifles student expression.

However, if a school system decides to institute prior review, the courts have offered a few gentle suggestions.

1. The U.S. Supreme Court has stated, "Any prior restraint on expression comes to this Court with a 'heavy presumption' against its constitutional validity." *Organization for a Better Austin.*

2. For a system of prior review to pass constitutional muster, it must contain "narrow, objective, and reasonable standards by which the material will be judged [and] precise criteria sufficiently spelling out what is forbidden so that a reasonably intelligent student will know what he may write and what he may not write." *Baughman, Nitzberg.*

3. The system of prior review must:

(a) Specify to whom the material is to be submitted for approval. *Eisner* .

(b) Limit the time the official has to reach a decision on whether to approve or disapprove distribution. *Baughman, Quarterman, Nitzberg, Eisner.*

(c) Provide for the contingency of a school official failing to issue a decision within the time specified. *Baughman.*

(d) Afford students the right to appear before the decision-maker and argue why distribution should be allowed. *Nitzberg, Leibner.*

(e) Provide an "adequate and prompt appeals procedure" if

the school official decides to ban distribution. *Eisner, Nitzberg*. A review procedure which lasts "several weeks" is too lengthy. *Leibner*.

APPENDIX

ACLU v. Radford, 345 F.Supp. 893 (W.D. Va. 1970)

Antonelli v. Hammond, 308 F.Supp. 1329 (S.D. Mass. 1970)

Baughman v. Freienmuth, 478 F.2d 1345 (4th Cir. 1973)

Bayer v. Kinzler, 383 F.Supp. 1164 (E.D.N.Y. 1974), *aff'd* 515 F.2d 504 (2nd Cir. 1975)

Bazaar v. Fortune, 476 F.2d 507 (5th Cir. 1973)

Brandenburg v. Ohio, 395 U.S. 444 (1969)

Brooks v. Auburn University, 296 F.Supp. 188 (M.D. Ala. 1969)

Cintron v. State Board of Education, 384 F.Supp. 674 (D.P.R. 1974)

Dickey v. Alabama, 273 F.Supp. 613 (M.D. Ala. 1967)

Eisner v. Stamford Bd. of Ed., 440 F.2d 803 (2nd Cir. 1971)

Fujishima v. Board of Education, 460 F.2d 1355 (7th Cir. 1972)

Gambino v. Fairfax County School Board, 429 F.Supp. 731 (E.D. Va. 1977), *aff'd* 564 F.2d 157 (4th Cir. 1977)

Jacobs v. Bd. of School Comm., 490 F.2d 601 (7th Cir. 1973), 420 U.S. 128 (1975) (dismissed as moot)

Joyner v. Whiting, 477 F.2d 456 (4th Cir. 1973)

Koppel v. Levine, 347 F.Supp. 456 (E.D.N.Y. 1972)

Lee v. Board of Regents, 306 F.Supp. 1097 (W.D. Wis. 1969), *aff'd* 441 F.2d 1257 (7th Cir. 1971)

Leibner v. Sharbaugh, 429 F.Supp. 744 (E.D. Va. 1977)

New York Times v. Sullivan, 376 U.S. 254 (1964)

Organization for a Better Austin v. Keefe, 402 U.S. 415 (1971)

Papish v. Bd. of Curators, 410 U.S. 667 (1973)

Peterson v. Board of Education, 370 F.Supp. 1208 (D. Neb. 1973)

Pliscou v. Holtville Unified School Dist., 411 F.Supp. 842 (S.D. Cal. 1976)

Poxon v. Bd. of Ed., 341 F.Supp. 256 (E.D. Cal. 1971)

Quarterman v. Byrd, 453 F.2d 54 (4th Cir. 1971)

Riseman v. School Comm. of Quincy, 439 F.2d 148 (1st Cir. 1971)

Schiff v. Williams, 519 F.2d 257 (5th Cir. 1975)

Scoville v. Bd. of Ed., 425 F.2d 10 (7th Cir. 1970)

Shanley v. Northeast Ind. Sch. Dist., 462 F.2d 960 (5th Cir. 1972)

Sullivan v. Houston Ind. Sch. Dist., 475 F.2d 1071 (5th Cir. 1973)
Talley v. California, 362 U.S. 60 (1960)
Thonen v. Jenkins, 517 F.2d 3 (4th Cir. 1975)
Tinker v. Des Moines Independent Community School District, 393
    U.S. 503 (1969)
Trujillo v. Love, 322 F.Supp. 1266 (D. Colo. 1971)
Vail v. Board of Education, 354 F.Supp. 592 (D.N.H. 1973)
Zucker v. Panitz, 299 F.Supp. 102 (S.D.N.Y. 1969)

SPLC Model Guidelines
For Student Publications

I. STATEMENT OF POLICY

It is undeniable that students are protected in their exercise of freedom of expression by the First Amendment to the Constitution of the United States. Accordingly, it is the responsibility of the school officials to insure the maximum freedom of expression to all students.

It is the policy of the_____Board of Education that_____(newspaper)_____, _____(yearbook)_____, and _____(literary magazine)_____, official school-sponsored publications of_____High School have been established as forums for student expression. As a forum, each publication should provide a full opportunity for students to inquire, question and exchange ideas. Content should reflect all areas of student interest, including topics about which there may be dissent or controversy.

It is the policy of the_____Board of Education that student journalists shall have the ultimate and absolute right to determine the content of official student publication.

II. OFFICIAL SCHOOL PUBLICATIONS

A. Responsibilities of Student Journalists

Students who work on official student publications will:

1. Rewrite material, as required by the faculty advisers, to improve sentence structure, grammar, spelling and punctuation;

2. Check and verify all facts and verify the accuracy of all quotations;

3. In the case of editorials or letters to the editor concerning controversial issues, provide space for rebuttal comments and opinions;

4. Determine the content of the student publication.

B. Prohibited Material

1. Students cannot publish or distribute material which is "obscene as to minors". Obscene as to minors is defined as:

(a) the average person, applying contemporary community standards, would find that the publication, taken as a whole, appeals to a minor's prurient interest in sex; and

(b) the publication depicts or describes, in a patently offensive way, sexual conduct such as ultimate sexual acts (normal or perverted), masturbation, excretory functions, and lewd exhibition of genitals; and

(c) the work, taken as a whole, lacks serious literary, artistic, political, or scientific value.

(d) "Minor" means any person under the age of eighteen.

2. Students cannot publish or distribute material which is "libelous", defined as a false and unprivileged statement about a specific individual which injures the individual's reputation in the community. If the allegedly libeled individual is a "public figure" or "public official" as defined below, then school officials must show that the false statement was published "with actual malice", i.e., that the student journalists knew that the statement was false, or that they published the statement with reckless disregard for the truth—without trying to verify the truthfulness of the statement.

(a) A public official is a person who holds an elected or appointed public office.

(b) A public figure is a person who either seeks the public's attention or is well known because of his achievements.

(c) School employees are to be considered public officials or public figures in articles concerning their school-related activities.

(d) When an allegedly libelous statement concerns a private individual, school officials must show that the false statement was published willfully or negligently, i.e., the student journalist has failed to exercise the care that a reasonably prudent person would exercise.

(e) Under the "fair comment rule" a student is free to express an *opinion* on matters of public interest. Specifically, a student enjoys a privilege to criticize the performance of teachers, administrators, school officials and other school employees.

3. Students cannot publish or distribute material which will cause a "material and substantial disruption of school activities."

(a) Disruption is defined as student rioting; unlawful seizures of property; destruction of property; wide-spread shouting or boisterous conduct; or substantial student participation in a school boycott, sit-in, stand-in, walk-out, or other related form of activity. *Material that stimulates heated discussion or debate does not constitute the type of disruption prohibited.*

(b) In order for a student publication to be considered disruptive, there must exist specific facts upon which it would be reasonable to forecast that a clear and present likelihood of an immediate, substantial material disruption to normal school activity would occur if the material were distributed. Mere undifferentiated fear or apprehension of disturbance is not enough; school administrators must be able to affirmatively show substantial facts which reasonably support a forecast of likely disruption.

(c) In determining whether a student publication is disruptive, consideration must be given to the context of the distribution as well as the content of the material. In this regard, consideration should be given to past experience in the school with similar material, past experience in the school in dealing with and supervising the students in the subject school, current events influencing student attitudes and behavior, and whether or not there have been any instances of actual or threatened disruption prior to or contemporaneously with the dissemination of the student publication in question.

(d) School officials must act to protect the safety of advocates of unpopular viewpoints.

(e) "School activity"—means educational activity of students sponsored by the school and includes, by way of example and not by way of limitation, classroom work, library activities, physical education classes, individual decision time, official assemblies and other similar gatherings, school athletic contests, band concerts, school plays, and scheduled in-school lunch periods.

C. Legal Advice

1. If, in the opinion of the student editor, student editorial staff or faculty adviser, material proposed for publication may be "obscene", "libelous", or "cause a substantial disruption of school activities", the legal opinion of a practicing attorney should be sought. It is recommended that the services of the attorney for the local newspaper be used.

2. Legal fees charged in connection with this consultation will be paid by the board of education.

3. The final decision of whether the material is to be published will be left to the student editor or student editorial staff.

III. PROTECTED SPEECH

School officials cannot:

1. Ban the publication or distribution of birth control information in student publications;

2. Censor or punish the occasional use of vulgar or so-called "four-letter" words in student publications;

3. Prohibit criticism of school policies or practices;

4. Cut off funds to official student publications because of disagreement over editorial policy;

5. Ban speech which merely advocates illegal conduct without proving that such speech is directed toward and will actually cause imminent lawless action;

6. Ban the publication or distribution of material written by nonstudents;

7. Prohibit the school newspaper from accepting advertising.

IV. NONSCHOOL-SPONSORED PUBLICATIONS

School officials may not ban the distribution of nonschool-sponsored publications on school grounds. However, students who violate any rule listed under II.B. may be disciplined after distribution.

1. School officials may regulate the time, place and manner of distribution.

(a) Nonschool-sponsored publications will have the same rights of distribution as official school publications.

(b) "Distribution"—means dissemination of a publication to students at a time and place of normal school activity, or immediately prior or subsequent thereto, by means of handing out free copies, selling or offering copies for sale, accepting donations for copies of the publication, or displaying the student publication in areas of the school which are generally frequented by students.

2. School officials cannot:

(a) Prohibit the distribution of anonymous literature or require that literature bear the name of the sponsoring organization or author;

(b) Ban the distribution of literature because it contains advertising;

(c) Ban the sale of literature.

V. ADVISER JOB SECURITY

No teacher who advises a student publication will be fired, transferred, or removed from the advisership for failure to exercise editorial control over the student publication or to otherwise suppress the rights of free expression of student journalists.

VI. PRIOR RESTRAINT

No student publication, whether nonschool-sponsored or official, will be reviewed by school administrators prior to distribution.

VII. CIRCULATION

These guidelines will be included in the handbook on student rights and responsibilities and circulated to all students in attendance.

Amendments to the U.S. Constitution

(The first 10 Amendments were ratified December 15, 1791, and form what is known as the "Bill of Rights")

AMENDMENT I

Congress shall make no law respecting an establishment of religion, or prohibiting the free exercise thereof; or abridging the freedom of speech, or of the press; or the right of the people peaceably to assemble, and to petition the Government for a redress of grievances.

AMENDMENT II

A well regulated Militia, being necessary to the security of a free State, the right of the people to keep and bear Arms, shall not be infringed.

AMENDMENT III

No Soldier shall, in time of peace be quartered in any house, without the consent of the Owner, nor in time of war, but in a manner to be prescribed by law.

---

* Amendment XXI was not ratified by state legislatures, but by state conventions summoned by Congress.

AMENDMENT IV

The right of the people to be secure in their persons, houses, papers, and effects, against unreasonable searches and seizures, shall not be violated, and no Warrants shall issue, but upon probable cause, supported by Oath or affirmation, and particularly describing the place to be searched, and the persons or things to be seized.

AMENDMENT V

No person shall be held to answer for a capital, or otherwise infamous crime, unless on a presentment or indictment of a Grand Jury, except in cases arising in the land or naval forces, or in the Militia, when in actual service in time of War or public danger; nor shall any person be subject for the same offense to be twice put in jeopardy of life or limb; nor shall be compelled in any criminal case to be a witness against himself, nor be deprived of life, liberty, or property, without due process of law; nor shall private property be taken for public use, without just compensation.

AMENDMENT VI

In all criminal prosecutions, the accused shall enjoy the right to a speedy and public trial, by an impartial jury of the State and district wherein the crime shall have been committed, which district shall have been previously ascertained by law, and to be informed of the nature and cause of the accusation; to be confronted with the witnesses against him; to have compulsory process for obtaining witnesses in his favor, and to have the Assistance of Counsel for his defence.

AMENDMENT VII

In suits at common law, where the value in controversy shall exceed twenty dollars, the right of trial by jury shall be preserved, and no fact tried by a jury, shall be otherwise reexamined in any Court of the United States, than according to the rules of the Common law.

AMENDMENT VIII

Excessive bail shall not be required, nor excessive fines imposed, nor cruel and unusual punishment inflicted.

AMENDMENT IX

The enumeration in the Constitution, of certain rights, shall not be construed to deny or disparage others retained by the people.

AMENDMENT X

The powers not delegated to the United States by the Constitution, nor prohibited by it to the States, are reserved to the States respectively, or to the people.

AMENDMENT XI

(Ratified February 7, 1795)

The Judicial power of the United States shall not be construed to extend to any suit in law or equity, commenced or prosecuted against one of the United States by Citizens of another State, or by Citizens or Subjects of any Foreign State.

AMENDMENT XII

(Ratified July 27, 1804)

The electors shall meet in their respective states and vote by ballot for President and Vice-President, one of whom, at least, shall not be an inhabitant of the same state with themselves; they shall name in their ballots the person voted for as President, and in distinct ballots the person voted for as Vice-President, and they shall make distinct lists of all persons voted for as President, and of all persons voted for as Vice-President, and of the number of votes for each, which lists they shall sign and certify, and transmit sealed to the seat of the government of the United States, directed to the President of the Senate;—The President of the Senate shall, in presence of the Senate and House of Representatives, open all the certificates and the votes shall then be counted;—The person having the greatest number of votes for President, shall be President, if such number be a majority of the whole number of Electors appointed; and if no person have such majority, then from the persons having the highest numbers not exceeding three on the list of those voted for as President, the House of Representatives shall choose immediately, by ballot, the President. But in choosing the President, the votes shall be taken by states, the representation from each state having one vote; a quorum for this purpose shall consist of a member or members from two-thirds of the states, and a majority of all the states shall be necessary to a choice. [And if the House of Representatives shall not choose a President whenever the right of choice shall devolve upon them, before the fourth day of March next following, then the Vice-President shall act as President, as in the case of the death or other constitutional disability of the President.—]* The person having the greatest number of votes as Vice-President, shall be the Vice-President, if such number be a majority of the whole number of Electors appointed, and if no person have a majority, then from the two highest numbers on the list, the Senate shall choose the Vice-President; a quorum for the purpose shall consist of two-thirds of the whole number of Senators, and a majority of the whole number shall be necessary to a choice. But no person constitutionally ineligible to the office of President shall be eligible to that of Vice-President of the United States.

AMENDMENT XIII

(Ratified December 6, 1865)

SECTION I. Neither slavery nor involuntary servitude, except as a punishment for a crime whereof the party shall have been duly convicted, shall exist within the United States, or any place subject to their jurisdiction.

SECTION 2. Congress shall have power to enforce this article by appropriate legislation.

AMENDMENT XIV

(Ratified July 9, 1868)

SECTION I. All persons born or naturalized in the United States, and subject to the jurisdiction thereof, are citizens of the United States and of the State wherein they reside. No State shall make or enforce any law which shall abridge the privileges or immunities of citizens of the United States; nor shall any State deprive any person of life, liberty, or property, without due process of law; nor deny to any person within its jurisdiction the equal protection of the laws.

SECTION 2. Representatives shall be apportioned among the several States according to their respective numbers, counting the whole number of persons in each State, excluding Indians not taxed. But when the right to vote at any election for the choice of electors for President and Vice-President of the United States, Representatives in

---

*Superseded by section 3 of the twentieth amendment.

Congress, the Executive and Judicial officers of a State, or the members of the Legislature thereof, is denied to any of the male inhabitants of such State, being twenty-one years of age,* and citizens of the United States, or in any way abridged, except for participation in rebellion, or other crime, the basis of representation therein shall be reduced in the proportion which the number of such male citizens shall bear to the whole number of male citizens twenty-one years of age in such State.

SECTION 3. No person shall be a Senator or Representative in Congress, or elector of the President and Vice-President, or hold any office, civil or military, under the United States, or under any State, who, having previously taken an oath, as a member of Congress, or as an officer of the United States, or as a member of any State legislature, or as an executive or judicial officer of any State, to support the Constitution of the United States, shall have engaged in insurrection or rebellion against the same, or given aid or comfort to the enemies thereof. But Congress may by a vote of two-thirds of each House, remove such disability.

SECTION 4. The validity of the public debt of the United States, authorized by law, including debts incurred for payment of pensions and bounties for services in suppressing insurrection or rebellion, shall not be questioned. But neither the United States nor any State shall assume or pay any debt or obligation incurred in aid of insurrection or rebellion against the United States, or any claim for the loss or emancipation of any slave; but all such debts, obligations and claims shall be held illegal and void.

SECTION 5. The Congress shall have power to enforce, by appropriate legislation, the provisions of this article.

AMENDMENT XV

(Ratified February 3, 1870)

SECTION I. The right of citizens of the United States to vote shall not be denied or abridged by the United States or by any State on account of race, color, or previous conditions of servitude—

---

*Changed by section 1 of the twenty-sixth amendment.

SECTION 2. The Congress shall have power to enforce this article by appropriate legislation.

AMENDMENT XVI

(Ratified February 3, 1913)

The Congress shall have power to lay and collect taxes on incomes, from whatever source derived, without apportionment among the several States, and without regard to any census or enumeration.

AMENDMENT XVII

(Ratified April 8, 1913)

The Senate of the United States shall be composed of two Senators from each State, elected by the people thereof, for six years; and each Senator shall have one vote. The electors in each State shall have the qualifications requisite for electors of the most numerous branch of the State legislatures.

When vacancies happen in the representation of any State in the Senate, the executive authority of such State shall issue writs of election to fill such vacancies: *Provided,* That the legislature of any State may empower the executive thereof to make temporary appointments until the people fill the vacancies by election as the legislature may direct.

This amendment shall not be so construed as to affect the election or term of any Senator chosen before it becomes valid as part of the Constitution.

AMENDMENT XVIII

(Ratified January 16, 1919)

[SECTION I. After one year from the ratification of this article the manufacture, sale, or transportation of intoxicating liquors within, the importation thereof into, or the exportation thereof from the United States and all territory subject to the jurisdiction thereof for beverage purposes is hereby prohibited.

[SECTION 2. The Congress and the several States shall have concurrent power to enforce this article by appropriate legislation.

[SECTION 3. This article shall be inoperative unless it shall have been ratified as an amendment to the Constitution by the legislatures of the several States as provided in the Constitution, within seven years from the date of the submission hereof to the States by the Congress.]*

AMENDMENT XIX

(Ratified August 18, 1920)

The right of citizens of the United States to vote shall not be denied or abridged by the United States or by any State on account of sex.

Congress shall have power to enforce this article by appropriate legislation.

AMENDMENT XX

(Ratified January 23, 1933)

SECTION I. The terms of the President and Vice President shall end at noon on the 20th day of January, and the terms of Senators and Representatives at noon on the 3d day of January, of the years in which such terms would have ended if this article had not been ratified; and the terms of their successors shall then begin.

SECTION 2. The Congress shall assemble at least once in every year, and such meeting shall begin at noon on the 3d day of January, unless they shall by law appoint a different day.

SECTION 3. If, at the time fixed for the beginning of the term of the President, the President elect shall have died, the Vice President elect shall become President. If a President shall not have been chosen before the time fixed for the beginning of his term, or if the President elect shall have failed to qualify, then the Vice President elect shall act as President until a President shall have qualified; and the Congress may by law provide for the case wherein neither a President elect nor a Vice President elect shall have qualified, declaring who shall then act as President, or the manner in which one who is to act shall be selected, and such person shall act accordingly, until a President or Vice President shall have qualified.

SECTION 4. The Congress may by law provide for the case of the death of any of the persons from whom the House of Represent-

---

*Repealed by section I of the twenty-first amendment.

atives may choose a President whenever the right of choice shall have devolved upon them, and for the case of the death of any of the persons from whom the Senate may choose a Vice President whenever the right of choice shall have devolved upon them.

SECTION 5. Sections I and 2 shall take effect on the 15th day of October following the ratification of this article.

SECTION 6. This article shall be inoperative unless it shall have been ratified as an amendment to the Constitution by the legislatures of three-fourths of the several states within seven years from the date of its submission.

AMENDMENT XXI

(Ratified December 5, 1933)

SECTION I. The eighteenth article of amendment to the Constitution of the United States is hereby repealed.

SECTION 2. The transportation or importation into any State, Territory, or possession of the United States for delivery or use therein of intoxicating liquors, in violation of the laws thereof, is hereby prohibited.

SECTION 3. This article shall be inoperative unless it shall have been ratified as an amendment to the Constitution by conventions in the several States, as provided in the Constitution, within seven years from the date of the submission hereof to the States by the Congress.

AMENDMENT XXII

(Ratified February 27, 1951)

SECTION I. No person shall be elected to the office of the President more than twice, and no person who has held the office of President, or acted as President, for more than two years of a term to which some other person was elected President, shall be elected to the office of the President more than once. But this Article shall not apply to any person holding the office of President when this Article was proposed by the Congress, and shall not prevent any person who may be holding the office of President, or acting as President, during the term within which this Article becomes operative from holding the office of President or acting as President, during the remainder of such term.

SECTION 2. This article shall be inoperative unless it shall have been ratified as an amendment to the Constitution by the legislature of three-fourths of the several States within seven years from the date of its submission to the States by the Congress.

AMENDMENT XXIII

(Ratified March 29, 1961)

SECTION I. The District constituting the seat of Government of the United States shall appoint in such manner as the Congress may direct:

A number of electors of President and Vice President equal to the whole number of Senators and Representatives in Congress to which the District would be entitled if it were a State, but in no event more than the least populous State; they shall be in addition to those appointed by the States, but they shall be considered, for the purposes of the election of President and Vice President, to be electors appointed by a State; and they shall meet in the District and perform such duties as provided by the twelfth article of amendment.

SECTION 2. The Congress shall have power to enforce this article by appropriate legislation.

AMENDMENT XXIV

(Ratified January 23, 1964)

SECTION I. The right of citizens of the United States to vote in any primary or other election for President or Vice President, for electors for President or Vice President, or for Senator or Representative in Congress, shall not be denied or abridged by the United States or any State by reason of failure to pay any poll tax or other tax.

SECTION 2. The Congress shall have power to enforce this article by appropriate legislation.

AMENDMENT XXV

(Ratified February 10, 1967)

SECTION I. In case of the removal of the President from office or of his death or resignation, the Vice President shall become President.

SECTION 2. Whenever there is a vacancy in the office of the Vice President, the President shall nominate a Vice President who shall take office upon confirmation by a majority vote of both Houses of Congress.

SECTION 3. Whenever the President transmits to the President pro tempore of the Senate and the Speaker of the House of Representatives his written declaration that he is unable to discharge the powers and duties of his office, and until he transmits to them a written declaration to the contrary, such powers and duties shall be discharged by the Vice President as Acting President.

SECTION 4. Whenever the Vice President and a majority of either the principal officers of the executive departments or of such other body as Congress may by law provide, transmit to the President pro tempore of the Senate and the Speaker of the House of Representatives their written declaration that the President is unable to discharge the powers and duties of his office, the Vice President shall immediately assume the powers and duties of the office as Acting President.

Thereafter, when the President transmits to the President pro tempore of the Senate and the Speaker of the House of Representatives his written declaration that no inability exists, he shall resume the powers and duties of his office unless the Vice President and a majority of either the principal officers of the executive department or of such other body as Congress may by law provide, transmit within four days to the President pro tempore of the Senate and the Speaker of the House of Representatives their written declaration that the President is unable to discharge the powers and duties of his office. Thereupon Congress shall decide the issue, assembling within forty-eight hours for that purpose if not in session. If the Congress, within twenty-one days after receipt of the latter written declaration, or, if Congress is not in session, within twenty-one days after Congress is required to assemble, determines by two-thirds vote of both Houses that the President is unable to discharge the powers and duties of his office, the Vice President shall continue to discharge the same as Acting President; otherwise, the President shall resume the powers and duties of his office.

AMENDMENT XXVI

(Ratified July 1, 1971)

SECTION I. The right of citizens of the United States, who are eighteen years of age or older, to vote shall not be denied or abridged by the United States or by any State on account of age.

SECTION 2. The Congress shall have power to enforce this article by appropriate legislation.

Index